FUN FACTS

Ripley's

Believe It or Not!®

Kids

3 SILLY STORIES 3

D0117303

Consultant Barbara Taylor
Design Rocket Design
Reprographics Juice Creative

Published by Ripley Publishing 2014
Ripley Publishing, Suite 188, 7576 Kingspointe Parkway
Orlando, Florida, 32819, USA

10 9 8 7 6 5 4 3 2 1

ISBN 978-1-60991-116-4 (US)

Library of Congress Control Number: 2014939815

Manufactured in China
in June/2014
1st printing

PUBLISHER'S NOTE
While every effort has been made to verify the accuracy
of the entries in this book, the Publishers cannot be held
responsible for any errors contained in the work. They
would be glad to receive any information from readers.

WARNING
Some of the stunts and activities in this book are undertaken
by experts and should not be attempted by anyone without
adequate training and supervision.

First published in Great Britain in 2014 by
Young Arrow, Random House,
20 Vauxhall Bridge Road, London SW1V 2SA

www.randomhouse.co.uk

Addresses for companies within The Random House
Group Limited can be found at
www.randomhouse.co.uk/offices/htm

The Random House Group Limited Reg. No. 954009

A CIP catalogue record for this book is available from
the British Library

ISBN 9780099596622 (UK)

For information regarding permission, write to
VP Intellectual Property
Ripley Entertainment Inc.
Suite 188, 7576 Kingspointe Parkway
Orlando, Florida, 32819, USA
Email: publishing@ripleys.com
www.ripleybooks.com

Pretty in pink

Flamingos are pink because of the food they eat.

In the doghouse!

Believe it or not, these houses are for dogs!

Some of them even have air conditioning and running water!

Now, where did I bury my bone?

Cheeky Monkey

Female baboons bring up their young alone.

Six-year-old Emily Bland is best friends with Rishi the orangutan. They met when they were very young, and have stayed friends ever since.

TIGER FACTS

Tigers can kill prey over twice their size.

12

They have **striped skin,** as well as striped fur.

Tigers are the **largest wild cats** in the world.

SWEET DREAMS

A piglet sleeps with a tiger in a zoo in Bangkok, Thailand, where they have lived happily together from an early age.

14

Japan has roads that play music as you drive over them at the correct speed.

You can't hum while holding your nose. Try it!

Monster Munch?

Stuffed olive eyes

Tomato tongues

Salamiese Twins

Artist Kasia Haupt from New York creates scary monster sandwiches!

Green chilies

Rice teeth

Sandwich-saurus

Olive feet and head

BICYCLE SPECTACLE

The owners of a bicycle shop in Germany attached 120 bikes to the building to advertise their shop.

It measured 43,000 square feet (4,000 sq m)!

Don't look down!

French artist François Abélanet created this giant 3-D street artwork.

WEEE... SPLAT!

A farmer from Holland set up a slide for his muddy pigs!

Dull in Scotland is the sister town of Boring in Oregon.

Your brain is often more active when you are asleep than when you are awake.

ZZZZ..

FLYING FOOLS!

These crazy contestants have made their own aircraft for a flying competition. They jump from a platform into the sea, and the machine that travels the furthest wins!

The Fish

LOONY LOADS!

Have you ever tried carrying lots of things at once? Probably not as much as these heavy loads...

Phew, this cycling is thirsty work!

Plastic bottles on the back of a rickshaw in India.

Lanterns on the back of a motorcycle in Sri Lanka.

A sofa on the back of a motorcycle in Kenya.

TAXI!

Cats can't taste sweetness.

They do not have the sense organ for sweetness.

People with Alice in Wonderland Syndrome see objects much smaller or larger than they really are.

THAT'S POTTY!

Janey Byrne lives with her pot-bellied pigs, Molly and Meeka, in her home in the U.K.

It's crumbs again Meeka.

ABOUT **80%** of all the animals on Earth are insects.

Er, waiter...

...there's a worm in my soup!

Earthworm soup is popular in China and is thought to cure fevers.

These cuddly mascots took part in the world's largest gathering of mascot characters in Japan.

The giant squid has the world's largest eyes. They are the size of a **dinner plate!**

Grrrrr!

Walt Disney, creator of Mickey Mouse, was afraid of mice!

Your heart beats about **40 million times** a year. That makes **2.5 billion** times by the time you are 70.

This Hide-N-See TV for hamsters, gerbils and mice lets your pet star in its own TV show!

EYES ON THE PRIZE

Gostra is a traditional game played in Malta. People climb up a greasy pole to pull out a flag and win a prize!

SCRAPE

SLIP

Your lungs are roughly the same size as a

tennis court

if you flattened them out.

THE APPLE OF MY EYE...

Special Valentine's Day apples featuring love messages were sold at a supermarket in China.

GENTLE JAWS

Mother crocodiles often carry their babies in their mouths after they have hatched so they reach the water safely.

Eeek, don't swallow me!

THE GREEN MAN

Can you spot him? Artist Liu Bolin hides in this store display by painting himself covered in vegetables.

Cranberries are sorted for ripeness by bouncing them. A ripe one can be dribbled like a basketball.

Elephants NEVER stop growing.

felineFUN

Check out this cool furniture for cats!
They can explore the walkways and
beds attached to the walls and ceilings.

That doesn't look very comfy!

Help me!

Mudskippers, a type of fish, can drown underwater. They need to be able to poke their heads above the water to breathe.

BEST BUDS!

Grizzly bear cub Bam Bam and Vali the chimp are best buddies!

They live in Myrtle Beach Safari Park in South Carolina.

SMILE!

This watermelon carving was made by a student in China using only a spoon.

Palm trees grew in Antarctica 50 million years ago.

ANTS **STRETCH** when they wake up in the morning.

Little Miss Cuddly

Jo Black from the U.K. has 2,700 pieces in her Mr. Men and Little Miss collection.

57

ONION FACTS

If you rub an onion on your foot, within an hour **you will taste it.**

This is because it travels through your skin and into your bloodstream.

Eating onions will make you **sleepy,** but you'll have to eat a lot of them!

Chewing gum while peeling onions will stop you from crying.

TONGUE TALENT

Giant Anteaters' tongues are about two feet (0.6 m) long.

You'll have to take my word for it, it's rude to stick your tongue out!

The ancient Aztecs ate tortillas stuffed with

TADPOLES

for dinner.

Are you fur real?

Mohawk

Designer Leah Workman has created these wacky wigs for dogs!

Pink Wig

Blue 'do

Smokin'!

John Ward from the U.K. has created the world's smallest working fire truck!

LITTLE BERNING
FIRE BRIGADE

'You've not been put out until we put you out!'

P204 KEY

An average person laughs **TEN** times a day.

Strewth!

There are more than 60 kinds of kangaroo.

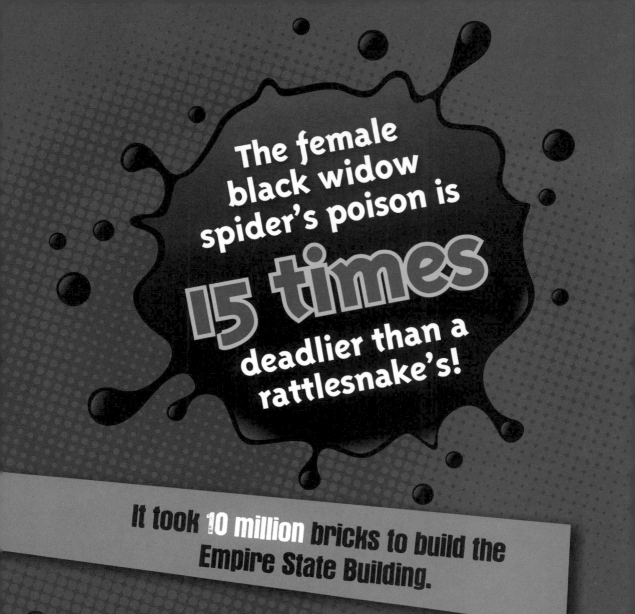

The female black widow spider's poison is **15 times** deadlier than a rattlesnake's!

It took **10 million** bricks to build the Empire State Building.

GULP!

In your lifetime you will drink enough water to fill 20 swimming pools.

So, by the time you are 80, you will have drunk over 1.5 million gallons (5.7 million l) of water.

GEEZER!

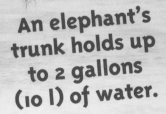

An elephant's trunk holds up to 2 gallons (10 l) of water.

Rats laugh when tickled

Tickle me, tickle me!

ONE tree produces enough oxygen in one year to keep TWO human beings alive.

A bunch of bananas is called a **HAND.**

A single banana is known as a **FINGER.**

The word

SWIMS

when written upside
down still looks like

SWIMS

Most crabs grow a new
claw when they lose one.

Do flying fish fly?

No, they just glide on wind currents. Some glide 20 feet (6 m) above the water.

Big-hearted beasts

A waterbuck with a heart-shaped nose!

A fluffy penguin with a heart-y chest.

A cat with a heart on its chin!

Rhys!

SCISSORS!

ROCK,

NUTS!

The Rock, Paper, Scissors Championships were held in the U.K. in 2013. Rhys Parkey beat 249 other competitors to be crowned champion.

PAPER, SCISSORS!

Some worms in Australia are over four feet (1.2 m) long!

Giant pandas spend up to 16 hours a day eating bamboo.

Why did a man wear **70 ITEMS** of clothing to a Chinese airport?

So he didn't have to pay the extra baggage charge!

79

PERISCOPES!

Elephants can swim, and they use their trunk like a snorkel to breathe when they're in deep water.

The founder of McDonald's has a degree in Hamburgerology.

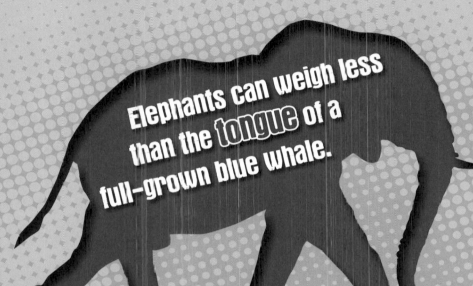

Elephants can weigh less than the tongue of a full-grown blue whale.

Horses can only breathe through their nostrils, not their mouth.

What do you call a lizard with a bright blue tongue?

A blue-tongued lizard!
It uses it to scare off predators.

when you tell a lie your nose heats up.

HORSES CAN SLEEP

STANDING UP!

They lock their knees so they don't fall over.

FISH SUPPER

A black swan feeds carp at a wildlife park in China.

BIG TANK!

A Boeing 747 airliner holds 57,285 gallons (216,847 l) of fuel.

Vending machines kill 4 times more people each year than sharks.

A group of bunnies is called a fluffle.

Did someone say carrots?

Gentoo and Adélie penguins give their mate a pebble as a way of proposing.

chicken poop was used as a cure for baldness in 17th-century England.

Dogs are banned from Antarctica.

Santa Claus received nine votes in the 2008 U.S. presidential election.

It's almost **IMPOSSIBLE** to sneeze with your eyes open.

Hagfish have four hearts.

POP!

Believe it or not, this is what an exploding balloon full of water looks like! It was photographed by Shimon Mentel from Israel.

This is the world's biggest glass Christmas tree bauble!

It measures 65 inches (165 cm) across and weighs 44 pounds (20 kg)

Your left side is your best side

Scientists think people find it more attractive.

twyndyllyngs is the longest English word without a vowel. It's another word for "twin."

Astronauts get taller when they are in space.

They grow about 2 inches (5 cm) taller during long missions due to the lack of gravity that pulls them down on Earth. When they return home, they shrink back to normal.

Do sheep enter beauty contests?

shall I bother entering?

YES! In Senegal there is a televised beauty contest for sheep.

101

An average person eats about 60,000 pounds (27,216 kg) of food in their lifetime.

That's the weight of about **six elephants** or **30 small cars.**

Cows can be identified by their noseprints.

SMASH, POP, BOUNCE!

Bubble soccer is a sport played all over the world—it's the same as soccer but every player is inside an inflatable bubble

It would take

4,000

helium balloons to lift a 110-pound (50-kg) person off the ground.

DUCK SOUP!

12,000 rubber ducks took part in a duck race in Germany.

Las Vegas would be the **BRIGHTEST** city if you looked down at Earth from space at night.

Night-flying tropical butterflies have **EARS** on their wings to avoid crashing into bats.

Lungfish can survive without water for as long as **four years.**

Scientists can't agree why ice is slippery.

Really?

The ultimate
BRAIN FOOD!

Andy Millns made a miniature copy of his brain out of chocolate... and then ate it!

Astronauts in space often lose their sense of smell and taste.

112

Woodlice drink from both ends of their body.

ZZZZZZZZZZZ...

In Germany, there is a snoring museum.

One inch
(2.5 cm)
of rain =

= **10 inches**
(25 cm)
of snow.

Winging it!

Flying is the new way to get to work, with this flying bicycle. The bike can reach heights of up to 4,000 feet (1,200 m).

Dang! who stole my parking space?

BANANA MAN

Humans and bananas share **50 percent** of the same genes.

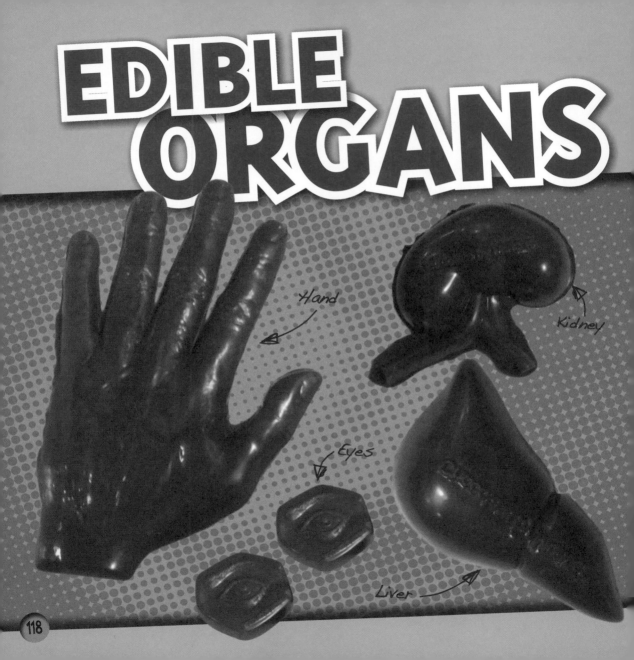

The company "Chocolate by Mueller" make chocolate body parts, including ears, eyes, hearts, and brains!

Brain

Ear

Lungs

Heart

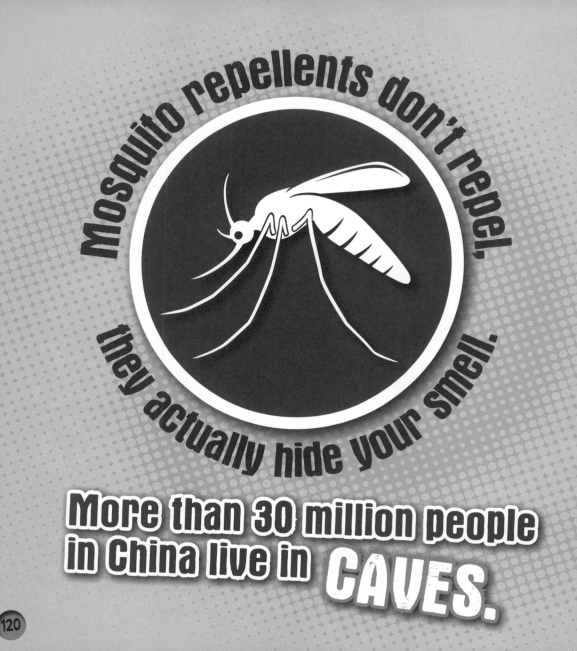

Mosquito repellents don't repel, they actually hide your smell.

More than 30 million people in China live in **CAVES.**

120

BEST MATES

Cows have best friends and can get stressed when they are separated.

121

sticky corner

Thousands of pieces of chewed gum have been stuck to a wall in Seattle, Washington.

Dolphins "name" each other by using unique **whistles.**

Big nose!

Stinky!

Sometimes the tuatara lizard of New Zealand breathes only **once an hour.**

Venezuela almost ran out of toilet paper in 2012.

WHOSE A PRETTY BOY THEN?

chuckle!

These bright pooches belong to Catherine Opson, a professional dog groomer from California.

I'm not leaving the house like this!

Time for your walk Sebastian!

CAN YOU FIGURE IT OUT?

Guess which body parts these odd-shaped vegetables look like?

A. Curvacious carrot

Ewww, get a bath!

B. Extraordinary eggplant

C. Curious cucumber

Super Snails!

Twenty four snail sculptures made from recycled plastic were placed all around Sydney, Australia.

Are watermelons SQUARE?

Not usually, but in Japan they are sometimes grown in cubes so they stack better.

FLAME THROWER!

Anybody got a fire extinguisher?

Meet Fanny the world's largest walking robot! The robotic dragon measures 51 feet (16 m) long, has a wingspan of 40 feet (12 m), and can even breathe fire!

AMAZING ANTS

Ants started farming long before humans.

LIGHT DELAY

It takes 8 minutes for sunlight to travel from the Sun to the Earth. This means if you see the Sun go out, it actually went out 8 minutes ago!

If you raise your legs slowly, and lie on your back, you can't sink in quicksand.

Cows have four stomachs.

Well, not exactly!

It's one stomach

with four chambers in it.

"Get down" with the fishes

This band performed for visitors in the sea tunnel at Ocean World in China.

Mini monarch!

Would your majesty like her breakfast?

ZZZZZ...

Mary, Queen of Scots, became queen in 1542 when she was just **SIX** days old.

A dog has **220 million** smell receptors in its nose...

a rabbit has 100 million...
you have just 5–6 million.

I can smell a rabbit!

Do thirsty plants scream?

If a plant is thirsty it will make a high-pitched sound, but it is too high for us to hear.

Eeeeeek!

Speak up!

Termites eat wood twice as fast when they feel musical vibrations through it.

Cool, I love this tune!

"Wooden Heart" by Elvis?

Thorny devil lizards drink water through their **FEET.**

Yee Haa!

Bottlenose dolphins sometimes take rides on the heads of humpback whales.

SHREK LOOKALIKE!

This flower looks like Shrek the ogre!
The rare bee orchid was found in Spain.

Q

Who asks over 400 questions a day?

A four-year-old child. Many of them are just "Why?"

Why? Leave it!

RAINBOW MAGIC

This tree in Hungary is covered in a rainbow of spiderweb crochet designs! Known as "Yarnbombing" the knitted webs took three months to stitch together!

FORK LIFT

Eat-Fit cutlery helps you exercise while eating! The knife and fork weigh 2 pounds (1 kg) each—the same as a bag of sugar—and the spoon is twice as heavy.

Try a "lighter" meal!

Einstein, a fourteen-inch-tall (36 cm) miniature horse, plays with Hannah, a St. Bernard dog!

Toy Plane?

This plane is actually a kindergarten classroom! The plane, in the Georgian city of Rustavi, is full of desks, games and toys.

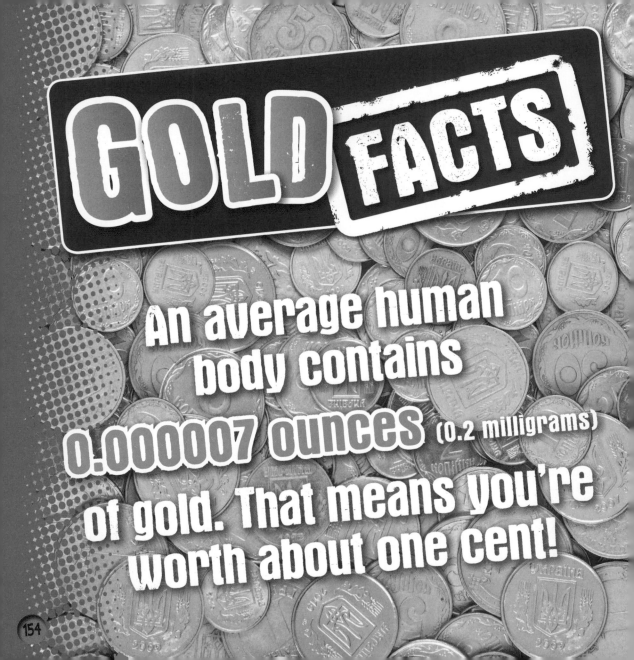

GOLD FACTS

An average human body contains **0.000007 ounces** (0.2 milligrams) of gold. That means you're worth about one cent!

154

All the gold mined in the world in a single year would **only fill the living room** in an average house.

Olympic gold medals contain only **1.3 percent gold.** They are actually 92.5 percent silver and the rest is copper.

Jumbo bunny

Ralph the giant rabbit weighs 56 pounds (25 kg) and measures three feet (1 m) in length.

OOOF!

Take a look at the size of those feet!

156

BZZZZZZZ

whoa, headache!

Woodpeckers peck up to 20 times a second.

Hangin' around

Bats hang upside down because their legs are too weak to support their weight in an upright position.

YUMMY!

Americans started eating popcorn for breakfast in the 1800s.

Your head ages faster than your feet.

This is because time moves faster at higher levels, as the Earth's gravity is weaker up there.

Catching flies

Sticking out your tongue when you are concentrating helps your brain deal with information.

Careful though, you might catch a big, juicy fly!

LillyBelle the dog has an amazing skill... she can sniff out nuts! She's been trained to find nuts and keep them away from seven-year-old Meghan Weingarth, who has a severe nut allergy.

LillyBelle raises her paw if any of Meghan's food contains nuts.

WHICH ANIMALS TIE THEIR TAILS TOGETHER?

Groups of South American Titi monkeys. Scientists think they do it as a sign of affection.

GUIDING STAR

Dung beetles use the stars in the sky as a guide to help them move in straight lines at night. This stops them going round in circles.

NO WAY!

A woman in Boston paid $560,000 for two parking spaces in the city.

The worst game EVER!

Bokdrol Spoeg

is a South African sport where competitors spit antelope dung as far as possible.

That's just revolting!

Mr Stink!

Skunks can spray their smelly fluid as far as 15 feet (5 m).

oh yeh!

Censored!

charming!

LOOPY!

Aaron Homoki from Arizona completed a 15-foot-high (4.6-m) skateboard loop.

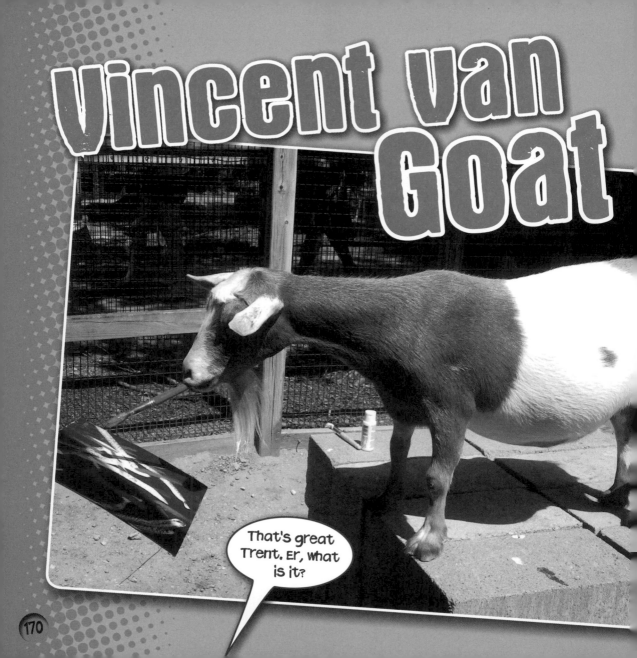

I just love painting!

Trent the goat loves painting!

The creative creature picks up the paintbrush in his mouth and makes beautiful art!

The sheep-eating plant uses sharp spines to catch passing sheep!

OUCH!

Why?

When the trapped sheep dies and decays, it becomes food for the plant, like a fertilizer.

WATER RATES

Over $1,000,000 (£600,000) in coins is thrown into the Trevi fountain in Rome, Italy, every year.

$4,000 (£2,500) is taken out everyday and given to the poor.

Super Ted

Teddy bears were named after the 26th U.S. President Theodore Roosevelt, who was called Teddy.

WOODEN WONDER

KNOCK!

This car is made out of wood! Momir Bojic spent a year hand-building the VW Beetle replica in his garden workshop. It can even drive like a normal car!

Yes! Particularly DogTV, a television channel for dogs based in San Diego, California!

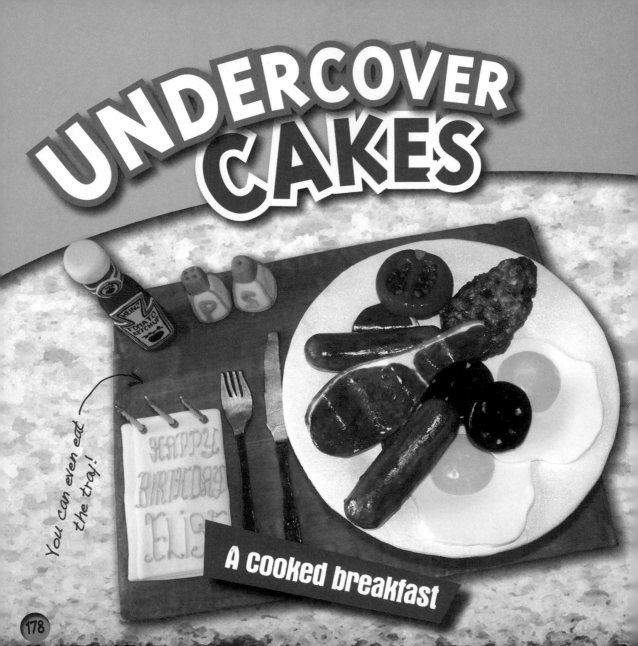

UNDERCOVER CAKES

You can even eat the tray!

A cooked breakfast

Believe it or not, these are made of cake!

Chef Paul James from the U.K. can create anything using icing and sponge.

Delicious sponge roofs and trees

A fairytale castle

Longest lick?

wow!

Giraffes clean their eyes and ears with their **21-inch** (53-cm) tongue.

Counting one billion seconds would take you about **31.7 years.**

Er, don't try it!

Some bees in Thailand drink HUMAN TEARS.

It's a source of water, protein and salt for them!

The pilot
and co-pilot on a
plane always eat
different meals.

If they were both to
get sick from food
poisoning there would
be no one to fly
the plane!

SLOPPY CHOPS!

Dairy cows can make up to 50 gallons (190 l) of saliva a day to help digest their food.

184

ERASER EXTRAVAGANZA

Seven-year-old Hannah Walker was given 1,500 erasers by her aunt! When Hannah decided to collect erasers, her aunt Alice dug out her 30-year-old collection.

Choc Frock

This dress is covered in chocolate!

Chocolate, in the form of cacao beans, was used as money until the late 19th century in parts of South America.

The average chocolate bar has about 8 insects' legs in it.

what?

187

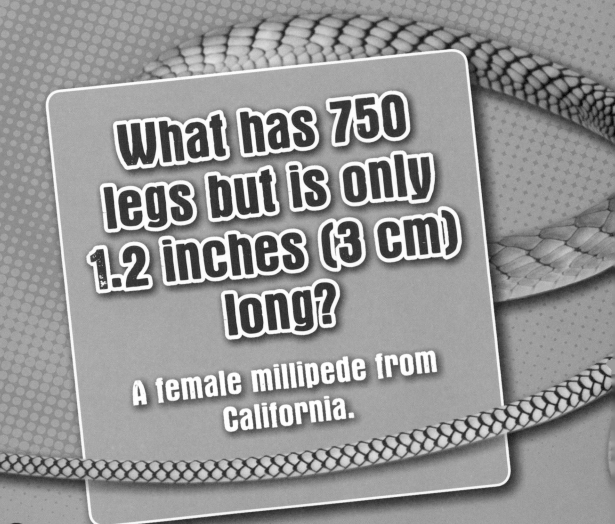

What has 750 legs but is only 1.2 inches (3 cm) long?

A female millipede from California.

Scientists think that if you lived on Earth 1,900 million years ago, it would have smelled like

rotten eggs.

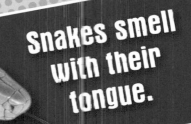

Snakes smell with their tongue.

Horsemaid

Get off me foot!

Alex Wells from the U.K. had her horse Toffee as one of her bridesmaids on her wedding day.

25 percent of the bones in your body **are in your feet.**

Lightning is five times **HOTTER** than the surface of the Sun.

Some seals in Norway have red faces!

The iron particles in the sea can stick to the hairs on their face causing it to turn red.

Yes, and you've got nothing on!

Salamanders use their lungs to hear sounds!

You would have

33,554,432

direct ancestors...
If you traced your
family tree back
25 generations.

WATER MUSIC

OK, who stole my guitar?

This surfer, dressed as a rock star, competes in the ZJ Boarding House Halloween Surf Contest in California.

Aaron Bling can hold a note on his saxophone for 39 minutes 40 seconds.

LOVE AND FLEECE

Hi man!

Long-haired sheep Bobbie Marley has curly dreadlocks!

An average person grows **590 miles** (950 km) of hair in a lifetime!

Which animal has see-through blood?

The ocellated ice fish.

Some farmers in Africa use

chili peppers

to keep elephants away from their crops.

Lightning strikes the Earth about **8 million** times a day.

An average person will walk the Earth during their lifetime. the same as four times around the Earth during their lifetime.

Only 1 percent of the water on Earth is drinkable.

202

OUT COLD!

Hippos sleep underwater. They rise to the surface to breathe without waking.

STRANGE CARGO

The first passengers in a hot-air balloon were a sheep, a duck and a rooster.

They flew from Versailles, France, in 1783.

I think we're gonna crash!

It's OK for you two, you can fly anyway!

SNOW BOATS

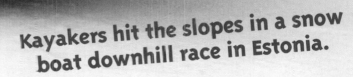

Kayakers hit the slopes in a snow boat downhill race in Estonia.

CHRISTMAS COLLECTION

Sylvia Pope from the U.K. has a collection of more than 1,750 Christmas decorations.

Can you roll your tongue into a tube?

At least 65 percent of the population can.

HOT PANDA

Wei Wei the panda cooled down in summer by hugging a giant ice block!

Ahhhhhh!

DOG DUDES

Surfing dogs compete in the Surf City Surf Dog competition in Huntington Beach, California.

The wipe out...

...as we see the front of the board start to go under, disaster is just moments away—and he knows it!

Text book

Cool, calm and collected. Way to go!

The doggie double

Nicely done, although "number 2" seems to be having a hard time—maybe it's the view?

A praying mantis can turn its head ALL THE WAY AROUND.

It is the only insect that can do this.

FLAMIN' TUBA

Christopher Werkowicz entertains people in London, U.K., by playing a tuba on fire!

Your **left** lung is smaller than your **right lung** to make room for your **heart.**

BAD HAIR DAY?

An ancient Roman hair dye formula included **pickled leeches, sea urchins and lard.**

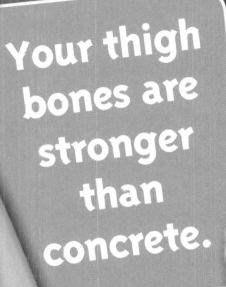

CLINK

Your thigh bones are stronger than concrete.

Rope climbing was an Olympic sport until 1932.

More than half of the world's population has never made or received a phone call.

Anybody there?

218

CAT BURGLAR!

Norris the cat creeps out at night and steals clothes, slippers and food from nearby houses! He sneaks in through cat flaps and comes home the next morning with the stolen goods. He has even taken a bath mat and towel set!

INDEX

PHOTO CREDITS

We hope you enjoyed the book!

Have you seen books one and two? They're packed with even more fun facts and silly stories!

Race

transitions

General Editor: Julian Wolfreys

---

transitions Series
Series Standing Order ISBN 0–333–73684–6
(*outside North America only*)

You can receive future titles in this series as they are published by
placing a standing order. Please contact your bookseller or, in case of
difficulty, write to us at the address below with your name and address,
the title of the series and the ISBN quoted above.

Customer Services Department, Macmillan Distribution Ltd
Houndmills, Basingstoke, Hampshire RG21 6XS, England

---

transitions

R a c e

Brian Niro

First published 2003 by
PALGRAVE MACMILLAN
Houndmills, Basingstoke, Hampshire RG21 6XS and
175 Fifth Avenue, New York, N.Y. 10010
Companies and representatives throughout the world

PALGRAVE MACMILLAN is the global academic imprint of the Palgrave Macmillan division of St. Martin's Press, LLC and of Palgrave Macmillan Ltd. Macmillan® is a registered trademark in the United States, United Kingdom and other countries. Palgrave is a registered trademark in the European Union and other countries.

ISBN 0–333–75312–7 hardback
ISBN 0–333–75313–5 paperback

This book is printed on paper suitable for recycling and made from fully managed and sustained forest sources.

A catalogue record for this book is available from the British Library.

Library of Congress Cataloging-in-Publication Data
Niro, Brian.
    Race / Brian Niro.
        p. cm. – (Transitions)
    Includes bibliographical references and index.
    ISBN 0-333-75312-7 — ISBN 0-333-75313-5 (pbk.)
        1. English literature—History and criticism. 2. Race in literature.
    3. American literature—History and criticism. I. Title. II. Series.
    PR408.R34N57 2003
    820.9'355–dc21   2002193090

10 9 8 7 6 5 4 3 2 1
12 11 10 09 08 07 06 05 04 03

Printed in China

Contents

General Editor's Preface

Transitions: *transition-em*, n. of action. 1. A passing or passage from one condition, action or (rarely) place, to another. 2. Passage in thought, speech, or writing, from one subject to another. 3. a. The passing from one note to another. b. The passing from one key to another, modulation. 4. The passage from an earlier to a later stage of development or formation . . . change from an earlier style to a later; a style of intermediate or mixed character . . . the historical passage of language from one well-defined stage to another.

The aim of *Transitions* is to explore passages and movements in critical thought, and in the development of literary and cultural interpretation. This series also seeks to examine the possibilities for reading, analysis, and other critical engagements which the very idea of transition makes possible. The writers in this series unfold the movements and modulations of critical thinking over the last generation, from the first emergences of what is now recognised as literary theory. They examine as well how the transitional nature of theoretical and critical thinking is still very much in operation, guaranteed by the hybridity and heterogeneity of the field of literary studies. The authors in the series share the common understanding that, now more than ever, critical thought is both in a state of transition and can best be defined by developing for the student reader an understanding of this protean quality.

This series desires, then, to enable the reader to transform her/his own reading and writing transactions by comprehending past developments. Each book in the series offers a guide to the poetics and politics of interpretative paradigms, schools, and bodies of thought, while transforming these, if not into tools or methodologies, then into conduits for directing and channelling thought. As well as transforming the critical past by interpreting it from the perspective of the present day, each study enacts transitional readings of a number of well-known literary texts, all of which are themselves conceivable as having been transitional texts at the moments of their first appearance. The readings offered in these books seek, through close critical reading and theoretical engagement, to demonstrate certain possibilities in critical thinking to the student reader.

It is hoped that the student will find this series liberating because rigid methodologies are not being put into place. As all the dictionary definitions of the idea of transition above suggest, what is important is the action, the passage: of thought, of analysis, of critical response. Rather than seeking to help you locate yourself in relation to any particular school or discipline, this series aims to put you into action, as readers and writers, travellers between positions, where the movement between poles comes to be seen as of more importance than the locations themselves.

Julian Wolfreys

Acknowledgments

I am eternally grateful to Julian Wolfreys for the extensive support, both professional and personal, that he has consistently provided since we first met seven years ago. At that meeting, I was an absolutely bewildered postgraduate. Although it will be for others to decide exactly what I am now, I consider myself extremely fortunate to have had his guidance in my own transition between then and now. Cheers mate.

For their invaluable editorial assistance, I would also like to thank James E. Sojoodi, Christopher R. P. Laney, and T. Adrian Lewis. In particular, I would like to extend my warmest gratitude to Stephanie King for her editorial comments, questions, and corrections. It is more than likely that any clever turn of phrase, sharp observation, or meaningful insight contained in these pages is in some direct way related to her efforts. Undoubtedly, everything mundane, academic, or obvious is my own. Stephanie also deserves considerable thanks for putting up with me during the creation of this volume. Cheers again.

I would like to thank the people at DePaul University for their support, interest, and encouragement. Thank you Janie Isackson for the kindness you showed me during the last effort in the completion of the manuscript.

Finally, I would like to thank my parents, Raymond and Judy Niro, for making everything, and I mean everything, possible

Brian Niro

Introduction

> In short, beginning is *making* or *producing difference*, but – and here is the great fascination in the subject – difference which is the result of combining the already-familiar with the fertile novelty of human work in language. (Said 1985: xxiii)

Race is a monster. It is tremendous and terrible and astonishingly resilient. Race changes shape, size, and color as the need arises. It is a monster because of the manner in which it has been employed for the justification of systematic oppression and for the wholesale murder of huge populations. Race is also a monster because of the exacting tenacity with which it survives despite more than a few deliberate and sophisticated attempts to remove the concept from our ideological lexicon. Alas, the concept of race, like the word itself, is here to stay. More than merely resting in its resilience, however, race seems to be growing in stature, from end to end, both in terms of its presence in the commonsensical appreciation of "ordinary" folk, and in the dizzied minds of the intellectual elite. Race is on the lips and in the minds of the politicians, the pundits, the general population, the active, and the apathetic alike. Indeed, for many academics, politicians and professionals, race is a scary business. And to be sure, race is also big business for the editors and publishers of scholarly tomes (bless them); a simple survey of the sheer number of recent articles and books is testament to that fact. But what of value have we gathered from this scholastic archeology, and where did this monster come from? Who created it, and why? More importantly, why are we so ambivalent about our belief in it? We know it is terrible, but why do we consistently place so much stock in its continued existence? Why does this ambivalence lend the concept so much power?

Race is scary work for politicians and academics alike. As suggested above, attempts to theorize the nature of race from within the hallowed confines of the ivory tower often means little in terms of the actual application of the word. This, along with the progressive atti-

tude of those within the academy, has inspired a great deal of trepidation in the mere acknowledgment of the word itself. Take, for
example, Robert Ferguson's *Representing 'Race': Ideology, Identity and
the Media* (1998). Ferguson insists upon using the word with inverted
commas for two specific reasons. The first is that the term has "no
reliable scientific status," and the second "is to guard against any
intellectual complacency as I attempt to engage with a field which,
though primarily discursive, has had and continues to have real material consequences and correlates" (Ferguson: 1). He continues, "It is
important to resist any attempt to *normalise* the term 'race'"
(Ferguson: 1). Despite Ferguson's best and most benevolent intentions, it seems largely "academic," if you will excuse the term, to
suggest that he has arrived several hundred years too late in his resistance to normalization. What Ferguson seemingly both accepts and
wants to deny is that all the inverted commas in the world will not
amend the fact that the word race is alive and well. Nor will the theoretical discussion of race transcend the "material consequences and
correlates" that insist that race is marked on and under the skin,
instantly recognizable by those who pass us on the street. The very
title of this volume presumes the genuine presence of race – the validation of its existence occurs through the mere printing of the word
itself and its recognition by those who read it. There is also a limitation in the recognition of the printed word, for the word has not
always existed. Nor has the concept merely lain dormant, patiently
anticipating its discovery by adventurous and "civilized" people. To
presume such a thing is both to ignore the variation of the word
across temporal landscapes (over, say, five hundred years), and to
diminish the possibility of variation across ideological landscapes.

If race is a monster, it seems reasonable and rational to dismiss the
concept (as many would like) in the same manner we exorcise other
monsters, by recognizing that they do not exist and that they are mere
figments of our collective, cultural imagination. We need merely to
turn on the lights, open our eyes, and check beneath the bed to realize
that race is not here. To paraphrase James Joyce, we must simply
wake up from the nightmare of our racial history. In this regard,
however, the persistence of race is not unlike the persistence of superstition. For instance, very few people actually *believe* that the number
thirteen connotes bad luck and common sense tells us it should not.
And yet, you would be hard-pressed to find the thirteenth floor in any
of the countless soaring towers of the Chicago metropolitan area. Are

we really suggesting that the fourteenth floor is anything other than what we know it actually is? Or are we so deeply immersed in the significance of what we name our surroundings that, indeed, the thirteenth floor magnificently fails to exist? But perhaps the trouble with common sense – and race certainly entertains a commonsensical status – is that it does not necessarily need empirical proof for sustenance. Common sense has a momentum all its own.

This begs the question: What specifically is our collective motivation behind our resistance to the abandonment of a term we know to be both so significantly empty and so dramatically unconstructive? There must be a reason – or, more likely, reasons – for the doggedness of race. Surely, it must be something more than the cautious suggestion not to push our skepticism too far. There is a desire to view the insidiousness of race, or rather our belief in it, as really no more than a symptom of our cultural immaturity. An enlightened child, or an enlightened society, would not trifle with such nonsense. But enlightened rationality and reason play an integral role in the fabrication of race. To dismiss race under the inhospitable scrutiny of such reason and rationality may very well ignore the implicit nature of the relationship between the rise of rationalism and its role in the construction of race. If we are to trace the plentiful confusion that surrounds the term race, then it seems an obvious point to suggest that any rigorous interrogation might begin at the beginning, with the origin of the term.[1]

Race is not always where we think it may be. Ironically, race is a product of rationalism. The Enlightenment fabricated race, but the simple equation of cause and effect is unhelpful and reductive. Certainly, the Enlightenment shaped race into a form readily recognizable in the modern experience of the concept. Race as a fledgling concept, however, existed before the Enlightenment; at least the theorists who helped solidify the term during the Enlightenment were consistently of this disposition. For this reason, the Greeks tend to get a great deal of attention when commentators consider the origin of race. Certainly, the odd exoticism of some Greek writing resonates with bigotry. Moreover, the societal networks described by several key philosophers, Plato and Aristotle in particular, appear to the modern eye to be radically charged with the potential for racist thought. Although not entirely compatible with one another, the ideal social construct of both Plato and Aristotle would appear to represent much of what is deplorable about the more recent history of the West's encounter with foreign people. But this is an awkward proposition, and one that is steeped in revisionist history that inappropriately applies modern convention to the past.

A counterclaim to this line of reasoning suggests that the Greek antagonism between political and barbaric people precluded the need for race. Instead, the Greeks are credited only with creating the discursive tools that will later fabricate race. This line of criticism, which supposes Greeks did not have a concept of race, focuses critical attention on the nature of the Greek interaction with the exterior world. The Greeks, it seems, deduced that the world can be organized and classified according to natural types, a technique which both Plato and Aristotle apply to the social world. The result of this application speculates the existence of natural slaves, those incapable of self-government and best employed as beasts of burden for their contribution to the greater good of the community. To the modern mind, it is hardly surprising that slavery reeks of the racist practices that stem from the early European encounter with West Africa and the Americas. But the one need not necessitate the other. For their part, the Greeks never seem to have fully employed the tools of their own making. This is an odd conundrum for those who would discuss the origins of racial thought, as race seems oddly present, and yet not entirely so, in the precursor to much of Western thought and civilization. This conundrum, therefore, exemplifies what we will call a false origin.

Race has more than one false origin. The word race existed in European languages for several hundred years before the Enlightenment, and within this time period enjoyed a wildly variable connotative span. Within that span, the word race did not have the connotation most familiar to the one it offers today. Instead, race could signify an unstable scope of ideas from the wake of a boat, to competition, to (most pertinently) national or noble lineage. Thus, race enters Western languages with a meaning only tangentially related to what it eventually becomes. Add to this a discursive landscape that allows for only biblical accounts of human origin, and we can readily see an opportunity for a broad spectrum of imminent confusion. Because of these facts, there are more than a few moments when one can observe the concept of race becoming muddled in competing registers that mark color, foreignness, religion, nobility, and national allegiance whereby an individual's race (lineage) could preclude his/her foreignness or complexion in terms of the primary signifier of identity. One such example is William Shakespeare's *Othello*. Thus, as late as the Elizabethan period, we can read a second false origin in literal racial origins because the word race is present while the concept of "race" is not, or at least not entirely.

The construction of race required a community effort. The racial account of human variety seems almost inevitable when considered next to the number of individuals who played some role in its fabrication. The Enlightenment project of natural philosophy signals a more genuine construction of racial thought than the examples cited above, but it may not necessarily represent malice so much as cultural arrogance. As suggested earlier, many commentators have taken the coincidence of this project and the explosion of slavery and colonial conquest as a sign that the two concepts are explicitly united and that race was developed as a justification for the wholesale subjugation of Africa and the Americas. The two incidents obviously do assist one another in a multitude of ways, but to fabricate a simple cause and effect relationship offers little in terms of substance or understanding. Certainly, race helped slave traders deny the humanity of their cargo. But the matter is not quite so simple and to presuppose malevolence overlooks the complexity of Enlightenment theorists' view of the natural world. Moreover, as Robert Bernasconi points out, the fact that many instrumental theorists in the construction of race resided "in Germany rather than in Britain or America suggests that it was not specifically the interests of the slaveowners that led to its introduction, but rather . . . an interest in classification and above all the attempt to provide a theoretical defense of monogenesis" (Bernasconi: 2001, 21). Monogenesis held firmly to the notion that humanity descended, as in the biblical account, from a single couple. All variation of humankind, therefore, needed to be accounted for within the discursive barriers raised by the biblical narrative. And so here we have a fledgling scientific discourse united with biblical history in a manner that demands some form of racial explanation to account for the variety of human specimen. Moreover, European experience of the outside world became increasingly one of military dominance and Enlightenment theorists needed to explain the one-sided nature of their expansive conquest. Add these discursive pressures to an advantageous reading of Greek philosophy that suggested strict and unsympathetic socio-cultural hierarchies, and the racialization of the world seems an almost inevitable, if terrible, eventuality.

Race is tenuous and threatening. Moreover, race is threatening because it is tenuous. Throughout the gradual solidification of racial theory in the Enlightenment, race remained a contentious idea. Although we discuss the "solidification" of the idea, we must remember that complete petrifaction never, nor has ever, occurred. The recognition that the categorical demarcation of race may be impermanent and malleable suggested a threat to the presupposed fortitude of European society. The natural conclusion of these European theorists' logic demanded that exposure to lesser peoples ultimately would sow the seeds of European degeneration. Had the precious European society already begun to decline? Or, could the colonial experience work in the other direction? Does exposure to the demanding severity of Africa, Asia, and perhaps America actually increase racial fortitude *via-à-vis* the over-urbanization and corruption of European cities? The answers were not, and are not, willingly apparent, but the cultural and racial fears that operate beneath the questions are readily so.

Race is a biologically unsound concept. After the exhaustive contributions of the Enlightenment theorists, we can perceive the scientific foundation for race theory. It is interesting, then, that almost as soon as scientific discourse was able to apply its rigid methodology to the term, a key figure in the evolution of science summarily argued against its existence. Darwin exhausted considerable effort demonstrating that racial categories simply do not work within the realm of taxonomic division. Thus, what is probably the most persuasive and formidable discourse to emerge from European expansion and conquest systematically refutes the validity of race. Like Frankenstein, however, the construction of the monster race, although dependent on the progress of natural philosophy, does not need the approval of its creator to wretchedly enter the world.

So despite Darwin's efforts to remove special categories for individual varieties of the human subject, a preeminent vein of scientific discourse nevertheless embraced race not only as valid, but also as the primary method for discerning the worth of human variation. The forceful rhetoric of Darwin, therefore, was subsumed under the more popular paranoia that converted race into the central component of human evolution and the history of civilization. Social progress and failure could thus be measured by a conventional wisdom that saw race as potentially both the source of the most civilized advancement and of its terrible decline. Thus, theories of degeneration (in which an individual literally regressed into a more savage state of being) and eugenics (in which Darwin's theory of natural selection was applied to social structures), appropriated scientific observation and solidified the notion that race was a fundamental divisionary device for isolating portions of humanity. And it is these theories of social progression and regression that provide Europe the template for the horrors of the twentieth century.

If race is biologically unsound, then it must be little more than a social construct. Indeed, many theorists would take advantage of this simple fact to significantly diminish or dismiss it. If we can construct an object socially, we may naturally dismantle that same object. There are, of course, those who would take this a step further by insisting wholesale that the substantial object of race cannot be investigated. For these detractors, the advent of a more enlightened scientific community has exposed the inconclusive, contradictory, and empty nature of the term. According to these critics, we cannot treat race as a conceptual entity in and of itself without participating in an abject defiance of reason and rationality. While this is undeniably compelling, it ignores a simple and fundamental political truth: race *does* exist as an object. The distinction here, however, is sound in that it attempts to define between theory and practice. Solomos, for example, notes "two main programmatic conclusions: (a) that 'race' cannot be the object of analysis in itself, since it is a social construction which requires explanation; (b) that the object of analysis should be the process of 'racialization' or 'racial categorization', which takes place within the context of specific economic, political and ideological relations" (Solomos 1986: 99). To suggest that race itself cannot be treated as an object in preference to a treatment of the process of racialization seems to imply an impressive method of research, and to deny any real engagement with any significant degree of lexical (un)certainty. Interestingly, the potential conclusion from this logic asks us to read backward into the manner in which race is fabricated, while, of course, maintaining an essential distance from that process, which we know to be false. The shift that Solomos suggests may be compelling for more reasons than the obvious benefit of dispelling the material object of race. The act of shifting critical attention from the tangible reality of race toward the social pressures that inspired it may be a rewarding venture if our goal is only to illuminate how race can be used as a social tool, for oppression or otherwise. This Marxist response posits race in terms of a class struggle first, and as a social reality only afterwards. Again, this approach is both advantageous and perhaps rather unhelpful. Making race solely a function of class struggle subsumes race within that struggle.

This becomes rather tricky ground, for if we are to abandon the concept of race, which has been so intimately tied to so much dread, we seem obligated to tear a great deal more than the misnamed fourteenth floor from the cloak of rationalism. Once we begin to tug the strings, we are left to wonder what else might unravel. No one should need to debate the difference between the tangible tragedies inflicted through the belief in race and the persistence of, by now, mostly benign linguistic idiosyncrasies. Counterintuitively or otherwise, race is very, very real.

Race and its erstwhile partner racism are phenomenologically real. Put simply, the vast majority of conversation about race deals either with European conceptual origins or the North American abuse of those original racial templates, and particularly the latter. In doing so, however, these discussions often miss a great deal else that is relevant to the future of the term, including its past. If, as Michael Shermer asserts, "Traditional popular racial categories are literally skin deep," one might wonder as to how far exactly we have come since those theoretically simplistic times when such traditions were being established (Shermer 1997: 247). Again, the answer seems to be two-pronged. We have traveled both very far from and no further than where we began, as contemporary ideas about race seem often to remain simply skin deep. And the superficial nature of early and recent race theory has not stopped race from influencing human interaction. As suggested above, the history of the practical application of race has consistently had little to do with either the social construction or biological invalidity of the concept. Attempts to supersede race often neglect the very real experience of what has become the marked racial subject. This is problematic because it helps silence the legitimacy of an individual at the precise moment that her/his legitimacy has finally been allowed a voice. To argue that race is a construct and that it works only in terms of the imagined, deliberately distracting, struggle within the proletariat places class over race at the precise moment that racially marked individuals have gained the ability to speak for themselves. In other words, denying the existence of race also raises the political barrier. A recent commentator has suggested that "The main task facing racial theory today, in fact, is no longer to critique the seemingly 'natural' or 'commonsense' concept of race – although that effort has not by any means been entirely accomplished. Rather, the central task is to focus attention on the *continuing significance and changing meaning of race*" (Winant 2000: 181–182). To this we might add the changing "experience" of race.

If we consider race as a phenomenon that is experienced and also normalized, we must also consider the potential for response allowed to the racialized subject. Here it is essential that we move our discursive perspective away from those that have helped create and deny race, toward the subject that has been marked by race. Predominantly since the turn of the twentieth century there have been a growing number of critics and philosophers who have worked to re-orientate the cultural exchange between dominant and subjugated parts of the globe. In Africa, Aimé Césaire and the Negritude movement worked toward an aesthetic of blackness in an attempt to unite the experience of the black and vocal subject in an oppressive and silencing white social dynamic. Likewise, Franz Fanon helped investigate the material and psychological interdependency in the formation of an empire of white and black binary positions, an opposition that is mustered for the psychological oppression of the black mind. To this end, Edward Said has played an integral role in the formation of a postcolonial response that reacts to the troubled exchange between East and West. This perspective, known as Orientalism, helps move racial discourse away from the black/white binary systems that have come to dominate the critical response to imperialism, particularly in the United States. Instead, Said considers the significance of race under the more broad notions of dominant discourse and the "others" that it creates. The culmination of these responses has been a radical revaluation of Western social preeminence.

As one might expect from evaluation that emerges from the visual, for many of these original observers the question was primarily an aesthetic one. For this reason, it is not uncommon to encounter an evaluation of racial difference that orientates beauty with, expectedly, the observer's race, and ugliness with all the others, albeit to varying degrees. With the advent of Said's Orientalism, mentioned above, we can also see the way in which this dynamic can be reversed between the sexes so that opposite race/sex can become the site of colonial desire at the same moment that same race/sex individuals are denigrated and fixed as vulgar. This dynamic, along with fears of degeneration and supposed purity, has led the racial discourse of the United States to become fixated on the potential for miscegenation.

Race is a catastrophe in the United States. From the first grand encounter between the Americas and Europe, the ability to distinguish the relative varieties of humankind has been something of an obsession. From the Spanish conquests and the eradication of the Native Americans to the prevalence of slavery in the United States, this encounter has been one of abject failure. Now, in the United States, the perpetuation of this failure has taken on a variety of troubling new guises. Indeed, the United States may represent the most voracious and expansive modern commentator on race, a fact that is mostly disconcerting.

The history of the United States is marked with racial opportunism and counterintuition. Beginning with the three-fifths compromise (see Chapter 5) through to the 2000 census, devising official methods of racial identification has been somewhat of an American obsession. While original census forms considered only three potential responses for the question of race, the 2000 census has reached absurd proportions owing to an unintelligible conflation of race and its cousin ethnicity. Between these two dates, race has continued, often forcefully, to mix and muddle in the United States, as in the rape of slave women, and despite attempts to articulate an aesthetics of race, as in the Harlem Renaissance. Race, therefore, is both polarized in American discourse and radically undermined in its stability.

The division between what we have come to accept with our modern sensibilities (which suggests that the concept of race is a cultural construction and therefore significantly empty) and the actual practice of race as experienced in modern subjectivity, politically or otherwise, opens before our feet like a profound chasm. On the one hand, there is the common-sense nature of the term. It makes some social sense and, besides, we know it when we see it. On the other hand, race does not enjoy a scientific status, which means that it is not quantifiable in terms of our most rigid discourse. Race is an American fixation, however, and perhaps nowhere else is race quite so phenomenological and real. Again, this merely serves to announce a chasm between theory and practice. As Kwame Anthony Appiah suggests, "much of what is said about races nowadays in American social life, while literally false if understood as being about biological races, can be interpreted as reporting truths about social groups" (Appiah 1995: 285). The same might be said were we to reverse the components of Appiah's formulation and it is precisely this slippery ambiguity that allows the term to consistently reappear attached to multiple guises.

Perhaps, then, the most advantageous point at which to examine race is the crossroads between theory and practice. Here we find the most redeeming aspect of the American experience of race in the form of two companion theoretical movements, Critical Race Theory and White Studies. It has often been intuitively and explicitly suggested that whiteness is the blank canvas upon which all other races add color. In the United States, this has largely meant the polarization of a black/white binary with little room for genuine engagement with "other" others. Critical Race Theory recognizes the need to address the legacy of this binary construction, and the reductive nature of the structure, but helps to mend that limitation of racial discourse in America through an inclusive program. Although White Studies needs to be woven into the more ambitious Critical Race Theory its initial mission, which is to mark whiteness in the same manner that other races are marked, temporarily precludes its participation in Critical Race Theory. The value of Critical Race Theory, therefore, lies in its ability to perform this kind of inclusiveness not by emphasizing a specific racial category, but by focusing on the limits and oppressive potential of legislative discourse.

By situating the point of contention between the law and its creators and subjects, Critical Race Theory returns our debate very nearly to the site of our first false origin, the point of intersection between the political and the individual. Critical Race Theory, however, does not eradicate race by doing so. Instead, theory and practice are treated as equal counterparts and thus the movement is not so far removed from either official discourses or popular sites of resistance. Politics does not precede race, but the success of the movement partially lies in its ability to speculate a day when this might be the case.

Race exists in literature. There may appear to be a fixation with liminal or borderline characters in this volume, and there are several equally compelling reasons for this fact. (1), as suggested above, race is a social construct and thus the supposed barriers that might mark racial absolutes do not, in practice, exist. (2), literature is often the place where we test our social constructs. (3), by testing the value of our social constructs in literature we betray our hopes and fears. Narratives are both the substance of our culture and the place where the borders of that culture can be drawn. For this reason, this volume traces significant texts from across the historical timeframe discussed: from the travel writing of Sir John Mandeville, Shakespeare's *Othello*,

Defoe's *Robinson Crusoe*, Shelley's *Frankenstein*, Kipling's short stories, Conrad's *Heart of Darkness*, Achebe and Cheikh Hamidou Kane's response, Jean Toomer's *Cane*, to Nella Larsen's *Passing*. In this volume, these texts are treated next to others that are not explicitly fiction in order to demonstrate and test the value of the social mores and concepts we have created. Thus, as suggested in the discussion of *Robinson Crusoe* in Chapter 2, reading a character like Xury next to the Enlightenment philosophers who diligently outlined a scientific basis for race, tests the discursive boundaries of that conceptualization because he comprises a variety of racial characteristics in varying social circumstances. Xury, in other words, acts as the literary test that demonstrates the sliding contextual scale of social, cultural, and racial registers. He demonstrates the method of construction.

To trace these formative discourses and their manifestations in literature from race as political civility, race as origin, race as generation, race as inheritance, race as family, race as biblical heritage, race as nation, race as biology, to race as the simple mark of skin color, and then back to race as some aspect of an ambiguous, even tautological, ethnicity, is to negotiate (hopefully) the boundary between a theoretical disposition and a practical application of the term. The mistake that this volume attempts to mend, therefore, is the damaging notion that absolutes exist in our ideological landscape, and that race is not, as Ivan Hannaford suggests, a "historyless given" (Hannaford 1996: 6). Instead, this volume reads race as it undermines its own discursive legitimacy over the course of several dramatic strands of its evolution.

Note

1. Edward Said describes the difference between the terms "origin" and "beginning" as the difference between passive and active methods of describing creative impulses. Said states, "thus 'X *is the origin of* Y,' while 'The beginning of A *leads to* B'" (Said 1985: 6). Said suggests, therefore, that beginning denotes a causal mechanism with will or intent, while origin implies a link that is imprecise. The difference is significant in this discussion because of the muddled origin/beginning of racial thought. Put simply, Enlightenment (and many subsequent) theorists felt that race originated with the Greek philosophers and, at the same time, that their own efforts represented its beginning. Both origin and beginning will be employed to signify this confusion.

1 False Origins: The Greeks, Methodology, Etymology, and Shakespeare

> One of the great problems of modern-day race relations is that few people have the slightest idea of the origin of the ideas and concepts they employ with such profligacy. (Hannaford 1996: 15)

> Travelers with closed minds can tell us little except about themselves. (Achebe 1989: 16)

Theory, practice, and origins

And now, let us look closely at the original object/subject of race itself. A compelling point of departure for such an endeavor, as one might expect, is the beginning. And indeed, there are at least two distinct (although imprecise) beginnings that deserve our attention. We must observe not only the conditions within Western cultures (European in particular) that cultivated a necessity for the word, but also the word's practical entry into Western languages. The aim of this chapter, therefore, is to question the context and history of both the fundamental dispositions that cultivate the need for the word's existence, and the word in its earliest manifestations.[1] The isolation of two basic elements, the word as a material object that has passed through Western languages (most pertinently for this discussion, English) and its compositional principles, is central to treating the twofold archeology of race's history, conceptually and pragmatically. The goal here is to isolate the theoretical framework of race, and to trace its practical application. (In stating this ambition, we must also fully recognize the mythical nature of origin. Because isolating origins is an act of recovery, they must always/already be speculative or even partially fictional.) To isolate the framework (to draw the boundaries of the field, as Pierre Bourdieu might venture), is also to define the criteria for racialized thought and the principles that would allow the concept to be applied in the political world.

This is, however, an inverse proposition, as we are defining race largely through the observation of where it is not yet developed, or at least not developed with proficiency. Essentially, we are looking for the concept before it had a label. Our definition also questions the relationship between racial thought and its material practice. This is not to say that material practice signifies solely tangible examples of oppression, or dehumanizing behavior. It is not viable to suggest that we may locate the original racialized community, for example, if we simply locate the first community of slave owners. Although slavery represents a system of exploitation and oppression based implicitly on one's standing as a human agent and the applied (real) manifestation of the oppression that accompanies a denial of that humanity, we must note that the existence of a system of oppression does not, *per se*, denote the existence of racial thought. Generally speaking, we know race when we see it. But here, we are also trying to locate race by observing where it is not, or where it exists only partially and by observing the transition of those elements into a genuinely tenable construction.

It seems pertinent to begin with an investigation of the more distinctly ideological, structural foundations of racial thought and work toward the more conventional, etymological history of the word itself. Of course, the relative merits and detractions of an attempt to actually isolate these two complementary components must be acknowledged. The effort alone reveals the distinction between theory and practice, the pitfalls of reading any history, and the impossibility of side-stepping the critical limitations of our own temporal location, i.e., the danger implicit in not recognizing that we are irretrievably composed by our limitations. The value of this approach lies, therefore, in the admission that we will never completely know the history of race, and in the realization that we are at least capable of outlining inherited false starts, misreadings, and misappropriations, of renegotiating those readings, and of re-appropriating a distinct historical perspective from this performance. As one might imagine, already, we are in something of a conundrum.

The original conundrum stems, at least in part, from the manner in

which race evolved from an abstraction to a pragmatically fixed, institutional piece of Western cultural exchange. This transformation
began with a misreading of ancient ideological and philosophical
musings on rational thought and the individual's responsibility within
the political world. This misreading involves, primarily, seventeenth
and eighteenth-century theorists who borrow the basic tenets and
authority of the ancient Greeks in order to shore up the radical expansion of racialized thought, which comfortably (although not necessarily intimately) coincides with the expansion of Western imperial
influence and domination. This is our original false start. Race seems
to stem from the Greeks because the men who (actually) created and
disseminated race believed that it did. Their authority to explicate
racial theory resided in their just and appropriate interpretation of it.
However, several significant theorists have recently begun to reread
the Greeks and, in so doing, have redefined the criteria that denote
racial thought. This redefinition, as suggested earlier, relies heavily on
noting the combination of the theoretical and practical applications
of race.

Now, conventional wisdom suggests, almost unequivocally, that
race is a European construction. Likewise, this construction has been
vehemently tied to several moments of European progress: the rise of
rationalism, the Enlightenment, and the advent of imperialism and
industrialization. Indeed, a few critics have gone so far as to suggest
that Western society is fundamentally a racial society and is therefore
explicitly responsible for the term and its subsequent spread across
the globe. The rather odd significance of this gesture, however, lies in
the implicit insistence that race is a relatively recent (historically
speaking) construction. To this end, scholars have repeatedly argued
over the precise moment that the word race appears in the Western
lexicon. Ivan Hannaford broadly suggests that "Between the expulsion of the Jews and Moors from Spain and the landing of the first
Negro in the North American colonies in 1619, the word 'race' entered
Western languages" (1996: 147). More directly, Michael Banton
heralds the exact moment of the word's entry into our specific
lexicon, stating, "the word race entered the English language in 1508
in the poem *The Dance of the Sevin Deidly Sins* by the Scotsman,
William Dunbar" (1987: 1). Although the placement of precise dates is
often sketchy, mythological work at best, Hannaford and Banton's
two basic assertions seem appropriate. The specificity of the word
race entered Western languages somewhere in the sixteenth century.

Moreover, the denotative, connotative scope of the word relates only distantly to the word as we currently understand it. Rather, race could denote a trove of disparate ideas, some more relevant than others, and some more persistent than others. One need merely consider the second most common use of the word race, as a contest (e.g., horse race), to note the malleability of the term. Indeed, upon its entrance into English, race could signify "running, mathematical or astrological lines, millstreams, ships' wakes, marks, and courses," as well as "being of good, noble, and pure lineage" (Hannaford 1996: 147). More than merely the broad scope of referents, however, a key component in understanding the movement of race from there to here is the malleability allowed in being of good, noble, and pure lineage. Here, the term waited, sufficiently readied and pliant, for the time in which it might assume its present shape.

What is odd and somewhat disconcerting in Hannaford and Banton's accounts, however, is the necessary repetition of the word "entered" to describe the emergence of the term. Without deliberately misappropriating either Hannaford or Banton's metaphor, one might easily wonder from where the word entered, for if the word race enters Western languages from this specific point, a logical presumption demands that it entered from somewhere. To deny this would suggest a bizarre spontaneous origin (tellingly, an origin that is not claimed by those who helped the term gain much of its momentum in Western languages), and a seemingly random occurrence. At first glance this may appear as meaningless hairsplitting, for there seems little point in contending that race is a Western construction, given the common-sensical critical acceptance of the premise. Perhaps one of the most confounded aspects of this paradox stems directly from this confu-sion. Race is either a seventeenth or eighteenth-century fabrication developed in response to profoundly disparate cultural contact, or it was inherited from earlier conventions of cultural exchange. As ever, the most obvious response to this conundrum is the most difficult to develop and substantiate. Put simply, the word race, as it most closely resembles our contemporary conceptualization, *did* originate some-where across the seventeenth or eighteenth-century. This fabrication, however, relied heavily on a misrepresentation and misappropriation of earlier cultural theoreticians, primarily the Greeks. It has, however, been convincingly argued that the Greeks entertained no notion of race, as we shall investigate at greater length in a moment. And indeed, many early racial theorists used the isolation of these apparently exterior/causal elements to legitimize their own construction of race. The focal point of this debate, therefore, resides outside of the Greeks, but also claims to locate the Greeks as its foundation and center. Here we can see how highly political such a contest must be.

There is no lack of theories suggesting alternative sources for the original, ancient fabrication of racial thought. As suggested, the quest for isolating origin remains something of an indistinct notion for both the intellectual conditions that inspire it, and, most importantly, for the contemporary material consequences. These consequences, however, often trace a keenly sharp political edge. It is with this political single-mindedness that the ultimate and often insidious side to the debate over origin muddles the genuine questioning of the origin of race with dubious concentration on accountability. As ever, and as suggested by the first epigraph of this chapter, (re)reading history is always a political act, but one with varied levels of jaded cynicism. And there is no shortage of potential resources for those who would trace the lineage of race to founts outside the borders of Western thought. Although receding in number and prominence, there is a significant body of scholarship that has consistently claimed "to find the idea of race 5,000 years ago, in India, and among the early Chinese, Egyptians, and Jews" (Boxill 2001: 10). Such research, valid and insightful, can also be quite disarming, or at least distracting to those who hold fast to a culpability that is purely Western. For those uneasy with the suggestion, it seems a purely academic exercise (excuse the expression) to postulate whether the Incas conceived racial differentiation independently of the European encounter when it remains rather improbable, quite simply, that we could ever trace any material consequences of that disposition. The matter becomes purely conceptual and significantly removed from the pragmatic. And here is the rub. An integral part of our working definition of racial thought is that it must accompany practice. The distinctly pragmatic dimension to the advent of racial research leaves racial theorists out in the political cold. As Glenn Jordan and Chris Weedon clearly state, the concept of race, and more importantly racism, "is a cultural politics, producing its effects in the conjoined spaces of culture, power and subjectivity" (Jordan and Weedon 1995: 161). Because race embodies this direct and significant political dimension, the concept must be married to pragmatic, active, tangible, bodies of information. To put it simply, if we are to find race in earlier cultures, we must find it active in early cultures, or we have not found it at all. Moreover, it is not enough simply to suggest that ancient Indians were capable of noting that some people were of a different colored skin. This alone does not constitute race. The simple, practical policies of base social exclusion do not constitute race either, even when such practices closely resemble a bigotry we have since experienced racially. To clarify, perhaps contentiously, while the ownership of a slave certainly makes an individual socially parasitic, the practice itself does not intuit racism, *per se*. To condemn all exclusionary social policy as racially motivated, or as evidence of the practice of racial ideology, threatens to cheapen the idea through grossly expansive definition, and may very well miss the more significant opportunity to criticize racial *practice*. All cultures, and many interactions that we would not even deem worthy of the title cultural, have mechanisms that protect the familiar and resent the exterior. While this practice may resemble it, this is not racism, pure and simple. To suggest otherwise is to condemn racialized thought to each and every living human being as fundamental as social organization and familial structures. This may explain why evidence of other racialized cultures is so easy to find elsewhere, but this ultimately confuses and distorts the definition of race. We will encounter this confusion again in a moment with the more intrinsically conceptual and concretely practical misreading of racial origin and the Greek arts of philosophy and politics.

Before moving forward, it must be noted that what can be so disarming in such a debate is the tremendous, but often spurious, political relevance in arguing the origins of racial thinking. When performing such a dramatic rereading, we must also consider what is at stake today in denying or maintaining the theoretical status quo. It would be rather naive to suggest that were we to attribute the concept of race to, say, the ancient people of India, that there would be little, if any, impact on its current postcolonial position. India's position in the world today is a result of its history as the *oppressed* and not the oppressor, but to attribute this oppressive mechanism to its ancestors would have a profound effect on our ability to sympathize with its political standing today. The somewhat cynical effort in such thought lies in either shifting entirely, or at least diluting, the perceived responsibility of an almost exclusively traditional Western social theory. An attempt to relinquish its own culpability explicitly demonstrates the obvious stake that the West now has in the absolution of its social conscience. Nonsensical or otherwise, for better or for worse, there is a great deal on the line in playing out the political blame-game and isolating those responsible. When placed under this light, the rhetorical finger-pointing, however, fails in its ability to articulate what exactly these cultures did with the concept of race. As Imtiaz Habib states, "Even if . . . racial formations may be said to be anterior to early modern European colonialism, since they can be detectable in earlier historical epistemes such as the classical and the medieval periods . . . it is in the potency they acquire in the latter moment that gives them their greatest, and from the standpoint of our own temporal location, their most significant discursive visibility" (2000: 3). And so, again, we point away from antiquity and toward the advent of European progress to locate "racial formations" because of the practical significance of that period. To discuss race before then seems pointless as it held no explicit ideological currency, either culturally or politically, until this point in any other culture. However, we still have not resolved either the original conundrum or the "entered" puzzle and, in continuing the pursuit, we approach the most impressive false start yet. The issues here are how we define racial thought and how those who created it justified doing so.

The Greeks: Plato and Aristotle

Now, a more grounded pitch for discussion in the creation of a racial revelation revolves around the role of the ancient Greeks, those forefathers of Western thought. At least part of what makes this arena so enticing is that, if sufficiently decisive, the scholar may potentially resolve the original, and origin-ary, conundrum posed at the outset of this chapter. If we attribute the origin of racial thought to the Greeks, then we have simultaneously isolated the disposition necessary to create the need for the term, and potentially the object of race itself. In other words, by locating race in ancient Greece, the scholar is able to marry the ideological origin to a relatively more precise etymological one. In this line of thinking, one need not bother with the specifics of how, where, or from whom the term race entered Western languages in the sixteenth century, because the conditions necessary for the entry (or perhaps re-entry) lay dormant in the unconscious of Western thought, full stop. This dormancy becomes merely an ideological memory repressed through the bad old days of the Dark Ages, waiting patiently to re-emerge in the enlightened European man.

Ivan Hannaford must be credited for his grand rereading of Greco-

Roman thought and his historicizing of racial thought in the West. His work has gone to exhaustive lengths to challenge the inherited account of the Greek role in race. Simply, the line of thought suggests that Europeans used reason to create race and the Greeks gave us the impetus to value reason. Race, therefore, is the always/already child of Hellenic influence on Western civilization. In going beyond the general resistance to traditional interpretation, Hannaford more directly confronts the antagonism between Greek civics and barbarism. Indeed, Hannaford builds fundamentally upon Foucault's assertion in *The History of Sexuality*, that "it is unhistorical to consider that the antipathy between Greek and barbarian presupposes a certain racial resentment" (Hannaford 1996: 41). Instead, Hannaford quite usefully insists that "Antiquity was, in fact, riven by slavery and barbarism – but not by race, and for that reason the classical idea of politics still has something to say in our time" (Hannaford 1996: 9). Can we read the Greeks on their own terms? The mental maps that we apply to the world, knowingly or otherwise, are problematic because of our relative inability to accommodate other maps, independently or in hindsight, without (mis)appropriation.

There is, admittedly, some fertile pasture from which we might gather the racist dispositions of several key Greek theorists. A great majority of Greek philosophers and scribes often entertain a strong, near-oppressive, cultural arrogance that undoubtedly grates on our current, postcolonial sensibilities. In particular, there are moments where it seems effortless to attribute racist thought to a chain of Greek philosophers linked to Plato and Aristotle, perhaps two of the most significant figures in Greek philosophy. Among others, however, Hesiod's *Theogony* and *Works and Days* has been interpreted as containing a division of the world into races, Herodotus' *Histories* was regarded by "the great historian Barthold Georg Niebhur, as the precursor of modern ethnography," while Hippocrates' *Airs, Waters, and Places*, was manipulated by Johann Gottfried von Herder and Alexander von Humboldt as "proof of their newly invented cultural and climatic theories of existence" (Hannaford 1996: 20). The sum of these parts would seem to suggest, irrevocably, that the Greeks were fundamentally a society imbued with race as an integral part of their cultural exchange.

The interpretation of Hesiod that situates his work as racially moti-vated, however, relies on a substantial variety of misinterpretations, particularly on a translation of the word "*genos*" as synonymous with race rather than genealogy, and an awkward ability to ignore the simple notion that the Greeks never presumed themselves a people "possessed of distinctive characteristics and qualities – physical, intellectual and cultural – that mark them as superior" (Hannaford 1996: 22, 25). Instead, all individuals, Greek or otherwise, participate in the rather desperate state of the human condition, whereupon the Greeks salvage themselves through their subsequent participation in a well-legislated and ordered body politic. As such, Herodotus' focus on the litany of differences to be found in the people of the world would seem to explicitly add physiology to the puzzle to generate race. The fascination for Herodotus resides in the disparity of human language, custom, and appearance, similar to our current catch-all term ethnicity, which he works diligently to reconcile. Herodotus' interest here lies, in part, with the reasonable division of relative value systems (Long 1999: 301). Moreover, Herodotus was by no means entirely convinced of the ultimate superiority of the Greeks as an historical constant. The relativism found in Herodotus keenly attributes much of what may be applauded in Greek authority to the Egyptians, who are a shining example of political fortitude and order. Societal success finds, for Herodotus, "those who, whatever their origin, have risen above the vagaries and vicissitudes of the natural world and have demonstrated a judgment able to turn events to human advantage" (Hannaford 1996: 28). Again, an opportunity to transform Greek antagonism toward the foreign and unfamiliar fails to affirm distinct racial bias, *per se*.

Although still contentious, Hannaford's position has gained considerable ground among prominent scholars. Kwame Anthony Appiah appears to be in some agreement with Hannaford, noting that among the ancient Greeks, while there was a general understanding that "the black Ethiopians to the south and the blonde Scythians to the north were inferior to the Hellenes, there was no general assumption that this inferiority was incorrigible" (Appiah 1995: 275). The distinction here is significant. To this statement Hannaford adds, "What matters most for the Greek is not whether people are Ethiopian or Scythian, Greek or barbarian, but whether the moral standards set in the Hesiodic myth about the political idea – the right conduct of human affairs and the proper ordering of the universe – are met or not" (Hannaford 1996: 26). When posited against the other, therefore, Greek culture seems to embody arrogance only in as much as it embodies the values of political organization and order. While we may find such arrogance chafing to contemporary sensibilities, it does not necessitate any distinct racial formulation because the foreign is neither inferior – nor, we must not forget – superior, as such. The exterior becomes such based only on its inability to participate in an ordered political state, a notion that simply does not acknowledge race.

In Plato, however, we witness a rather dramatic change in focus for those who would attribute racial awakening to the Greeks. Thus far, we have operated within the intuitive understanding that the location of, and inspiration for, racial theory should emanate from a base, bigoted encounter with other cultures and physiological types. As opposed to cultural exchange outside of the Greek body politic, however, Plato's writing often grates on contemporary nerves because of the social interaction he posits *within* the Greek social hierarchical structure. Plato remains so offensively disconcerting to many contemporary commentators primarily because he is "frankly and unapologetically inegalitarian" (Annas 1981: 172). His division of an ideal society into three distinct classes (Guardians, Auxiliaries, and producers) resembles any reasonable observation of a class system, with the exception that Plato ascribes dramatic rights and responsibilities to each. And it is within these rights and responsibilities that we can see the gross division of power allowed in Platonic thought. This aspect of Plato's philosophic discourse has generated a fair amount of attention because of his apparent proposal and endorsement of an ambitiously eugenic society in which the "unfit" are relegated to the extreme exterior of political life while the superior enjoy a protected, governing privilege.

The protection of privilege is not merely for nepotistic sport or for the oppression of the mentally weak. In fact, privilege is not protected at all in terms of a caste system, where one may be born into privilege. In this sense, Plato is refreshingly meritocratic though nonetheless succinct in his division. Instead, he argues, "It's not that we suppose the slave must be ruled to his own detriment . . . but that it's better for all to be ruled by what is divine and prudent, especially when one has it [divine wisdom] as his own within himself; but, if not, set over one from outside, so that insofar as possible all will be alike and friends, piloted by the same thing" (Plato, *Republic* 590 d-590 (hereafter: Plato); Bloom 1968: 273). It is essential that we comprehend the benevolent intentions of the perhaps vulgar inequality to be found here. The lives of the producers are, for the most part, their own, excepting where it comes to the decision-making of state matters. There is an odd and revealing incongruity with contemporary thought concerning the master/slave dynamic that must be noted here. Plato does not position social rank as exclusive of social interaction. Indeed, the passage above insists that the advantage of this arrangement lies in the ability for all to be "alike and friends," with the added benefit of a singular communal direction, the word "friends" in particular supporting the communal "solidarity" of this mandate (Annas 1981: 174). While the slave is not allowed to protest or participate in social decisions, the otherwise impotent producers also own all the property and wealth (Plato 416d–417b, 419e–420a; Bloom 1968: 95–97). Indeed, the "producers" may also be translated as the money-making class, which provides for a potentially less offensive interpretation of Plato's social mission. Here the distinction lies between two different modes of power, one financial (producers), the other political (Guardians). This also suggests something about the nature of supremacy as lamented by commentators such as Annas, for example, who cringes at the inequality of power proposed in Plato's would-be eugenic society (1981: 175–176). Plato's systems, according to Annas, "contain no basis for self-respect" (Annas 1981: 174). A rather ambitious specu-lation, there is some difficulty in its justification. Speculative criticism of Plato's proposed social structure on the basis that it allows no room for the experience of self-respect overlooks Plato's ultimate social mission. Again, we must remember that Plato's proposal works toward the greatest good for all individuals as members of a societal whole that places the political participation in that society above the family, the notion of ethnicity, and the barbaric practices of a cruel and wild exterior world.

If Plato describes a societal ideal, in which all parties are asked to contribute and compromise, then we must measure that society with an eye to the principles that guide the construction. Certainly, the Guardians exercise privilege in their ability to shape the course of society, their removal from base labors, and their access to non-economic avenues of power. The Guardians must earn their position, however, by demonstrating their beneficence and by relinquishing a fair amount of personal, independent value to the greater demands of the state. The Guardians, for example, must live communally and without family. It is here that we find the kernel of Plato's potentially eugenic society. Socrates insists that among the Guardians, "All these women are to belong to all these men in common, and no woman is to live privately with any man. And the children, in their turn, will be in common, and neither will a parent know his offspring, nor a child his parent" (Plato 457d; Bloom 1968: 136). This leads to the passage of Plato's text upon which his dubious reputation as the precursor of racial theory rests. In Book V of the *Republic*, discussion turns to the general treatment of wives and children, the status of the family, and particularly to the consideration of selective breeding. "On the basis of what has been agreed . . . there is a need for the best men to have intercourse as often as possible with the best women, and the reverse for the most ordinary men with the most ordinary women; and the offspring of the former must be reared but not that of the others, if the flock is going to be of the most eminent quality" (Plato 459d–e; Bloom 1968: 138; also Hannaford 1996: 32). Again, this reputation relies on a mixture of Plato's concise division of class and his desire to ensure the continued success of the social structure.

Plato appears to loosen the foundation of his meritocratic society by introducing a hereditary dimension that, when considered along-side basic eugenic tenets, resembles the racially based construction of a master/ruling class. The problem here is which aspect of the society one chooses to prioritize. Plato did not propose that the most sophis-ticated, learned, and benevolent Guardians should procreate to breed out or otherwise remove the subjugated classes. Nor does lineage guarantee position in this society. As Hannaford notes, "The empha-sis is always upon the concept of an entire community based upon an assumption of individual Virtue, which must by definition be inde-pendent of race and sexuality, however much we may want it to be otherwise in our transliteration" (Hannaford 1996: 33). If we alter Hannaford's word "assumption" to "presumption," we find the site for the cynicism of some detractors of Plato's proposed society. As with Annas, speculative interpretation denies the ideal nature of Plato's theory and grounds it in the more suspicious reality of a supposed human nature. Our inability to genuinely trust individual virtue in the face of extreme political power helps negate the possibil-ity of Plato's abstract idea of the most just and rational society in an *a priori* gesture of skepticism.

Ultimately, the tension between the nurture and training of the Guardian class and the breeding of such a class seemingly contradicts itself. Hannaford suggests that "Plato's discussion of breeding of flock at the highest pitch of excellence . . . is only a contribution to the history of the idea of race if we subordinate and trivialize the importance of the love of knowledge in the *Republic*" (Hannaford 1996: 34). Knowledge, in this sense, represents what the Greeks believed to be the unique art of philosophy and its end, the political state. In familiar territory, and as expressed repeatedly by Hannaford, Plato's value system resides distinctly with the interest of the social order, the city. The pronouncement of "extreme evil-doing," or injustice, may stem from the mixing of class responsibility, but only inasmuch as this mixing could do the greatest harm for the city, were, say, the tailor to replace the warrior and vice versa (Plato 434c; Bloom 1968: 113). There is no harm in a shoemaker exchanging responsibilities with a carpenter, for example, because there is no movement in class, nor any threat to the well-being of the state (Plato 434a; Bloom 1968: 112).

While Plato may neglect or comprehensively deny the basic "natural rights" of an individual, he does so within his social structure, a structure that acknowledges and insists upon the relative nature of these rights. Annas is helpful here because she understands that Plato has no word "corresponding to 'rights'" (1981: 176). And yet, she fails to realize that there is no value in either the rights of humanity or the sanctity of human life outside of a system of law that provides and creates the possibility for such value. The creation of laws governing social order and the value of human life is a distinctly human characteristic and the source of our arrogance in regard to the "natural" world, a world which may resemble in its brutal nature Plato's ideal republic. While Annas laments the lack of a programmatic safety net that might forbid certain oppressive behaviors by the Guardian, she ignores the significance of Plato's mission in that it defies savagery or barbarism where there is no interest in law and order. These are precisely the criteria that merit Greek supremacy, according to the Greeks, and will act as the ideal balance to what worries Annas so. Oddly, Annas' cynicism here lies in a simultaneous value of human rights based on the mere condition of being human while also anticipating the worst expression of the human potential based upon an implied understanding and skepticism with regard to human nature. This is an almost identical line of thought that helps marry the *Republic* to an original racial thought process. Plato sidesteps this through his distinct and very clear lauding of philosophy, knowledge, and the state. As Hannaford suggests, "To understand Plato in terms of race is to misunderstand him in all that he says about the state of well-being" (Hannaford 1996: 41). The well-being of the individual exists only within the well-being of the state, which

values a unique philosophical investigation and political order foremost, and these two points must not be divorced in Plato's conceptualization of his ideal society.

In terms of this argument, the condition of the state is particularly
important for Aristotle as it comes into contact with his theory of
natural kinds. For Aristotle, the world is divided into two primary
classes: "those that exist by nature and those that exist for other
reasons" (Barnes 1995: 120). The natural, or natural objects and
phenomenon, embody their own principles of growth, movement,
and rest. The other objects are derivative and contain internal principles not as an embodiment of those principles, but only as an aspect
of the thing(s) from which they are made. In other words "if we
planted a bed we should not expect it to sprout baby beds, – if
anything, it would produce a tree" (Barnes 1995: 120). The idea of
natural essence and the methodology formulated by Aristotle for the
organization and classification of the world around him are the
primary reasons why we must not read race into Aristotle's work, and
also the primary reasons why later commentators felt justified in
doing so. And here we come to a rather perplexing point in our
attempt to define original racial thought and practice.

Aristotle's division of species and genus merits some consideration
as it acts later as a basis for taxonomic organizations and the categorical forms of natural philosophy. In an attempt to work backward
toward original form by contrasting the imperishable and eternal
material with that subject to decay, Aristotle notes in *Parts of Animals*
that "the former are excellent beyond compare and divine, but less
accessible to knowledge" (1.5.644b; Aristotle 1941: 656). The theory is
to gather information about more general and immutable forms, and
therefore the divine, by observing broad similarities in the structure of
the physical world. In so doing, Aristotle directs us to look at functions
first (the pen is made for writing and not the other way around, therefore writing is the function). The point is rather abstract, but Aristotle
is extremely clear on a number of matters, particularly pertaining to
the division of mankind. Aristotle suggests that "we have to describe
the attributes common to all animals, or assemblages, like the class of
Birds, of closely allied groups differentiated by gradation, or to groups
like Man not differentiated into subordinate groups. In the first case
the common attributes may be called analogous, in the second
generic, in the third specific" (1.5.645b; Aristotle 1941: 658). In
Aristotle's formulation, genus is the more abstract category and there-

fore closer to the divine. This is the standard inverted-triangle
formula for the taxonomy of plants and animals. What is significant
here is where exactly Aristotle places the human subject.
Subcategories of genus, or species, because they demonstrate increasingly precise variations from the original form signify a greater
distance from divinity by their own exclusivity. The term species,
therefore, applies to the genus that has subordinate groups that are
both closely allied, in function and appearance. Species, therefore,
denotes the bottom point of the inverse triangle, an irreducible quantity. Although outlining the basic organizing principles that will ultimately become the basis for a quasi-scientific ordering of the races,
Aristotle clearly argues that humankind is a *species* that cannot be
broken down any further into differentiated categories. It is only
through the removal of cause, function, and the essences of Aristotle's
systematic organization that allows Carolus Linnaeus and Friedrich
Blumenbach (each of whom will be discussed in Chapter 2) to manipulate Aristotle's "genus and species," which "were ingeniously
adapted and materialized to work out an arrangement by which the
natural realm could be radically separated from the metaphysical and
reordered into divisions or classes – termed 'races' – within a natural
order of things" (Hannaford 1996: 45). Currently, the presentation of
Aristotle's system seems moot as species will become race in the
hands of later theorists, but when observed in this light, the translation cannot be substantiated. Even more, the term "subordinate"
ominously signals the hierarchy that racial thought will later embody
as priority is placed upon the primary object as being that closest to
divinity. The subsequent movement from genus to species, therefore,
is an imperfect copy of the essential form. Again, an attentive reading
of Aristotle's organizational system must insist that race does not exist
as of yet.

As with Plato, a significantly disconcerting aspect of Aristotle stems
from his treatment of the organization of class and family structures.
However, in his *Politica* (*Politics*), Aristotle arrives at several distinctly
different conclusions as to the system of individual relation to the state.
Aristotle conserves the significance of individual property familial relation, and private residence, which is not found in Plato's supposedly
proto-eugenic society (see Chapter 3 for a more complete discussion of
eugenics). Nevertheless, Aristotle's social order provides little relief for
those who would like to find race in his writing. Hannaford laments
that a number of passages within the *Politica* "have been vigorously

massaged since the sixteenth century by writers to infer a racialist disposition" (Hannaford 1996: 45). The first excerpt here is Aristotle's fortification of the naturalness of politics and the state. Aristotle concludes, "Hence it is evident that the state is a creation of nature, and that man is by nature a political animal. And he who by nature and not by mere accident is without a state is either a bad man or . . . the natural outcast [who] is forthwith a lover of war" (1.2.1252b–1253a; Aristotle 1941: 1129). This statement brings both man and state into the realm of investigation and methodology prepared by the physical sciences.

The next section of Aristotle's *Politica* to receive a fair amount of critical attention deals primarily with the nature of social order within his natural state, and in particular, the position of slavery. Here, again, the difference between Aristotle and Plato is quite telling in that Aristotle insists on the maintenance of individual household as a natural digression from the state. When combined with several passages concerning slavery, however, the imposition of material possession not found in Plato's Guardians appears perhaps more sinister. Aristotle writes:

> A slave is a living possession, and property a number of such instruments; and the servant himself is an instrument which takes precedence of all other instruments . . . he who is by nature not his own but another's man, is by nature a slave (1.4.1253b; Aristotle 1941: 1131); for in all things which form a composite whole and which are made up of parts, whether continuous or discrete, a distinction between the ruling and the subject element comes to light . . . it originates in the constitution of the universe; even in things which have no life there is a ruling principle . . . this principle, of necessity, extends to all mankind . . . It is clear, then, that some men are by nature free, and other slaves, and that for these latter slavery is both expedient and right. (1.5.1255a–1255b; Aristotle 1941: 1132–1133)

To a version of this Hannaford adds, "Ergo, Aristotle recommends slavery, which resembles race, and hence he is a racist" (Hannaford 1996: 45). The sum of these pieces reads that the state is a natural phenomenon, as is the political aspect of humankind. Within the entirety of the natural world, one can find the principle of rule and subjection. This principle must also apply, therefore, to the nature of humankind and the political state. Therefore, slavery is natural and right. Although Hannaford's final exclamation is deeply sardonic, he is not merely being pedantic in his insistence on allowing Aristotle's natural phenomenon to speak more of the naturalness of the political world embodied in the state. There is a distinction between race and slavery that must be recognized outside of the connotation that they have earned in the last 400 years.

Hannaford's rethinking does not rest easy with some recent, although more traditional, interpretations that oddly depend upon a kind of pragmatism as the source for validation. Christian Delacampagne, for one, offers a less than forgiving account of race and racism in ancient Greece, suggesting instead that Aristotle was fully capable of racism on account of his most basic divisionary techniques. Delacampagne argues, "Racism, in the modern sense of the term, does not necessarily begin as soon as one speaks of the physiological superiority, or cultural superiority, of one race or another; it begins when one makes (alleged) cultural superiority directly and mechanically dependent on (alleged) physiological superiority, that is when one derives the cultural characteristics of a given group from its biological characteristics" (Delacampagne 1990: 85). And while Delacampagne acknowledges that the Greeks may not have been "racist in the sense this term has had since 1930," he also undermines this concession with the simple observation that "the only individuals allowed to enjoy the title of citizen . . . were propertied Greek adult males. Failure to meet any one of these four conditions was enough to disqualify one from 'normal' humanity" (Delacampagne 1990: 85). This is to say that even if the Greeks did not express race as we know it (and despite Delacampagne's protestation, particularly as we know it from the 1930s), they embodied it and meant it in much more fundamental ways. One does not, so the logic goes, need to be able to utter the word race in order to be a racist. Part of what remains so disconcerting in Delacampagne's argument is his specific focus on racism, rather than the seemingly more abstract term race. By centering his argument thus, he presumes the existence of race in ancient Greece and moves directly to the observation of its practical application.

As a response to Hannaford's central tenet that politics usurped the opportunity to arrive at racial distinctions, Delacampagne focuses simply on the apparent practice of racial exclusion. And indeed, this gesture fits very well with the proposition mentioned throughout this book. In particular, the opening of this chapter argues that in order to find race, one must find the practice of race. Delacampagne's argument (which is basically if it quacks like a duck, etc.) attempts to side-step Hannaford's political abstraction by contesting the privilege of those who are allowed within the political sphere of influence. In practice, the organization of citizenship, and thereby the opportunity to act politically, means simply that "women and slaves were quite simply *by nature* unqualified to be human" (Delacampagne 1990: 85). The express exclusion of a portion of the population from participation in the utmost social achievement most certainly resembles the direct practice of racial exclusion. Delacampagne, however, harmfully conflates racism with sexism and, while he relies on the exclusionary, oppressive sexual, sexist distinctions made by the Greeks to arrive at the crucial "physiological" component of his argument, he does not explain how such physiology translates into the practice of slavery. In other words, we are left to wonder exactly what aspect of physical composition demands that a slave remain such, as one might expect to find in the racial supposition of slavery. Aristotle, however, always insists that the relationship between master and slave must be mutually beneficial, and even delineates the two common uses of slave and slavery to note that while Greek arrogance might afford a reluctance to call a Greek slave with the same ease that the term is afforded to a barbarian, the reality (nature) of the situation is precisely that (1.6; Aristotle 1941: 1133). Aristotle continues, "Hence, where the relation of master and slave between them is natural they are friends and have a common interest, but where it rests merely on law and force the reverse is true" (1.6; Aristotle 1941: 1134–1135). Aristotle's emphasis on the natural relation of master/slave as ultimately beneficial subsequently helps his apologists avoid the fact that slaves were removed from participating in politics, and thereby denied a fundamental principle of greatness as viewed by the Greeks. With this in mind, Delacampagne's conflation is damaging because it muddles two forms of oppression, isolating a piece from each to reach "racism" in summation: the exclusion of the female subject based on physiology, and the nature of slavery. Furthermore, it denies Aristotle's impressively mobile and uncensored use of the term to describe both the interior and exterior of his cultural preference that Greek slaves, although Greek, are still slaves.

Hannaford consistently and vehemently counters that the issue for the Greeks, and particularly Aristotle, resides in political embodiment, as opposed to anything resembling the physiological. Hannaford reiterates, "It is this absence of a free class practicing politics, and governing in turn, which is the cause of the uniform condition of slavery among the barbarians and the *ethnos*, and it is this feature [that is] the real cause of the Greek feeling of superiority" (Hannaford 1996: 54). Delacampagne's confrontation is strong because it isolates the practice of oppression, but fails in that it muddles oppression with race.

Aristotle's apologists, who would recover him from racialist accounts, find secondary support in Aristotle's displeasure with physiological differentiation. Bernard Boxill agrees, but adds a level of complexity to the distinction made by Hannaford concerning the political man, particularly to the manner in which the Ancients have been interpreted and re-interpreted. In Boxill's ultimate concurrence, he states, "I am persuaded . . . that Aristotle did not have the idea of race," and "Since Aristotle failed to invent the idea of race, although he had the tools and opportunity to do so, we can only suppose that he saw no reason to" (Boxill 2001: 15). Boxill's statement invites an impressive continuation of Hannaford's basic logical negation. If the Greeks possessed the fundamental logic and tools necessary to create race, and indeed, that race was the "natural" conclusion of their logic, we must presume that they had no practical disposition that required racial thinking. The stage was set, but no actors made the call. Instead, Boxill "emphasize[s] the naturalness of the European invention of the idea of race at this point in *their* history. They fancied that reason and experience could be used to solve all puzzles. The Aristotlean theory of natural kinds and essences was available to them and leads naturally to the idea of race when it is used to solve the puzzle of the physical differences between Europeans and Africans" (Boxill 2001: 17, emphasis added). And so, if we are to suggest that the Greeks created the method for gunpowder, we must also concede that they never reached the material manifestation of the substance nor the ensuing, explosive conclusion. This retraces our conversation to the original conundrum. Again, the significance of the word "natural" here remains both a revealing and a compelling stitch in the fabric of this ideological disposition.

So far, we have suggested that the Greeks possessed the tools and the insight but did not do so because they lacked the need and disposition necessary to reach the logical, "natural" conclusion of their own intuition. So the immediate question emerges, what happens between the ancient Greeks and the dates that Banton and Hannaford suggest for the "entry" of race into Western languages? What creates the ideological disposition that, in turn, necessitates the construction of racial thinking? While we have not entirely uncovered the actual origin of race, we have at least set the stage for the concept's pre-development. As we will see in Chapter 2, in an odd reversal of Hannaford and Banton's proposal, commentators attempt to (re)define racial thought using the fertile soil of history to fabricate legitimacy. In essence, a denial of historicism concurrently allows for the misunderstanding of the term and its direct engagement. This manipulation of historical authority legitimates those who would fabricate race. Indeed, as we shall see below, there is a strong tradition of dependence and appropriation of authority in the early history of the European encounter with its exterior.

Methodology and travel writing

At this juncture, it is quite tempting to jump directly to the seventeenth and eighteenth-century Enlightenment theorists who have received so much attention, yet so far have been relegated to the margins of this chapter. It is during this period that race is galvanized in the fires of rationalism, science, and colonialism, until it reaches a form readily recognizable today. In an argument that, at times, closely resembles this one, Robert Bernasconi feels that the early instances of what might resemble racial thought "were not sustained by a scientific concept of race," and are not, therefore, really examples of racial thinking until we arrive at the eighteenth century (Bernasconi 2001: 11). The activities in and of fifteenth and sixteenth-century Spain (the expulsion of the Jews, the conquest of the Americas, and the systematic denial of Native American humanity) may all resemble racial thinking, but fail to meet Bernasconi's criteria on account of that fundamental scientific principle. There is, however, another significant moment of transition that must be noted before moving to the advent of the Enlightenment. Bernasconi is both accurate in his assessment and missing an integral piece of the puzzle that precludes *scientific* racial thought. Although scientific processes of nominalization fortify and legitimate the practice of race, there is also a transitory period where the material object of the word race enters into Western languages, say English, while the rigor of the concept has not yet been established. This leads to moments of odd muddling of cultural exchange that both demonstrates the initial malleability of the term race and sets the stage for what it will become. In a rather unconventional twist, the literal denotative space of the word, particularly as it refers to the lineage of kings, interrupts the base dehumanization of others. Quite the opposite, race in this sense more directly refers to a type of purity or direct descent from original, biblical personalities. Race, therefore, can be considered a benign, nepotistic mixture of religious and genealogical inheritance that speaks more to the class structure of the time than what we could consider race. Moreover, note the manner in which race has already superseded species in the hierarchical appropriation of Aristotle's system. As we shall see, these conflicting impulses, most compactly embodied in religion, pre-science, nation, physical difference, and nobility come to a head in the tension of William Shakespeare's *Othello*, in the space between the word's entry into English and the dawning of the Enlightenment.

Moving to the familiar ground of the European (pre)construction of race during the pre-Enlightenment, late medieval period, we must focus on the dilemma proposed by three related movements. First, we must understand the early European encounter as deeply flawed, but not without pathos. It is easy, and ridiculously arrogant, to scoff at medieval tales of sea-monsters and a flat world when we are so confident of our own maturity and relative sophistication in these matters. Simply peering down our noses at these strangers gives us little in terms of our exchange with this history, and in fact mimics what we often deride in their failure to understand their foreign encounters. We must, therefore, work to remember how genuinely strange the outside world appeared to the medieval mind. Secondly, we must note that making the foreign ridiculous and fantastic might betray bias, but not race. Although the radicalization of the foreign runs an undeniably important course in the construction of race, it is not the totality of that construction, nor does it necessitate the need for the material object of the word race, as we have witnessed above. Thirdly, it is important to note exactly how radically fantastic descriptions of other places and peoples paves the way for later manifestations of dehumanizing bigotry. The authority garnished by repetition and reappearance plays a dramatic role in the perpetuation of a confusing and confused portrayal of the foreign subject. Here, the basic peculiarities described by medieval commentators demonstrate both a penchant for wild exaggeration and a fundamentally limited discursive arena in which to articulate the unfamiliar. They also serve as a template for the discursive scope well beyond medieval commentary.

The Crusades (1095–1291) marked the first grand European

encounter with the exterior world on an intense and extended scale. Far from finding in the heathen a savage or barbarian horde, the Christian Europeans discovered highly organized and much more sophisticated societies in the bloom of their existence. As a result, the Western pilgrim often appeared more like the uncivilized barbarian to a cautious Eastern eye. Saladin noted the "Venetians, the Pisans, and the Genoese all used to come, sometimes as raiders, the voracity of whose harm could not be contained and the fire of whose evil could not be quenched" (quoted in Lewis 2002: 26). Indeed, Europe benefited much more from the technological and civil advances gained through the centuries of conflict. Thus the impact of the Crusades was negligible in the East, a matter of architecture and strongholds, while supremely beneficial to the West. As important to the Western mind, the legacy of the Crusades fabricated a religious antagonism that was to shape the nature of cross-cultural exchange between East and West for a considerable length of time. The experience of the foreign, therefore, was almost exclusively articulated within the parameters of religious discourse as a primary source superseding notions of race. It is within this discourse that Pope Urban II prepared the soil of the first Crusade by appealing to the "race of Franks, race from across the mountains, race chosen and beloved by God" as his instrument against the "race from the Kingdom of the Persians, an accursed race, a race utterly alienated from God" (Peters 1971: 2–3). In the appeal, Urban II conveniently blends a petition to national identity and the Christian brotherhood based finely on the nation-state's relative proximity to divinity. His appeal remains free of racial epitaphs, as such.

The plague beginning in 1347 helped galvanize religious discourse by decimating the European population. A great deal of the intellectual progress gained from the years of conquest vanished underneath the terrors of the Black Death. Throughout the fourteenth and particularly in the fifteenth century, Europeans began to reacquaint themselves with the tremendous multiplicity of specimen offered in the greater world. Travelers, explorers, and pilgrims steadily brought back tales of distant encounters, often embellished with the bizarre, and thus created an urgent need to reconcile the foreign with the familiar. One such account, *The Travels of Sir John Mandeville* (1356) (Mandeville 1983), offers a fabulous relation of encounters across most of the available world. Mandeville's tales remain important for several reasons not only because they are largely indicative of early

European (mis)interpretation of the outside world, but also because they expose fundamental problems in the methodology and discursive resources required to reach appropriate interpretations of it. Moreover, Mandeville remains important because he acts as an archetype of travel writing, which plays a central role in shaping the experience of both subsequent travelers and the anticipated experience of the foreign for those who never leave Europe. The wide popularity of Mandeville's writings must be understood as influential in terms of its academic import and its commercial success. Indeed, by "1400 some version of the book was available in every major European language," while the next hundred years saw its reproduction spread into the more relatively obscure languages (Mandeville 1983: 10, 11). That some 300 manuscripts survive testifies to the endurance of the text and, as such, *The Travels of Sir John Mandeville* must not be underestimated in terms of its influence, direct or indirect, on the shape of the European world.

One of the fundamental peculiarities in reading Mandeville now lies in the rather bizarre and fantastic content of his experience. The uncanny events of his text actually serve to demonstrate a double complexity in the narrative structure, one that is not peculiar to Mandeville. His description, for example, of passing through the Vale Perilous with its distractions and "marvelous things, and gold and silver and precious stones and many other jewels on each side of us," certainly seems unlikely in the literal sense, just as on the isle that rests beyond the valley where "folk are as big in stature as giants of twenty-eight or thirty feet tall," can no longer be taken at face value (Mandeville 1983: 174). Returning to the Vale Perilous directly, the demons that appear to Mandeville and his companion in "different guises" and "the multitude of dead men's bodies that lay" in their path, are not likely to be details that rest comfortably with a modern reader (Mandeville 1983: 174). Presently, the accumulation of these details leads only to skepticism in terms of literal value of the text. But Mandeville's sources for these stories actually describe a great deal about the movement of knowledge in the time. As Giles Milton suggests, "despite all Mandeville's claims, his Travels actually added very little to the world's storehouse of knowledge" (Milton 1996: 214). Rather, Mandeville borrowed heavily from earlier sources (in this case Odoric) and did not hesitate to embellish upon those tales from which he borrowed heavily.

Let us consider first the borrowing of the material. This phenome-

non is not an isolated affair culminating with Mandeville. Indeed, the
acquisition, repetition, and perpetuation of earlier sources demonstrate a fundamental methodology in the transportation of valid information, a methodology that depended upon *auctoritas* (authority).
Interestingly, Mandeville's engagement and appropriation of previous
material has allowed at least one critic to suggest that his "longest
journey was to the nearest library" (Mandeville 1983: 12). Travel
writing clears a strange path for those initial, misguided adventures
into distinct cultural exchange. Secondly, Mandeville's tales highlight
the difficultly in processing information and experience outside the
limitations of known patterns of experience, a phenomenon that is
not foreign to any human subject. Mandeville's adventures, therefore,
highlight the differences between his and our own modern mental
maps. While Odoric might have only been able to articulate a bizarre
phenomenon, perhaps the singing sands of the deserts of Asia, in
terms of the supernatural call and threat of demons, the tale as appropriated comes to life with rich detail and, as importantly, a concise,
sardonic moral message (Mandeville 1983: 20–21). The value of
auctoritas as the written reflection of reality could be appropriated
and manipulated to claim experience, and to reimburse the validity of
this experience, both in terms of its objective reality and, more importantly, its base moral message. Mandeville is not immune to participation in or subsequent appropriation by the precise authoritative
function described above. Mandeville then becomes a source for such
authority and his "memorable fanciful trope" becomes the site of
both a moral and a fantastic truth (Mandeville 1983: 20n). If
Mandeville's primary function is to repeat and reinvigorate several
fundamental misconceptions of the foreign, he also does so with a
distinct moral agenda that resides within the nugget of his tale. In
other words, his writing may not be about the experience of travel at
all, but rather a series of fabulous stories *designed* to critique the
social structure that has produced it. The fabulous stories, therefore,
are exactly that, fables. One need only consider the much more extensive travel and detailed description contained in Marco Polo's writing
to note a worthy counterclaim to Mandeville's narrative. Marco Polo's
tales may have been more factual as well as exotic, but they lack both
the moral purpose and the fabulousness of Mandeville.

Having mentioned the limitations prepared by methods of assimi-
lating information, we must also consider the major framework
within which the European, well beyond Mandeville, was prepared to

encounter the outside world. Thus, suggests Banton, race "was introduced into an intellectual world in which the bible was accepted as
the authority on human affairs" (1987: 1). As suggested in the moral
nature of Mandeville's tale, the bible acted as the fundamental arbiter
with which all information and experience must be reconciled. The
predominance of biblical influence is, not surprisingly, prevalent in
Mandeville's discussion of Genghis Khan. Here, Mandeville highlights
perhaps the primary concern in the reconciliation of the outsider with
scripture by relating a simple narrative history, one which was largely
commonsensical and obvious. Tellingly, this has absolutely nothing
to do with the Great Khan. In the narrative, Mandeville is able to trace
and explain the disparity of human form as well as account for creatures that are perhaps not members of the human species. Mandeville
writes:

> These three sons of Noah divided the earth between them after the
> Flood. Shem, because he was the eldest, chose the best and largest
> part, which is towards the East, and it is called Asia. Ham took Africa,
> and Japhet took Europe. Ham was the richest and mightiest of the
> brothers; and from him came many more descendants than from his
> other brothers. From one of his sons called Chus came Nimrod the
> giant, who was the first king there ever was; and he began to build the
> Tower of Babel. In his time many devils came in the likeness of men
> and lay with the women of his race and begat on them giants and
> other monsters of horrible shape – some without heads, some with
> dog's heads, and many other misshapen and disfigured men.
> (Mandeville 1983: 145)

In this statement, Mandeville summarizes the lineage of the entirety
of humankind. In doing so he highlights the primary, of three, biblical
explanation for what would later become racial variation. The need
for an overarching narrative stemmed predominantly from an inability to account for such dramatic human variation and the common
ancestry of Adam and Eve. The first recounts the tale of Cain and Abel,
where Cain is marked for his transgression against God's will; the
second relates to Noah's descendants as described above; the third
narrative recalls the tower of Babel and the dispersion of language
through the nations. Taken together, these narratives formed the
foundation for thought about human variety for a considerable span
of history. The tension between experience of the foreign and the

need to reconcile this experience with biblical structure thus greatly influences the form and detail of Mandeville's narrative. The acuity of Mandeville's narrative lies in its ability to speak both metaphorically and literally. The odd description of men with dog's heads, for example, was a common metaphor for heathen that becomes literalized in this explanation. Likewise, the narrative provides a simple explanation for the disparity of types within the human form based on geographically isolated parentage.

From the biblical narrative then, the earlier manifestations of the word race more closely resemble lineage than one's physical appearance (as in Pope Urban II's appeal to the race of Franks). Thus, one might mention the Jewish race, based on the perceived progeny of those people, or the race of Abraham under the same pretense. This would not have been necessarily a comment on physical appearance, although perhaps a factor, as much as a comment on the direct lineage from Adam. As importantly, this source allows for only a single pair of human ancestors. To this end, Banton continues, "To understand what happened to the various sections of humanity . . . it was necessary to trace their histories back genealogically through the links in the ancestral chain" (Banton 1987: 1). This will be referred to in Chapter 2 as the monogenesis account of human history and lineage, in which Adam and Eve are the sole parents of humanity whose descendants spread across the globe in several thousand years. God, therefore, becomes the ultimate source of differentiation, and lineage directly reflects an individual's distance from this source. One could refer to nobility, therefore, in terms of a race of kings. The intellectual coup here suggests the noble individual's embodiment of royal exclusivity, protected in the limited exchange of royal blood, and the direct link to divinity. In a familiar, unfortunate, and perhaps forgivable human gesture, the experience of physical difference was explained as the punishment of God meted out among an entire people. So, *physical* difference existed simply as *physical* proof of God's punishment of Cain or a curse on the descendants of Ham.

The growing contact between Europe and the outside world meant simply that the cloistered mindset would be increasingly called upon to deal with the unfamiliar. Indeed, in the sixteenth, seventeenth, and for the greater portion of the eighteenth century, resolution of the foreign with the familiar was theological in composition. As a brief exposition, the tumultuous example of Spain may be of use. Spain's exposure to Christian, Muslim, and Jewish antagonism remains much more intense than the vast majority of other nations in this time period. In these confrontations, there was still a dramatic political restraint on the formation of a genuine race theory despite the increasingly prominent use of the word. In fact, "we quickly forget that the Jews had achieved a significant, honorable, and recognized place in Spain for almost fifteen hundred years and the Moors for eight hundred years that was not determined 'racially,' but in accordance with acknowledged political ideas, practices, and procedures" (Hannaford 1996: 100). Instead, the word race was enlisted as a counterclaim to the Jewish and Muslim histories, and as a demonstration of the direct lineage of Christian European "membership in an ancient and exclusive order of kings and bishops that had its authority and origin in a historical past stretching back to Rome" (Hannaford 1996: 147).

A more striking application of this biblical authority appears in the Spanish encounter with the new world. In the new world, there is a notable lack of counterclaim that might presuppose a civilized and righteous society. There is no history of interaction between these two civilizations, so there is no tradition or even history of cultural exchange that could soften the severity of the collision between the two. For the Europeans, the new world exposes them not only to a new form of physical difference, but also, and more significantly, to the genuinely foreign. The one-sided nature of this contact (unlike similar excursions into the East and during the Crusades) leaves the European to speculate as to the grounds for his surpemacy. The most vivid clash between Europe and the new world is articulated by Bartolomé de las Casas (1474–1566). The debate, grounded in theological considerations, as structured by las Casas revolves around the humanity of the native. If one cannot reconcile the foreign savage with the timetable and account of creation, then there are two potential options at hand. The first incorporates the progeny of Ham to explain God's punishment and banishment of the various descendants of the original narrative. The other, more extreme option incorporates elements of the fantastic to declare that these specimens, if not accounted for in the narrative of the creation of humankind, simply are not genuine members of humanity. This final response proves to be quite beneficial to those interested in the wholesale exploitation and/or removal of those individuals.

Las Casas prepares a counter argument to the theories that negate the humanity of the Native Americans found in the new world. His argument runs that "Because he possessed reason, he should not be deprived of political liberty or title to property by force, and he should not be reduced to slavery because he had the potential to become not only a part of the body of the faithful in Christ but also a citizen of *respublica* [a political man]" (Hannaford 1996: 149). The response to this claim reaches back to Aristotle and finds the Indian to be, by nature, the inferior. The enslavement and exploitation of the Indian becomes simply a matter of due course and is justified by the natural order of the world. The explanation follows that God placed the savages in the new world in order that they might be discovered and exploited for this very purpose by their natural masters, the Spanish. This marks a convenient method of incorporating Aristotle with the biblical narrative without actually contesting the authority of the bible. To this end, las Casas is not in contest. He has no opposition to the strength of the biblical narrative. Rather, his defense of the Indian is predicated upon "the great hope and strong presumption that such unbelievers will be converted and set right against these errors" (las Casas [1552] 1996: 249). The lengthy defense prepared by las Casas remains significant for the manner in which it still appeals to the political agency, rather than racial identity, of its subject, as well as for the religious vigor that acts as the central, undeniable tenet. Thus articulated, las Casas helps solidify the grounds for the debate around the biblical narrative of origin. This debate is active well into the Enlightenment and helps to generate the ideological tension that later establishes the need for race, a need that counterintuitively operates in favor of the biblical narrative and against slavery. This will be covered in greater detail in Chapter 2.

Admittedly, we have yet to isolate within these examples a direct definition of the word race. The previous section instead outlines the development of racial thought and attempts to establish the limited, limiting methodology available to the European. As we move forward in time and away from the European continent, we begin to trace the material object of the word race itself. The appearance of race in the English lexicon during the Elizabethan period allows us to see the second major transition of race in a time when the slave trade is already a viable proposition, and England moves into Europe as a young and ambitious country experiencing the outside world.

Etymology and Shakespeare

Previously, we have commented on the odd and counterintuitive nature of the entry of the word race, as the material object, into the language *before* it begins to denote the concept of race as we have come to know it. Having arrived, however, a steady number of commentators on racial thought consistently remind critics of the need to consider race in its multitudinous forms, from the entry of the term into Western languages to its contemporary denotation. Perhaps chief among these scholars, Michael Banton repeatedly warns that "The failure to allow for changes in the sense in which the word race has been used has important consequences, for those who misunderstand the past of their society are likely to misunderstand the present, because people judge the present in the light of what they believe the past to have been" (Banton 2000: 52). Indeed, the multiple transitions of the word race deserve attention not only because of the current political climate, but also because of its tremendous range of manifestations. As previously noted, race entered Western languages with a multitude of denotative possibilities including those applicable to mathematics and astrology, millstreams, and the wakes of ships. While it is important to note these possibilities, the most significant denotation for our purposes focuses on direct noble lineage. In Christian Europe, the fortification of racial purity and noble privilege stretched back to Rome and served as a "resistance to any counter-claim from Trojan, Saxon, Arthurian, Celtic, Gallic, Frankish, Jewish, and Moorish sources," which were summarily dismissed as fabrication and fiction (Hannaford 1996: 147). The ability that the word race demonstrates both to shift across a wide range of discursive land-scapes, and to act as a political shield protecting the right of the privileged, is by now a familiar theme in this discussion.

The malleable, political phenomenon will become particularly important in Chapter 2 when we observe the fabrication of a (third and) more familiar personality of race. For now, however, it is worth-while to focus on what we consider the secondary origin of the term. For our purposes, the entry of race into the English language will receive primary critical attention. It is within this arena that we will heed the charge proffered by Banton's warning. There are at least two reasons for this eventuality. First and most obviously, English is the language of this text itself. Secondly, and more significantly, the entry of race into English roughly coincides with intense periods of transition for not only the English language and all written Western languages, but also for England as a nation increasingly ambitious in its experience of the world around it. So, on a simple level we can observe the etymological movement of the word as it accompanies England's emergence on the world stage, as well as the unprecedented reach of the written word through the invention and dissemination of the printing press. The importance of this broad transition cannot be underestimated.

Oddly, and perhaps poetically, given the role that the term ultimately plays in the machinations of British imperialism, race enters the English language directly from the French, but through a Scottish (colonial) mediator. We mentioned earlier Michael Banton's assertion that race appears for the first time in the English language in 1508, with the Scotsman William Dunbar's poem, *The Dance of the Sevin Deidly Sins.* At this time, however, race (or rather, "racis") contains a dramatically varied significance from the one we currently recognize. To a man of Dunbar's ilk, race potentially places the individual in a tribal, familiar, clan divination, and thereby denotes his/her proximity to the original couple. Likewise, Dunbar's need to qualify his "sindry racis," those who follow the sin of envy, makes race emblematic of a cultural sphere of influence and symptomatic of degenerative behavior (see Chapter 3).

The signifying scope of race persists in the muddle of lineage and religion for much of its early career in the English language. The course of this early career, however, coincides with the expansion, albeit relatively modest, of a literate public and the equally pertinent expansion of the printed word. Now, the proliferation of the written word creates the need for a more accessible and unified body of language. The Elizabethans advance this confusion by working between a cultural obsession with lineage, blood and nobility on the one hand, and the need to reconcile and explain the non-white individual within the limited scope of the scripture on the other.

Here, we also find a transition in the word, and in the English nation itself. Elizabeth I establishes Britain as an emerging colonizer, but does not overwhelmingly accomplish this task. As Matar points out, commentators on British history tend to "forget that in the Elizabethan and early Stuart periods, England was not a colonial power – not in the imperial sense that followed in the eighteenth century. Although England had colonized Wales and Scotland and was waging a colonial war in Ireland, at the time Queen Elizabeth died

[1603], England did not possess a single colonial inch in the Americas" (Matar 1999: 10).[2] While undeniably on the cusp of its imperial extension and domination, England has yet to emerge as the nation that it will become in terms of its presence on the globe. For *Othello*, England's relative humility is particularly relevant because it appears at a time when England is still prepared to stand in awe of the force of Moorish innovation and accomplishment. The position of Venice as the seat of the action of the play echoes England's emergent desire to enter the world stage and participate, as Venice did, in the triumph of the far-reaching, civilized nation-states. Put simply, Venice represents the culturally resilient and politically forceful ambition of England's blossoming rose. Situated between the four significant regions of the world, Venice is an emblem of commercial success, cross-cultural sophistication, and tolerance.

But we must be careful not to extend England too soft a hand. Elizabethan England was not by any means above or beyond racial conflict and prejudice. Elizabeth twice entreated the wholesale removal of blacks and Moors from England, although the need for two such treatises in a relatively short time suggests either the burgeoning of a grand cosmopolitan encounter, or the relative inefficiency of the first proclamation. However, "Elizabeth I's proclamation (1601) expelling Moors and Negroes from England . . . suggests also the topicality and relevance of the subject to the Elizabethans" (Ogude 1997: 154). For *Othello*, then, the tension inherent in the theoretical admiration and practical antagonism acts as a foundation for a racial politics that is both undefined and uncertain.

The uncertainty that follows from the lack of a working definition of race extends well into the basic English/non-English dynamic. For if, as suggested, England admires the civil accomplishments of the near east and North Africa, there seems to be no real method for establishing a difference between these foreign types and many others. Nabil Matar, for example, laments the manner in which many contemporary critics of the Elizabethans are content to assemble black Africans (sub-Saharan) on "the same pages where they have dealt with North African Muslims" (Matar 1999: 7). The fault, however, may not lie entirely in the intellectual insensitivity of contemporary commentators. The source may reside more readily with the confusion in the intellectual, discursive scope of the Elizabethans themselves. Habib adds a plausible level of complexity to the issue by noting that "what notions of race the Elizabethans had were hopelessly confused, as they routinely combined Africans with Arabs, Indians and south Asians, and pre-Colombian Americans" (Habib 2000: 2). This confusion extends beyond the mere interchangeability of racial types that we currently accept as quantifiably distinct. The Elizabethan concept of race runs the gamut of interpretive possibilities, from a familiar sentiment in our current concept of race as an exterior indicator, to a more directly traditional sense of lineage, to the potentially antagonistic opportunities allowed in a strict biblical application. To this end, Anthony Kwame Appiah aligns himself with the notion that, for the Elizabethan, race maintains the connotation of "natural or inherited disposition," apparently to the exclusion of all other possibilities (Appiah 1995: 278). So we have a situation in which, from the simple observation of physical difference that is loosely marked by race, one can infer quality of character, distance from religious enlightenment, disposition – or, less physically marked but more directly denoted in the literal word race – lineage (particularly significant if of noble descent), blood, and clan fealty. Note also Appiah's use of the word "natural" to describe something essential in the individual.

The choice of *Othello* here is deliberate and acts in complete awareness of Shakespeare's other highly racialized texts. Shylock from *The Merchant of Venice*, Caliban from *The Tempest*, and Othello each have acquired a significant amount of critical attention focusing on the varied manifestations of race and/or oppression. Interestingly, Shylock, the humanized Jew, acts out lineage and the clan or familial sense of the term race as one of several of the interpretive potentials offered. The Jewish race, then, is the easiest "race" to humanize because of the significance the term race entertains in this dynamic. This will become an important aspect of Othello's struggle to gain his humanity, as we shall see in a moment. When Shylock asks his famous questions, "I am a Jew. Hath not a Jew eyes? hath not a Jew hands, organs, dimensions, senses, affections, passions? fed with the same food, hurt with the same weapons, subject to the same diseases, healed by the same means, warmed and cooled by the same winter and summer, as a Christian is? If you prick us, do we not bleed?," he echoes a strong chord of common ancestry shared through descent from Adam and Eve (III.i.51–56). Shylock's appeal is not unlike that proposed by las Casas in his insistence on base humanity. The fact that these questions must be asked, however, testifies to the ease with which the foreign or unfamiliar could be demonized.

In juxtaposition with Shylock, *The Tempest*'s Prospero and Caliban have become a trope for the master/slave, colonizer/colonized dynamic. Prospero's unapologetically antagonistic relationship to Caliban acts out several of the key stereotypes found in the colonial dynamic. Caliban represents for Prospero the demonized subject who deserves to be ruled based on his fundamental nature. Caliban is "A devil, a born devil, on whose nature/ Nurture can never stick" (IV.i.189–190). By now, the contestation of natural inferiority has become the standard justification for the enslavement for any individual. Likewise, Caliban acts as the sexual aggressor, a symbol of savage incivility and further justification of his need to be ruled. The fact that Caliban attempts to rape Miranda reflects one of the fundamental fears of the colonial dynamic. The supposed lasciviousness of the colonial subject is a source of great paranoia not only for Miranda's sake, but also for the lineage of Prospero. As evidenced by Caliban's apparent lack of remorse for the deed, a significant portion of the transgression occurs because successful intercourse with Miranda could have had dramatic consequences for the rigid structure of their social dynamic. Thus Caliban states, "O ho, O ho! Would'st had been done!/ Thou didst prevent me; I had people else/ This isle with Calibans" (I.ii.348–350). Finally, Caliban enacts the loaded question of education for the savage. Here, it is crucial for the colonizer that the subjugated wretch remains so. Education, and particularly linguistic education and literacy, is the underlying mechanism that preserves the master/slave dynamic. Caliban's lament of his introduction to Prospero's language, therefore, is not surprising, nor is his reversal of that "gift" upon Prospero. Caliban states, "You taught me language, and my profit on't/ Is, I know how to curse. The red plague rid you/ For learning me your language!" (I.ii.363–365). Specifically, the function of speech is a vividly contested action in *The Tempest*.

Use of speech in *Othello* is rather limited, with one particularly significant exception. For the most part, the other characters engage the dialogue, of which a considerable portion describes the Moor in seemingly racist terms. The rhetoric employed is familiar. Othello endures a bevy of slurs and epitaphs, almost all of which serve to make him into a beast. We hear of Othello's "sooty bosom," and that he is a "black ram," who will "tenderly be led by th'nose/ As asses are" (I.ii.70; I.i.88; I.iii.394–395). Each of these remarks characterizes Othello as ignoble and in need of governance, as we have seen in Aristotle and las Casas. He is also a sexual threat. As with Prospero's fear that his lineage would more closely resemble the savage Caliban,

Iago plays upon the contagion of Othello's beastlike qualities. When provoking Brabantio, their coitus resembles "the beast with two backs," thereby suggesting that the act brings Desdemona into Othello's bestial sphere of influence (I.i.116). The various attempts to articulate Othello in the terms of a beast are familiar tools in accomplishing the removal or denial of the other's humanity, and when taken together, Shylock, Caliban, and Othello represent a considerable problem for those who would completely deny Shakespeare's awareness of race, or racially motivated thought. To gather these characters together as such, however, neglects the particular nuance and ambivalence found in Shakespeare and the significance that this ambivalence demonstrates about the transition of racial thought from medieval divisions to an early modern colonial experience.

What this means for a significantly racialized character like Othello is that he is by definition, and lack thereof, obligated to enact the impossible task of filling the significant void. For this reason, Othello is all racial things to all of his commentators, particularly, but not exclusively, those operating within the narrative. His lack of voice as the colonial subject only makes this eventuality all the more concrete and inevitable. In this sense, Othello is unknown in two distinct arenas. He is unknown in the vacant subjectivity of the Other, and he is unknown in the very definition of his own racial space. This is an initial source of frustration for the characters of the play and also a primary impetus for its action. As Habib states, "What Iago teaches others about Othello repeatedly and insistently is not that he knows Othello and the others don't, but that Othello is unknowable" (Habib 2000: 138). Of course, nature and interpersonal subjugation hates a void, and so others are more than willing to attempt to fill Othello's radically racialized space. The racialized subject then becomes the site for a flurry of connotative propositions. Each character interacting with Othello is allowed at least a single attempt to fill the void. We must not forget how impressively thorough Shakespeare is in the execution of this matter. As Habib states, "The indicting of the Othello – subject, the subaltern, is a community project" (Habib 2000: 136). For Roderigo, "Othello is the decadent libertine, the corrupt sensualist who carries off his sexual obsession in the scenario of a part romantic, virile, midnight abduction" (Habib 2000: 136). Brabantio chooses to elicit an equally demeaning myth with his denial that his daughter could engage in any serious consideration of the Moor. His "witch doctor" Othello acts out the mystical, mythical heathen who has access to potions and charms, and represents secret forms of power. For the Duke, the Moor general is the power of nobility and force. Habib suggests that "The exoticism of Desdemona's Othello is the allure of the unconventional and the foreign that is also the fetishing of difference, and that together to the ambitious young Venetian girl is the promise of the world. This allure is based . . . not on a preference of his racial complexion but on an avoidance of it" (Habib 2000: 136). In each of these examples, the character defining Othello does so in a manner that more directly reflects the inner state of that character than it reveals anything of substance about the Moor.

Even within the more abstract stereotypes there are subcategories of distinction that reveal nuanced layers of racial essences. In fact, that Othello's precise history is obscured helps to bring additional racial tensions to the text. Within the Moor, Turk, Oriental dynamic, there are additional connotations to be gathered in the Elizabethan mind. Matar writes, "The 'Turk' was cruel and tyrannical, deviant, and deceiving; the 'Moor' was sexually overdriven and emotionally uncontrollable, vengeful, and religiously superstitious" (Matar 1999: 13). Even within demonizing racial stereotypes, Othello has an oddly nomadic potential for becoming all things for all those who would proscribe his racialized position. And here we have perhaps the most basic dynamic in Orientalism and the colonial project (see Chapter 4 for a discussion of Orientalism). The ability to speak equates directly to a power that extends beyond discursive semantics. It matters little whether Othello is oversexed, savage, ambitious, deceitful, or anything else, compared to the significance of who speaks for him and the manner in which those words reflect the desires of the individual constructing the racial other. But the simple "othering" of racial binaries is not exactly what we have in Othello.

In noting the communal nature of this project, it would be difficult to entertain the notion that Shakespeare is not directly describing, if not rapidly approaching, a distinctly racist community. All of these articulations, combined with the relatively mute Othello, witness the imperial impulse and testify to the blossoming imperial power. As Habib notes, "Through this ventriloquist muting the play text will enact Venice–England's conquest of its native subject, by engineering his physical and moral subordination" (Habib 2000: 177). The act of speaking for Othello, therefore, echoes the burgeoning imperial ambition, which is tacitly acknowledged by the audience. The matter, however, is not quite so black and white.

There are at least three distinct reasons why the simple reading of race in Othello remains troubled, while ambitious. First, Desdemona's relationship with Othello does not act out any colonial fears, nor is it based on the exoticism of otherness. Second, Othello is of noble descent. Third, Othello does eventually speak, and moreover, vividly turns the bestial tables. How interesting, then, that Habib posits Desdemona's desire not as "preference of his racial complexion but on an avoidance of it" (2000: 136). Instead, her affections for Othello are based on the exact points that initially draw the other characters to him, including Brabantio. This attraction is not the base exoticism of otherness, but rather a denial of it. Desdemona falls for Othello out of respect for his accomplishments, and his presence. Indeed, his nobility, both inherited and earned, is the source of the Duke's advice that "If virtue no delighted beauty lack/ Your son-in-law is far more fair than black" (I.iii.289–290).[3]

It is precisely between these conflicting definitions that Shakespeare hits his mark, as evidenced not only in Othello's color, but also in the nobility of his blood. Here, blood does not represent a distinctly biological notion of inheritance. Instead, blood remains a mythical, magical essence maintained by and representative of noble lineage. Shakespeare was writing, after all, "both about and to his countrymen's feelings concerning physical distinction between kinds of people" (Jordan 1968: 37). The cultural split in Jordan's "kinds of people" need not necessarily refer to distinctions between varied complexions, but may include the quite dramatic social division within Elizabethan England. Othello's descent from "men of royal siege," therefore, brilliantly blurs the boundary between not only the foreign and familiar, but also between the social structures of class (I.ii.22). Butler-Evans adds, "As a Moor, he is clearly presented as Other, but not necessarily an offensive Other; the qualifier of noble Moor does not extricate him from the realm of the exotic, yet it undermines the perception of him as evil" (Butler-Evans 1997: 146). Put simply, Othello is racially over-determined. Reading Othello as Moor, black, and noble demonstrates not only the "contradictory cultural attitudes of his observers," but also the dramatically mobile nature of racial identification for Elizabethans (Butler-Evans 1997: 148).

That Othello is racially over-determined can be seen in the racial mobility he demonstrates during his time and through to our own. Indeed, current argument rages over the exact complexion of Othello, specifically whether he should he be "tawny" or "black" (Kaul 1997;

Benjamin 1997). Mythili Kaul offers a grand explication of when and how the emphasis of Othello's color changes. Coleridge argues that "it is Roderigo who, because of rivalry, willfully confuses *Moor* and *Negro*" (Kaul 1997: 7). Coleridge then proceeds to demonstrate bigotry of his own formulation stating, "can we imagine that Shakespeare is so utterly ignorant as to make a barbarous *negro* plead royal birth? . . . it would be something monstrous to conceive this beautiful Venetian girl falling in love with a veritable negro" (quoted in Kaul 1997: 7). The bitter impudence in this exclamation is indicative of what troubles Othello both inside the text and out. Simply, he is read in a way that demonstrates more about the reader than the character as such.

We must not ignore the final point that confuses traditional racial readings of Othello. Namely, he speaks, both dramatically and effectively. For the action of the play itself, Othello's action comes rather too late for his own fate, which is by that point decided. With nothing genuinely at stake, we must wonder what Othello accomplishes by his sudden reclamation of speech. Habib notes, "Othello's coming forward here is deliberately aggressive and unexpected. Indeed, the play has already ended, its necessary esthetics have been completed, and the Moor's aggressive intrusion violates the play's formalist teleogy and the moral satisfaction of its (presumably European) audience" (Habib 2000: 145). Othello's final speech is a grand reclamation of his dignity and personage:

> No more of that. I pray you, in your letters
> When you shall these unlucky deeds relate,
> Speak of me as I am; nothing extenuate,
> Nor set down aught in malice: then must you speak
> Of one that loved not wisely but too well;
> Of one not easily jealous, but being wrought
> Perplex'd in the extreme; of one whose hand,
> Like the base Judean, threw the pearl away
> Richer than all his tribe; of one whose subdued eyes,
> Albeit unusèd to the melting mood,
> Drops tears as fast as the Arabian trees
> Their med'cinable gum. Set you down this;
> And say besides, that in Aleppo once,
> Where a malignant and a turban'd Turk
> Beat a Venetian and traduced the state,
> I took by the throat the circumcised dog,
> And smote him, thus. [*He stabs himself*] (V.ii.340–356)[4]

The speech combined with his suicide removes Othello from the grasp of a destructive social order that reviles him and inspires the murderous results of the play. Thus, to speak of him as he is, is to oppose the malicious "voice of the colonial discourse that has written him and reclaim the passionate humanity of the distinguished black military servant from the implicit barbarity of his literary insculpture" (Habib 2000: 145). And, in an ironic but inevitable colonial twist, "the colonized subject finds his voice in silence, by canceling himself" (Habib 2000: 146). By executing this act, Othello recovers himself by negating the possibility of his own ventriloquist subjugation.

Before silencing himself, however, Othello does manage to tacitly turn the tables somewhat. Having noted the manner in which Othello is made bestial, it is worth observing the moments where Iago suffers the same fate. He suggests himself that he "would change [his] humanity with a baboon" long before Roderigo pronounces "O damn'd Iago! O inhuman dog!" (I.iii.317; V.i.62). To this Lodovico adds both "viper" and "Spartan dog" (V.ii.285, 361). After all this by now exhaustive bestial rhetoric, we see that the inscription of beast and man is a privilege not solely reserved for overtly racialized characters. Interestingly, Othello approaches this activity and then declines, demonstrating his superior understanding of racializing mythology. Othello states, "I look down towards his feet – but that's a fable./ If that thou be'st a devil, I cannot kill thee" (V.ii.286–287). Othello alone can distinguish the reality from the myth; he alone resists literalizing the metaphor.

Transition

To reiterate, the word race can be read as having several false starts, or ghosts, that linger in the margins of its history. While it may be convenient to read race back into these lingering specters and even seem appropriate, to do so, by definition, misses the subtlety with which these false starts illuminate the conditions that create race. Hannaford asks of us is that we not only approach the Greek philosophers on their own terms but also remain particularly alert to the subtle differences in their individual agendas. The result of stripping Aristotlean method of its essences prepares the ground for reading race into Aristotle during the misapplication of his most basic organizational principles. The genius of this perverse methodology is that by performing a reading in this manner, the commentator can muster the authority of the ancients to justify his/her own highly politicized discourse, even as he/she claims to simply apply the genius of others. Hannaford's argument presupposes the significance of investigating the origins of the concept, as does Delacampagne, but on the terms negotiated by that specificity. To evaluate the subject *exclusively* through our own criteria is, at best, to miss the inspiration for looking backward in the first place, and, at worst, to simply repeat the erroneous conclusion reached by the seventeenth and eighteenth-century commentators. This is race's first false start.

Likewise, once the word race actually enters Western languages, we must consider the nature and substance of the intellectual landscape at the time. The fact that medieval commentators were capable of creating wild and fantastic stories, ones that often demonized foreigners in a gesture of confusion, actually helps us recognize the manner in which writers often reveal more about themselves, deliberately or otherwise, than the subject on which they are supposedly reporting. For Sir John Mandeville, his comments on the Vale Perilous and his digression during his exchange with Genghis Khan, suggest much more about his cloistered mindset, his limited discursive window, and his moral agenda than they ever reveal about either encounter, fictional or otherwise.

Race has more than one false start. If we ignore the fact that the Greeks did not have the concept of race because their valuation of political man preceded the need for it, the limited scope of literal biblical narrative, and the malleability of the term race as it appeared upon its first entrance into the English lexicon, we are incapable of appreciating a considerable source of dramatic tension in Shakespeare's *Othello* – and, indeed, in other similar exercises. The menacing underbelly to criticisms that focus on the complexion of Othello as the primary source of his identity fails to recognize that Othello's race (his nobility) stands in direct opposition to the bigoted (racial) soubriquets he endures from his peers. As we clearly divine, the nature of such debate remains more indicative of contemporary fixations rather than a genuine investigation of Shakespearean complexity. Debates currently raging over the relative shade of Othello's complexion miss the more fundamental and significant tension of the text. It matters little, nor did it matter to Shakespeare, if Othello was tawny or black. The matter lies in the tension of his two racial marks, between some form of darkened complexion and his nobility.

Finally, we have exhausted considerable effort isolating where race is not, or at least not completely. As we move away from the sixteenth and seventeenth century, we also witness the considerable effort made by a communal gathering worthy of Othello's bigoted antagonists, of Enlightenment natural philosophers, to articulate a fully grounded theory of race, as race.

Notes

1. I will refer to the term "disposition" throughout this chapter with a deliberate and respectful nod to Pierre Bourdieu and his theorization of the term "habitus," for which he most often uses disposition as a synonym. With the habitus, Bourdieu articulates the contiguous relationship between theory and practice, with an emphasis on the precise way in which practice is embodied in the individual through an implicit, intuitive appreciation for the governing structure of symbolic exchange. This allows cultural tropes to shape individual practice while leaving room for the individual to apply a modicum of his/her own agency.
2. Virginia was not established until 1607, with over twenty more years until Massachusetts was established in 1629. Maryland followed in 1632 with Rhode Island and Connecticut forming in 1635 and 1639, respectively.
3. Anachronistically, Othello endures another potential slur. Although we will not discuss the phenomenon in detail until Chapter 3, Othello's epilepsy becomes indicative of degeneracy, a tenuous scientific attempt at criminology in the nineteenth century. While degeneration can be read only as a spurious medical concept that supposes deficiency in the human condition, it is interesting that Shakespeare should accidentally play so directly into later theoretical machinations. Lombroso states, "It must be added that moral insanity and epilepsy which are so often found in association with genius are among the forms of mental alienation which are most difficult to verify, so that they are often denied, even during life, although quite evident to the alienist" (Lombroso [1899] 1911: vii).
4. How appropriate that there is perhaps an error in transcription of line 347, where the first Folio reads "Iudean" while the first Quarto reads "Indian" (Shakespeare 1969: 1057n). While likely to be only the legacy of a scribal error, the uncertainty left in the wake of this error remains bizarrely telling. Interestingly, the man most singularly responsible for reinvigorating modern mass experience of Shakespeare, Kenneth

Brannagh, chose to include the word "Indian" in his recent film version of the play. One speculates that the reason for this lies in the contiguity, and apparent racial similarity, between the Indian subcontinent and Othello himself. The fact that Indian may so closely resemble Judean in a more conveniently interchangeable sense, however, oddly enacts the Elizabethan experience of foreign bodies, in both the physical and ideological sense.

2 The Enlightenment and the Fabrication of Race

God, in pity, made man beautiful and alluring, after his own image; but my form is a filthy type of yours, more horrid even from the very resemblance. (Shelley [1818] 1963: 110–111)

Alas! Why does man boast of sensibilities superior to those apparent in the brute; it only renders them more necessary beings. If our impulses were confined to hunger, thirst, and desire, we might be nearly free. (Shelley [1818] 1963: 79)

The Enlightenment fabrication of race

Having attempted to isolate a working definition of race by observing its traditional misinterpretations and misappropriations, we have spent a great amount of energy describing where race is not, or at least not exactly. In Chapter 1, we began by suggesting that the Greeks did not have a concept of race because their valuation of the political man precluded the need for genuine racial distinction. The conceptual tools, however, had been created and the framework built. Secondly, we noted the actual entry of the word race into Western languages, and specifically the considerable confusion that surrounded its earliest manifestations in English. Here we argued over Othello's "race" (meaning noble lineage) as it operated in contrast to the barrage of epithets, exclusions, and bigotry that have become the hallmark of our contemporary concept of race. In this chapter, then, we will tie together the two original threads of race, the concept and the word, in the age of Enlightenment, perhaps exposing a more familiar connotation. Ultimately, the movement away from the initial linguistic confusion we witnessed in Chapter 1 brings us toward a more distinctly scientific understanding of humanity and signals a familiar, but rather new phase in racial history. Attempts to reconcile the abundance of material gathered through travel writing within the limited realm of the biblical narrative begins to shape a culture increasingly obsessed with isolating and organizing the natural world. As the Enlightenment unfolds, the desire to classify experience within the discourse of science also signals a transition from muddling imprecision to increasingly precise, if misplaced, specificity.

The dominating point in the evolution of the term race lies in its manipulation by proponents of "natural history." And, on that note, it is worthwhile to cast one final glance back to our tragic Othello. Commenting on the Moor, Voltaire remarks of his capacity for jealousy and violence, "cet Othello, qui est un nègre, donne deux baisers à sa femme avant de l'étrangler. Cela paraît abominable aux honnêtes gens; mais des partisans de Shakespeare disent que c'est la belle nature, surtout dans un nègre" [this Othello, who is black, kisses his wife twice before strangling her. This seems abhorrent to honest persons; but devotees of Shakespeare say that this is true to nature, especially in a Negro] [quoted in Potter 2000: 11). How appropriate that Voltaire should manipulate both the word honesty (honnetês) and nature in fabricating his racial epitaph. The word honesty seems oddly fitting here because of the manner in which Iago abuses the term throughout the play, and nature because it betrays the source of truth for the authors of the Enlightenment (Potter 2000: 11). And if, as suggested in Chapter 1, the isolation of Othello was a community affair, the substantial fabrication of race is much more dramatically so.[1]

There has been considerable recent debate regarding who, individually, most significantly contributed to the idea of race, thereby earning the dubious title of progenitor of the concept. Immanuel Kant has gathered considerable, but relatively modest, attention as the single most essential contributor to the scientific construction of race. And although decidedly important, to limit the discussion thus ignores the multitude of other voices that contribute to its creation. For this reason, we will trace several key figures, again highlighting the European community effort that enabled race. Here, we suggest that the fabrication of race is an almost inevitable enterprise in Europe, not primarily as a means to justify the slave trade a priori (as has been argued), but as a "natural" conclusion to the Enlightened application of natural philosophy.

Undoubtedly, many will be familiar with Voltaire for reasons other than his literary analysis of Shakespeare. Nevertheless, his contribution to the origin of racial thought, although minimal, is representative of several significant problems facing those engaged in the task. First, Voltaire is indicative of several key points of confusion in the exchange of the familiar and foreign for the European commentator. Here, questions emerge as to the origin of different races – whether that origin must be reconciled with biblical accounts, and the number of races that may be isolated in a taxonomic exercise, as with all living creatures, plant and animal. Likewise, Voltaire demonstrates the familiar linguistic complexities involved in hammering out a distinct definition of race, particularly as it comes to more closely resemble the idea as it exists today.

To the first end, namely the reconciliation of objective, observed experience with the limited narrative of biblical history, Voltaire relies heavily on Isaac de la Peyrère, who in 1655 published *Prae-Adamitae*, where he concisely argues against the position proposed in monogenesis, which interprets the bible literally. La Peyrère's argument is aggressive in its valuation of relative narratives, as it "is largely dominated by the problem of writing a coherent narrative that reconciled the Biblical story with the more extended chronologies proposed by the Chaldaeans, Egyptians, Greeks and Chinese" (Bernasconi 2001: 19). La Peyrère, therefore, offers a challenge to two integral parts of the second biblical creation narrative. First, la Peyrère usurps the totality of single ancestors for the entirety of the human population. Second, by positing a time before Adam, la Peyrère counters the imposed timeline that results from such a select progeny. The problem for the monogenesis position lies in the need to account for the disparity found in the varied forms of humanity, while maintaining the rigid structural, historical limitations imposed by the bible. In terms of the construction of race, monogenesis cannot explain how all humanity descended from one couple over the course of only several thousand years.

There is an odd, perhaps counterintuitive, series of ironies in the monogenesis/polygenesis debate. One might expect proponents of the monogenesis theory to value the human brotherhood of a common ancestor, a view prepared by the literal interpretation of the biblical narrative. Likewise, the value of polygenesis might lie in its antagonism to religious dogma and the subsequent purchase of scientific observation and intellectual rigor in opposition to strict and limiting literalism. In other words, polygenesis might resemble a more genuine scientific enlightenment. This, however is not entirely the case. Indeed, biblical narrative may presume two ancestors for all of humanity and the fact of this common progeny should unite humanity within a familial structure. However, as seen with Spain in the sixteenth century in the tragedy of las Casas, biblical supposition of human brotherhood is not employed to include different races. If the racial subject is thought to have an ancestor outside of Adam and Eve, it is not necessary to consider the foreign subject human at all. This is a convenient logic for those unable to reconcile scripture with experience, and for those who would make a profound profit in enslaving the foreign subject.

It would be a grave misstatement to claim slavery as the primary reason behind the defense of monogenesis. It is perhaps more viable that proponents of the slave trade found help in the promotion of polygenesis and, in a supreme irony, that "the concept of race was introduced to buttress the case against polygenesis" (Bernasconi 2001: 19). Admittedly, it is difficult to digest the notion that polygenesis acquired the dehumanizing element once brandished in Spain by ardent supporters of a world steeped in monogenesis. Further still, it is unlikely that "within the context of the late eighteenth century the idea of race was a resource for those who opposed slavery just as polygenesis lent itself to the upholders of slavery" (Bernasconi 2001: 21). Likewise, that the scientific construction of race should be pursued and misappropriated by supporters of slavery seems an odd, ironic end for an enlightened society. Again, however, we must not confuse the defense of monogenesis with the impure capitalist agenda of the slave trade. As Bernasconi argues, "The fact that the scientific concept of race was developed initially in Germany rather than in Britain or America suggests that it was not specifically the interests of the slaveowners that led to its introduction, but rather, as Kant's essays themselves confirm, an interest in classification and above all the attempt to provide a theoretical defense of monogenesis" (Bernasconi 2001: 21). We will come to Kant's role later in this chapter. For now, the relevant point is that race emerges in the Enlightenment through the combination of scientific classification, order, and religion.

Although met with a rather resounding critical reaction, la Peyrère at least creates a space in which to consider human history outside the limited discourse ensured by biblical transliteration. Implicitly contained within this space is the re-evaluation of an emerging racial theory. For if we devalue the strictly literal biblical account of origin, we must also reconsider the origin of the difference found in human appearance, which had borrowed heavily from the biblical account. In his *Traité de Métaphysique* (1734) and *The Philosophy of History* (1766), Voltaire reinvigorates the polygenesis standpoint. As previously suggested, the concept of race is not directly the result of a rethinking of the biblical narrative, but an attempt to denigrate the alternative. This is by no means to suggest that either Peyrère or Voltaire was anything like the enlightened counterpoint to the racial formulation. Instead, the shortcomings of both sides of the debate, indeed the pitch of the debate itself, succinctly demonstrate the ideological missteps prevalent in the foundation of the concept.

As suggested in Chapter 1, there are moments when idle conjecture and rather odd propositions emerge as a remnant of earlier writing, whether or not those writings are interpreted diligently or as blunders. And here Voltaire becomes rather emblematic of several distinct manners of misapprehension, particularly when it comes to the Greeks. Voltaire, for example, speculates as to the viability of an encounter he discovers in Herodotus' description of his travels in Egypt. Apparently inspired by his consideration of the mulatto, Voltaire sees no reason to discredit the possible union and offspring made through a coupling of woman and he-goat supposedly witnessed in the province of Mendes (Voltaire 2000: 6). And having noted this repulsive tale, Voltaire betrays two distinct influences. He states, "It is forbidden in Leviticus, chapter eighteen to commit abominations with he and she-goats. These copulations must then have been common, and till such time as we are better informed, it is to be presumed that a monstrous species must have arisen from these abominable amours" (Voltaire 2000: 6–7). First, he demonstrates that the biblical narrative still holds a considerable sway over the scope of his vision through his near chapter and verse recitation. Secondly, he reveals the significant familiarity and influence that the Greeks have upon his contemporary theorists, both for the better and for the worse (and Voltaire is certainly not alone in this matter). In this regard, Voltaire also exposes the continued command that implausible travel writing has over the popular and academic imagination. Thirdly, and most importantly for the substance of the transition that is occurring, Voltaire's skepticism, although perhaps nowhere near objective, implies his stake in the rigors of scientific observation and renegotiation of received experience.

More importantly, Voltaire demonstrates some confusion not entirely dissimilar to that which we have witnessed in the emergence of the literal, material word race in the English language. Here Voltaire ambiguously employs race and species without any apparent consideration of a possible distinction between them. In the example of the woman and the goat, Voltaire freely laments the "monstrous species" that must have resulted from the union. Moments later, Voltaire breaths a sigh of relief that such a species, because it could not engender, "could not interrupt the course of nature in the other races" (Voltaire 2000: 7). This rather odd equation of species with race is by no means a unique example in Voltaire's writing. Again, there is a litany of half-truths and inherited blunders to note here. Particularly, Voltaire embraces the myth that mulattos were sterile, which helps to problematize the union of black and white races. While noting that "negro men and women, being transported into the coldest countries, constantly produce animals of their own species," he adds that "mulattos are only a bastard race of black men and white women, or white men and black women, as asses, specifically different from horses, produce mules by copulating with mares" (Voltaire 2000: 6). In both examples, the ordering of species and race seems quite compelling, for in both instances Voltaire adds the synonymous term race as an afterthought to the more general term species. It is difficult to say convincingly that this double usage and multifarious distinction stem from a continued understanding of race as somehow more akin to lineage than biologic classification, yet it is worthwhile to note the possibility.

Interestingly, we can locate a precise fount for Voltaire's confusion between the nuance dividing race and species. Returning to the prominence of travel writing, and the observation that such writing carries tremendous value in shaping the mental landscape of the European, we must note the significance of François Bernier in his preparation of the word race. Having traveled extensively in the middle period of his life, he returns to publish his account of Persia, Egypt, and India in his *Voyages de François Bernier* (1670), which is subsequently published in English as *Travels in the Mogul Empire*. Although by no means unique in either his description of foreign peoples or his particular concentration on physical difference, Bernier is the first to group the people he encounters into distinct races merely on that basis. For this reason, Bernier's travel narrative also participates in the increasingly prominent art of "natural history." Likewise, it can be argued that his essay "A New Division of the Earth According to the Different Species or Races of Men" (1684) acts as the first instance where race is used both as a description based solely on physiognomy, and as an equivalent to the word species.

Bernier's classification is quirky, and perhaps even offensive and awkward, but it is easily distracted by his (one gathers more pressing) emphasis upon where he encounters beautiful women. As with his aesthetic judgment of women, he continually relies on recognizable gradations of difference for the basis of his categorization. For this reason, he may be described as having accomplished the sum total of racial thought, although to do so would certainly ignore significant portions of its historical development. It must be noted, however, that even Bernier is not entirely confident in the authority of his group-ings, noting that there may be "four or five species or races of men" (Bernier 2000: 1).

If Bernier is uncertain as to the number of races that his divisionary system describes, he is in no doubt as to the primary subject. He opens his first category with what might be considered fairly familiar racial distinctions. In the specious category, he places the people of "France, Spain, England, Denmark, Sweden, Germany, Poland, and generally all Europe except a part of Muscovy" (Bernier 2000: 2). Unexpectedly, however, he expands this group to include "a small part of Africa, that is from the kingdoms of Fez, Morocco, Algiers, Tunis, and Tripoli up to the Nile; and also a good part of Asia" (Bernier 2000: 2). One might readily speculate that Bernier, when encountering *Othello*, would situate the tension almost exclusively in the condition of Othello's foreign, not racial, otherness. And Bernier does not stop with this initial muddling. While observing that the Egyptians and Indians are significantly "black," he undermines this evaluation by noting the exposure they must endure in the sun. When not in the sun, he adds, they are rarely much darker than the Spaniard, who presumably does not suffer the same exposure. Furthermore, Bernier weakens the very basis for his own categorical structure by admitting that while the color and the shape of the Indian face may be different from "us," this "does not seem enough to make them a species apart, or else it would be necessary to make one of the Spaniards, another of the Germans, and so on with several other nations of Europe" (Bernier 2000: 2). In this gesture, Bernier exposes the purely arbitrary nature of his distinction. Inasmuch as he divides the species of the earth into categories that broadly correspond to Europeans, Africans, Orientals, and Laplanders, with the Native Americans left somewhere in the balance, Bernier's divisionary system both relies upon and, at times, denies the pertinence of what are later considered fairly broad examples of physical difference. It would seem, therefore, that Bernier's system remains lost within its own criteria, a fact that has lead Robert Bernasconi to suggest that we should not value "the list itself, but the fact that he employed the term 'race' for the purpose" (Bernasconi 2001: 12).

There may, however, be some value that we can recover from Bernier. As well as marking the arbitrary nature of his distinctions, we might also note several secondary priorities that he clearly delineates. First, he plainly prioritizes Europeans and North Africans as belonging to a single species, reluctant to dissolve the tenuous foundation of his system. One might also speculate that, if we consider the case of our Othello from Chapter 1, this emanates in part from the supposed civil nature of these peoples, which he hesitates to merge too readily with the other species that he treats less kindly, on the whole. This is the first speculative clue that Bernier's divisionary system operates with more than mere authority of descriptive differentiation. Furthermore, the gesture toward civilization directly echoes the priority of Greek philosophers who were quite willing to entertain difference based on participation in an ordered and well-legislated society. In this sense, Bernier can be read as a bridge between the newer values of natural science and the ancient priorities of political organization. More directly, Bernier also performs the methodology, inherited from the Greeks, that posits the naturalness of various phenomena.

Now, if Bernier helps to instigate the transportation of the Greek valuation of "natural kinds" to the art of natural history (or philosophy), we must also note that the criteria for his inclusive procedure is, at times, just that: inclusive. And so, inadvertently, Bernier again exposes the genuinely subjective nature of racial distinctions. Although we have been stating that his primary purpose resides in the differentiation and division of the people of earth, it is worthwhile to note that his concentration often ambles toward the uniting principles of similarity in its desire to include disparate groups. His inability to decisively locate the American species lies in the fact that he is unable to locate a difference that is "sufficiently great" (Bernier 2000: 3). This is an important and often overlooked aspect of his newly scientific endeavor. Although his categories are ultimately arbitrary, his willingness to be both inclusive and exclusive inherently calls into question the manner in which one prioritizes categorical differentiation. In other words, what one sees depends entirely, in this case, upon whether one looks for similarity or difference in the applicable methodology. Where Bernier redeems himself, if at all, is in his trepidation when approaching this dilemma. He marvels that he may have to unravel his system if he were to include Spaniards as a race, and he remains uncertain what to do with the Americans precisely because he has not forgotten that these are categories that do not exist entirely as natural phenomena, even as he applies the ordering principles of natural history. When suggesting that it is impractical to create a new racial category for Indians, who are lumped in with the Europeans despite the difference in shape of head and skin color, Bernier laments that he must make (as quoted earlier) an inclusive gesture "or else it would be necessary to make one of the Spaniards, another of the Germans, and so on with several other nations of Europe" (Bernier 2000: 2). Although he opens the door for natural history, Bernier, at least, does not ignore that when musing over why we may have different types, he is creating those types in the first place. Bernier's apprehension accounts for the tension between the naturalness and the man-made "nature" of his subject. This trepidation demonstrates the still very loosely articulated sense of race and more pressing cultural concerns.

Bernier's equation of species with race reveals a lack of concise terminology despite the application of the term in an arena recognizable to the contemporary reader. The use of race thus does not preempt, or otherwise replace, the use of the word in its other denotations mentioned in Chapter 1. But, again, Bernier helps to propel the concept of race into a more focused and intense scientific discourse grounded in the observation of physical differences, the power of which continues to gain momentum. Oddly, the uncertainty Bernier does articulate resonates within contemporary conflations of race and culture in the catch-all term of ethnicity. Again, what remains so compelling about Bernier is that, at times, he seems to echo the sum total of the racial landscape that follows. Bernier's imprecise use of race and ambiguity about culture are remarkably emblematic of the manner in which the terms are conflated within the popular American lexicon today. This will be discussed at much greater length in Chapter 5, but for now it is valuable to note how consistently and tenaciously the inexact "nature" of race helps to maintain its longevity by being both natural and man-made.

Finally, in terms of his foresight, Bernier also participates in the exoticism that will become the perverse hallmark of the European imperial project. His fixation on the relative beauty of women remains a distraction, at best, and ominous, at worst. However, Bernier also finds amid his diatribe a subject matter that subsequently receives a great deal of attention. And it is here, almost accidentally, that Bernier provides the second of his most dramatic contributions to the development of race. Bernier notes that the beauty of women "arises not only from the water, the diet, the soil, and the air, but also from the seed which must be peculiar to certain races and species" (Bernier 2000: 4; Bernasconi 2001: 13). Thus, Bernier articulates two pressures that form race. First, he speculates that climate causes racial difference and, second, that there is another essential agent at play. Since the Greeks, there had been a tacit understanding that the black Ethiops had in some manner been scorched by the sun, and supported this notion with mythical reasoning. Subsequent theorists found the climate the most directly observable causality for the alteration of skin color, the most marked of racial signifiers. The second catalyst for racial difference, however, raises some interesting points of concern. What Bernier suggests is that there is some essence found in an elusive seed that informs racial signifiers. That this "seed" has yet to be discovered is not necessarily an obstacle at this point, if only because the entire enterprise is relatively underdeveloped at this time. Later, Kant picks upon this theory and presupposes a similar agent within the races.

The explanatory mechanism of seeds helps fortify race for a number of reasons. Perhaps most perniciously, its function suggests that a great number of possible cultural characteristics might be linked to this mechanism. It is through the integral seed that other base attributes, say genius or fecklessness, are united with simple racial factors that, in themselves, have not solidified sufficiently to be reliable. Hence, Bernier's relative hesitancy in actually structuring his categories, which can be juxtaposed to his confidence that each race contains an essential character. In other words, if race potentially shifts with prolonged exposure to new climates, the natural philosopher needs a functional system to keep races essentialized and therefore essentially different.

In direct response to the need to find essential characteristics and to assist in the solidification of race, Carolus Linnaeus applies the ordering principles of natural philosophy, traditionally reserved for plants and animals, in an attempt to fortify the precision of race. Linnaeus' *Systema Naturae* (1735), which he continually developed within twelve editions until his death, plays an extremely significant role in establishing the ordering principles of taxonomy as they apply to racial categories. Indeed, rigorous order and classification are Linnaeus' central motivation, and relate directly to his appropriation of Aristotle's genus and species and attempt to fill the gaps apparent in the Great Chain of Being, a popular proto-evolutionary theory. We must note that the Great Chain of Being is not proto-evolutionary in the sense that each species descends from the previous one; rather it proposes a linear organization of species. The Great Chain of Being suggests that all of creation can be ordered hierarchically, from lowest to highest. God sits at the apex of the chain and rules over humanity, as humanity, in turn, rules over all of the lower classes of animals and plants, stretching in a direct line away from divinity. Here, Aristotle's discussion of natural slaves becomes a rather useful tool in ordering the supposed proper servitude of all creatures lower in the chain. Race, applied in this sense, is also a convenient tool for closing the gap between humankind and the apes. Initially, Linnaeus uses his system to isolate four subspecies of the human type, a theory which he consistently re-evaluates. In a significant departure from Aristotle, Linnaeus shifts the location of humankind up the inverted triangle, mentioned in Chapter 1, from the general to specific. Thus, Linnaeus more specifically divides, in a manner that Aristotle clearly does not, the different races of humankind into subspecies. For Linnaeus, humanity is no longer an irreducible quantity. The suggestion that human variation actually represents individual species has profound consequences with regard to the way in which Enlightenment philosophers approach the subject.

As with Bernier, Linnaeus demonstrates a need not only to order the races into concise categorical structures, but also to essentialize those structures. That is, Linnaeus' argument binds simple physiological difference with more substantive differences of human potential, personality, and character. Linnaeus' subcategories have nearly as much to do with the medieval notion of the four humors as they do with the four/five (negotiable) geographical varieties tentatively established by the likes of Bernier. This is not to say that Linnaeus directly appropriates Bernier's exact divisions, but that he helps to solidify the general principle that there are four or five subspecies. For his part, Linnaeus mentions five species specifically, only four of which are distinctly geographical, creating some confusion. With a devious nod to Aristotle, Linnaeus articulates physical difference and behavioral constitution as an essence. Linnaeus' basic categories are as follows: "*Homo ferus*: wild, savage, cruel man; *Europaeus albus*: ingenious, white, sanguine, governed by law; *Americanus rubescus*: happy with his lot, liberty loving, tanned and irascible, governed by custom; *Asiaticus luridus*: yellow, melancholy. governed by opinion; *Afer niger*: crafty, lazy, careless, black, governed by the arbitrary will of the master" (Hannaford 1996: 203–204; also noted with significant differentiation by Bernasconi 2001: 15). By combining the distinct racial organization with the medieval humors, Linnaeus is able to describe the essential nature of each category. Likewise, Linnaeus structures his races in conjunction with the structure of the Great Chain so that white denotes the highest link, which then passes directly through red, yellow, and black, with *homo ferus* closing any remaining gaps in the Great Chain.

But there is a curious inconsistency immediately evident in this ordering principle. The *homo ferus* lacks several obvious categorical traits allotted to all the other divisions. What *homo ferus* possesses in cruelty, he lacks in both color and geographical place, thereby signaling an odd gap in the coherence of the system. And in a gesture less objective than his scientific principle suggests, Linnaeus helps to ground Bernier's tentative categories into a confident, descriptive order, but undermines his own rigor with the arbitrary *homo ferus*. Furthermore, competing translations of the five subcategories of man leave significantly varied impressions of the moral and cultural character of each race. While Hannaford describes *Americanus rubescus* as "governed by custom," Bernasconi interprets this as mere "habit" (Hannaford 1996: 203–204; Bernasconi 2001: 15). Although perhaps a minor example, the relative value of these two assessments is significantly varied. Custom might imply an adherence to culture and tradition, while habit is likely to invoke something closer to apathy, sloth, or a lack of innovation. Our impression of each race, therefore, remains considerably negotiable and this fact reduces the substance of Linnaeus' scientific system considerably. Moreover, Linnaeus' need to close the Great Chain leads inevitably to problems in its implicit demand that there be even gradation from highest beings to lowest. Unfortunately for theorists like Linnaeus, the gradation between humanity and the rest of the animal kingdom does not offer a concise transition. Bernasconi highlights the addition in later editions of *homo monstrous* and *homo troglodytes* as examples of Linnaeus' willingness to "accommodate . . . that for which he did not have clear evidence" (Bernasconi 2001: 15). Surely, the failure to unite objective observation with rigorous taxonomy is the cardinal sin for the blossoming precision of this scientific method. Moreover, the insistence on blending behavioral categories into geographic ones undermines the validity of either register. Geographic variance is obvious among the human population. Likewise, there is a broad spectrum of behavioral characteristics available to humanity. To weave both options into race is a fallacy of dramatic proportion.

Despite the inconsistency in Linnaeus' organization, the impetus of his thought is designed to isolate and fix race into a constant. Indeed, Linnaeus needs this stability in order for his system to work. Banton asks rhetorically, "the Linnaean classificatory enterprise depended upon the assumption that the various sets of individuals to be classified were stable, for how could they be classified if they were changing?" (Banton 1987: 5). How odd, then, that Linnaeus seems to undermine his own need for stability by continually renovating his system, adding fewer and fewer convincing classifications. Specifically, there is a gap in Linnaeus' operating logic and its shortcomings demonstrate a need to find a viable mechanism to account for change.

At times, Georges-Louis Leclerc, Comte de Buffon has been given the onerous title of the man who introduced the word race into the literature of Natural History in 1749. His thirty-one volume *Histoire naturelle générale et particulière* (1758–1769) is an exhaustive system of racial organization and classification. Moreover, Buffon helps considerably in the need to find the mechanism for change in the scope of human variation. The precarious distinction of Buffon's role in linking race to natural history aside, Buffon helps to solidify race in terms of its scientific grounding. There are avenues of Buffon's thought, however, where he stands out considerably from the classification systems we have observed thus far. Buffon's method is structured primarily around geographic placement. Thus, the differences in racial type, particularly skin color, can be readily attributed to environmental characteristics.

While Buffon's attribution of race to environmental conditions may not be entirely ingenious, his denial of species and genus as valid classification systems certainly opposes any theory one might expect from the man who supposedly brought race to natural history. As Eze suggests, for Buffon, "races as *classes* simply have no natural existence" (Eze 2001: 103). Instead, Buffon believes that individuals are primary. Thus, Buffon prepares his entire argument in contrast to the Linnaean system of racial order. Indeed, Buffon is quick to denounce Linnaeus' amendments to his categories as self-defeating, and to indirectly criticize his tenuous supporting evidence. Buffon thus "rejected the classifications of Linnaeus as arbitrary" (Bernasconi 2001: 16). Buffon's rejection remains significant because it steers the nature of the racial debate away from essentialist views of racial characteristics and toward the causal mechanisms that might inspire human variation.

Buffon arrives at his schema for climatic differentiation through admittedly simple, albeit compelling, observations. During his description of the "numerous race, who occupy Canada," Buffon suggests with almost furtive desire that this race in some manner shares common descent with the "Oriental Tartars, [and] that, if they were not separated by a vast sea, we should believe them to have sprung from the same nation" (Buffon 2001: 16). He repeats his desire to link the two races but retreats, suggesting, "if there were no embarrassment concerning the possibility of their migration we should conclude them to be the very same people" (Buffon 2001: 17).[2] The conclusion that Buffon's perspective precludes him from making is, of course, an accurate one. Having reached the limits of his ability to reconcile conflated observations, he must settle for the next possible course of action and seek an alternative solution. Thus, Buffon ascribes climate as the causal mechanism for the similarities he has observed, and cites the secondary example of the "Negroes and the Hottentots" where we can suppose no communication between "Africa and this southern continent; and yet we find there the same species of men, because the same circumstances concur in producing the same degree of heat" (Buffon 2001: 22). Content that the climate is the causal element of skin color, Buffon does not feel the need to look further into how the exact mechanism works, although he does propose that exposure to the air is central to the process and that bile in the blood perhaps assists it. Instead, Buffon insists that the cause is fixed, in that transplanted peoples will maintain their race, but speculates that over successive generations one might find an adjustment to the expected race. Thus, Africans in Europe, even if isolated, will eventually become fairer, while Europeans in Africa may eventually become semi-permanently darkened. Buffon solidifies this notion in his "On the Degeneration of Animals" (1766), in which he argues that an animal's diet, along with climate and geography, could affect a substantial and somewhat permanent change in that animal.

The problem in Buffon's logic is his belief that the races are fixed with room for some variation. On the one hand, he argues for permanence, but admits that this permanence is ultimately fluid. The contradiction inherent in this logic leads Buffon to suggest a gradation in the human variety, and also a need for a second register of special differentiation. To Buffon, the gradation of humankind follows the general and gradual alteration in climate so, "after being exposed to the action of the air, and the rays of the sun, which renders the Spaniards more brown than the French, and the Moors than the Spaniard, also renders the Negroes blacker than the Moors" (Buffon 2001: 25). Buffon, therefore, could not assert that races were genuinely or entirely distinct, and that:

> Upon the whole, every circumstance concurs in proving, that mankind are not composed of species essentially different from each other; that, on the contrary, there was originally but one species, who, after multiplying and spreading over the whole surface of the earth, have undergone various changes by the influence of climate, food, mode of living, epidemic diseases and the mixture of dissimilar individuals; that, at first, these changes were not so conspicuous, and produced only individual varieties; that these varieties became afterwards specific, because they were rendered more general, more strongly marked, and more permanent by the continual action of the same causes; . . . and that, lastly, as they were originally produced by a train of external and accidental causes, and have only been perpetuated by time and the constant operation of these causes, it is probable that they will gradually disappear, or at least that they will differ from what they are at the present. (Buffon 2001: 28)

By preparing a continuous and contiguous gradation of the human subject, Buffon needs to find a secondary register to describe differences in species. Buffon finds this distinguishing action in a species' constant lineage and ability to reproduce consistently. This is later known as Buffon's rule. If a pair can successfully procreate, and that ability continues through successive generations, then the two are of the same species. Thus, Buffon articulates, species can be identified as a "constant succession of similar individuals that can reproduce together" (Bernasconi 2001: 16). The significance of this secondary register cannot be understated. For Buffon, the criterion of procreation is the "most fixed point that we have in Natural History" (Bernasconi 2001: 16). Likewise, for subsequent theorists, Buffon's rule becomes tremendously significant and is often employed in arguments against miscegenation by suggesting that successive generations of mulattos are sterile, as we have seen. often compared to the example of the sterile offspring of a horse and a donkey.

Buffon represents a move away from the Great Chain of Being and toward a more complex and dynamic account of human variation. Buffon thus helps to shift critical priority away from the concise linearity of the chain and directs critical attenion toward the criteria needed to establish the claim of speciation in the first instance. Added to the need for appropriate criteria, Enlightenment theorists also need to find a causal mechanism to describe how such change can be created. Johann Friedrich Blumenbach published his essay, "On the Natural Variety of Mankind," as his doctoral dissertation in 1775. The text was republished the next year and enjoyed a few revisions and republications before its final edition appeared in 1795. In the context of our previous discussion in this chapter it is worthwhile to note that Blumenbach also struggles with the number of races that can be viably differentiated. Indeed, the numbers at least are familiar as the early editions of his text identify four races, while the final edition adds a fifth to account for reports from voyages into the South Seas. Among other distinctions, Blumenbach introduces the term "Caucasian" into the lexicon, to which he also adds the categories of "Mongolian, Ethiopian, American, and Malay" (Blumenbach 2000: 27).

By and large, Blumenbach refrains from the essentialist thinking that dictates Linnaean personalities to his classifications, limiting himself instead to exhaustive physical descriptions. There is, however, dissatisfaction to be found in Blumenbach's writing with regard to the rather inconsistent standard of critical analysis prepared by his predecessors and peers. For this reason he remains remarkably egalitarian despite his qualified preferences. Having said this. Blumenbach does betray distinct bias in his predilection, noting that the Caucasian race embodies features that "according to our opinion of symmetry, we consider most handsome and becoming" (Blumenbach 2000: 29). When noting the similarities to primates, Blumenbach is reluctant to engage in standard racist fare. Instead, Blumenbach insists on the relativity of such correlations, stating, "but how little weight is . . . to be attached to this sort of comparison is clear from this, that there is scarcely any other out of the principal varieties of mankind, which by one nation or other, and that too by careful observers, has not been compared, as far as the face goes, with the apes" (Blumenbach 2000: 33). Blumenbach's comment here opposes the often simplistic and arrogant centrism so prevalent in almost all of his contemporaries.

Nevertheless, Blumenbach's most significant contribution to the formation of race stems in part from his aesthetic preference for the white race. The Caucasian as "white in colour, which we may fairly assume to have been the primitive colour of mankind, since . . . it is very easy for that to degenerate into brown, but very much more difficult for dark to become white" (Blumenbach 2000: 31). Here, Blumenbach builds upon Buffon and earlier theorists who also speculate that white constitutes the most basic color from which the others descend (Bernasconi 2001: 24). More important than his aesthetic preference, Blumenbach develops his core idea that the source of racial differences stems from the manner in which they have degenerated from one another. By the term "degeneration," we are not necessarily meant to intuit lack or paucity as one might gather in relation to descent in the Great Chain of Being. Instead, Blumenbach appears to have used the term to suggest the ability for the human form to change, although there is little need to extrapolate upon how quickly others may manipulate his basic premise. Degeneration, to Blumenbach, helps to explain the unseen mechanisms that allow certain attributes to pass through generations while others do not. To Blumenbach, "the genital liquid interacted with other material to produce a formative force which resulted in the normal reproduction of the animal or plant unless it was deflected in some way; in which case it produced monsters, hybrids, or greater variation" (Banton 1987: 6). Thus, Blumenbach creates the opportunity for a grand variation, both positive and terrible, in the human form. As with previous theories, the climate plays an extremely significant role in the deflection of normal development.

In his suggestion that white must be the original color, Blumenbach's logic is precise and actively working to engage his subject. The development of the degeneration theory thus marks a shift in the momentum of the argument. While Blumenbach, as with those discussed above, does spend considerable effort marking the races, his method for explaining their differences suggests at least one profound departure from previous classifications. Blumenbach's theory of degeneration describes the human subject as varying, and continually so. This is problematic for natural philosophers who have, to this point, largely attempted to describe a subject that they believe to be static. By creating a continually dynamic theory of human variation, Blumenbach destabilizes the human subject but, more importantly, the supposed distinctiveness of the human racial varieties, which he felt "differed only by degree" (Banton 1987: 6).

Working almost simultaneously with Blumenbach, Immanuel Kant develops similar theories related to imprecise essences and the alteration of climate as causal mechanisms for human variety. Although Blumenbach and Kant appear to disagree on a number of central issues in their construction of racial variety, they are each an integral part of the other's progress on the matter. Bernasconi suggests, for example, "What brought Kant and Blumenbach together was Kant's recognition that in his notion of *Bildungstrieb* or formative drive, Blumenbach had gone beyond natural description and an account of mechanical forces to posit a teleology in nature" (Bernasconi 2001: 26). By focusing on teleology, Kant signals that the scope of the racial theory has moved beyond simple categorization toward an attempt to explain the purpose of observed difference. For Blumenbach, this formative drive suggests the move from "unformed generative matter" to a "determinate form," in which an organic body will attempt to maintain and reproduce that form where possible (Bernasconi 2001: 26). Blumenbach understands this as an argument against the notion of preformed seeds the likes of which we mentioned above with our discussion of Bernier. For his part, Kant is willing to entertain a version of germ or seed theory, but Kant's goal in describing race is not only taxonomic. Instead, Kant wants to reach beyond simple description toward a more general understanding of human difference. Thus, Kant suggests, "Academic taxonomy deals with classes; it merely arranges according to similarities; while a natural taxonomy arranges according to kinships determined by generation. The former supplies a school-system for the sake of memorizing; the latter a natural system for the comprehension; the former has for its purpose only to bring creatures under a system of labeling; but the latter seeks to bring them under a system of laws" (Kant 1997: 39). Thus, for both Blumenbach and Kant, the racial enterprise is one based on the ability to observe a conceptual mastery of the subject, to be able to construct a law that effectively governs the natural world. This form of explanation extends beyond allowing for simple cause and effect toward a genuinely nuanced understanding of the purpose of difference. This is a bold departure from the more superficially descriptive achievements of previous attempts to isolate the races.

For the wealth of critical material that covers Kant's thought, there is a relative dearth of material that genuinely or sufficiently treats Kant's construction of race. This neglect is all the more disconcerting on account of Kant's instrumental role in assisting in the solidification of the concept. The relative inattention in this matter may stem in part from much of Kant's more racist pronunciations. As suggested in the Introduction, there is distinct trepidation or indeed squeamishness in confronting more uncomfortable or politically volatile aspects of race. Taken in isolation, and indeed in context, we can understand the nervousness inspired by well-worn passages such as "this fellow was quite black from head to foot, a clear proof that what he said was stupid" (quoted in Eze 2001: 102). For commentators and critics of Kant this translates as "the current embarrassment many feel in regard to what are now called his 'noncritical' writings" (Eze 2001: 98). Thus, Kant earns attention for his epistemological *Critiques* and his investigation into the sublime, and not for his "noncritical" racial writing.

In many respects, Kant can be read as owing a great deal to Linnaeus, Buffon, Blumenbach, and others. Kant's distribution of races does not break radically from the basic outline established by these earlier theorists. Kant identifies four races based almost entirely on observation of skin color that are connected to broad geographic counterparts: white, yellow, black, and red, which correspond to European, Asian, African, and American. Kant himself refers to these races as "(1) the race of Whites, (2) the Negro race, (3) the Hunnic (Mongolian or Kalmuck) race, and (4) the Hindu or Hindustanic race" (Kant 1997: 41). That Kant should structure his taxonomy primarily by color may not be entirely surprising, if not also potentially problematic. To this end, Kant's thought is symptomatic of the increasingly intense and primary focus placed on skin color, second to facial features ranked as racial signifiers. However, Kant also adds to these divisions that the white race also includes, "the Moors . . . the Arabians . . . the Turko-Tartaric ethnic stock and the Persians, and all the other peoples of Asia who are not specially excepted by inclusion in the other divisions" (Kant 1997: 41). As with Bernier, this classification system leads to some obviously contentious groupings. Thus, Bernasconi notes that "It is ironic that at the very time that Kant was giving the concept of race intellectual coherence, his criterion for distinguishing the different races was collapsing" (Bernasconi 2001: 17). By Kant's time, many of the most basic attempts to explain racial difference rely upon coloration as the primary distinguishing characteristic of race, a lingering notion that persists to a large extent today. From the outset, however, color alone consistently demonstrates its deficiency as a viable racial marker. But we must remember the more generally ambitious nature of Kant's enterprise. His is not simply an attempt to locate difference, but to more fully explain and understand its function, purpose, and relevance.

One of the reasons that Kant has received so much attention as the individual responsible for solidifying race into a scientifically viable whole, as opposed to any of the other contributors in this chapter, is the manner in which Kant incorporates elements of varied theories into his own. In particular, Kant adopts several central components of each of these theorists and applies them in often unintended ways. Kant, for example, incorporates Buffon's rule as the basis for his "Degeneration of the Animals" (1776). Likewise, in his "On the Different Races of Man" (1775), Kant insists upon the primacy of Buffon's rule stating, "animals which generate between them fertile young (whatever the difference of bodily form they may possess) belong to one and the same physical genus, must be looked upon as the general definition for a natural genus of animals, in contradistinction to all academic definitions of genera" (Kant 1997: 38–39). However, he does not identify with Buffon's theory of race. While Kant agrees with many previous commentators that climate and particularly exposure to air act as a causal element in the creation of different skin types, he is not prepared to continue the thought completely. He does not, for example, limit the mechanism that causes racial variation to these elements. As with Bernier, Kant supposes that all individuals also contain elemental predispositions and seeds that might be activated by the climate. Once brought into being, however, the changes are permanent. Thus, changes cannot, as with Buffon, continue to be revised, provided that the causal pressures are removed or altered. This is a particularly cunning gesture on Kant's part. By allowing for the climate to act as a causal mechanism, he does not need to refute the previous observations that suggest that climate could continue to influence race. Kant suggests that climate activates a deeper "germ or natural disposition," stating, "Air, sun, and food can modify an animal body in its growth, but cannot at the same time supply this alteration with a generative force that would be capable of again producing itself without this cause" (Kant 1997: 43). The generative force that Kant describes reaches back to Blumenbach's notion of the *Bildungstrieb* mentioned above. However, Kant amends this by suggesting that the climate only triggers the generative force of the germ while remaining unable to sustain the force itself. With this suggestion, Kant does not need to speculate on the continued variability supposed by evolutionary theories. All possible variations of the human form are achieved and cannot be brought back to an original state. Thus, "For Kant the geographical distribution of races is a fact, and the differences among them are permanent, fixed, and transcendent of environmental factors; the differences, he argued, are founded in an immutable natural germ" (Eze 2001: 103). So, Kant reconciles the mercurial forces of climate as a causal mechanism, but maintains the essentialist notions of race that suggest more than mere color or physical variation.

Kant summarily believes in the existence of natural racial kinds. For Kant, these kinds are more than mere descriptions of physical difference. Instead, Kant feels that underneath physical difference lies a more fundamental essence that allows for the creation of a hierarchy of races. Kant structures the hierarchy of value in these races on the basis of what he considers the "only alternative to a worthless existence" (Hill and Boxill 2001: 450). That is, Kant organizes his hierarchy according to his own esteem of his white, European, educated, male standard of living. Kant, therefore, posits the "white brunette" as the "stem genus," from which all the other races descend in natural order, from European, to American, to African, and then Asian. Kant does not trifle with his pronouncement that as a result, his race dominates the others in almost every cultural phenomenon that one might imagine:

> The inhabitant of the temperate parts of the world, above the central part, has a more beautiful body, works harder, is more jocular, more controlled in his passions, more intelligent than any other race of people in the world. That is why at all points in time these peoples have educated others and controlled them with weapons. The Romans, Greeks, the ancient Nordic peoples, Genghis Khan, the Turks, Tamurlaine, the Europeans after Columbus's discoveries, they

have all amazed the southern lands with their arts and weapons. (Kant 1997: 64)

Kant's double emphasis on European weaponry goes a long way toward explaining the rationale behind his hierarchy. For Kant, the European conquest of the world raises the rather disquieting question as to why the Europeans were able to subdue huge portions of the globe, and with diminishing levels of resistance. Kant, and his contemporaries, "needed to explain why Europeans expanded into the other continents rather than the other way around" (Boxill 2001: 20). Again, we must keep in mind that the mission of these Enlightenment theorists was not one exclusively based on justification or rationalization for the enslavement of multitudes. As Boxill suggests:

> Given that we are supposing that the Europeans had already devised a theory of racial essences to explain the observable physical differences between themselves and non-Europeans . . . many of them would have found it natural to infer that their superiority in the arts of war over the peoples they conquered stemmed from the same general causes that explained their physical differences from these peoples. That is, they would have found it natural to infer that their superiority in the arts of war stemmed from their racial essences, and consequently that they were inherently more intelligent, and disciplined than other peoples. (Boxill 2001: 20–21)

Here at last, we have a coherent articulation of race as a scientific account of difference, not only of skin type, but also of the supposed superiority or inferiority of those types. Articulated as such, Kant's major contribution to race theory is his ability to employ the basic grounds of objective observation as the primary criteria for a defendable theory, to explain the mechanisms of race, to muster its presence in terms of a defense of monogenesis, and to tie all of these into a theory based on reason. Kant's ultimate conclusions about race are certainly misguided, as the example noted by Eze (on p. 70) clearly demonstrates, but we should not infer that the entirety of Kant's racial suppositions are thus tainted and invalid. Kant has forged race into both its popular and scientific identity.

Defoe and racial malleability

Each of these individuals contributes fundamentally to the fabrication of race. While removing a single individual will not cause the puzzle to collapse necessarily, to do so, or to shift the scales by delivering race solely into the hands of a single individual, misses the community effort that is the fabrication of race. When gathered thus, it is tempting to argue that race is almost the inevitable offspring of Enlightenment thought. To reiterate, while no single individual can be deemed solely accountable for the fabrication of race, each increases the momentum that the notion gathers throughout the course of the Enlightenment. While the movement of race begins to crystallize scientifically, the term also begins to gain a more profound significance in the popular mind as well. Particularly, race, or rather racial difference, becomes gradually more romanticized for the delectation of the reading public. More than the base exaggeration and exoticism of Mandeville and fantastical travel writers, race begins to occupy an increasingly clari-fied and significant position in the mind of many Europeans. As evidenced by both the number of commentators who contribute to the process and the number of varying interpretations of their source material, we can intuit that race was a fascination, certainly, but that it also remains a highly mobile discursive method.

In Chapter 1 we suggested that there was significant ambivalence and general confusion with regard to the British experience of the foreign, due in part to the conflicting notions of race as lineage and race as we have come to know it in the black /white binary that is the colonial paradigm. Specifically in *Othello*, this means that the charac-ter Othello's race (his noble lineage) stands as the source of tension when juxtaposed to the bigoted response for which his color acts as catalyst. As we argued in Chapter 1, Othello poses a problem because his blackness is not fixable and, more importantly, because his nobil-ity supersedes the supposed offensive baseness of his complexion. Othello, therefore, quite literally embodies the tensions at play in the synthesis of race, civility, passion, violence, ignorance, strength, poli-tics, etc., which become ever more dramatic and polarized as we move away from the seventeenth century. The movement into the eighteenth century does not dispel these tensions entirely. Instead, the tension becomes increasingly polar, intense, and insidious, but even as belatedly as the latter half of the eighteenth century, as Roxann Wheeler comments, "Ideologically . . . it was still possible for the British to subordinate dark skin color to high rank and the profession of Christianity in relation to some populations" (Wheeler 2000: 139). She continues, "The way the [mid-eighteenth century] novels resolved this sometimes awkward exceptionality was either not to assign characters from other climates darker complexions, to erase the significance of nonwhite color through Christian conversion, or to show that what was believed to be actual color difference was really racial masquerade" (Wheeler 2000: 139). Increasingly, the contest between race and lineage was being won by race, and particularly, race as described by the likes of Linnaeus whose descriptive/proscriptive formula wove race conveniently into the fabric of sociological essentialism. Thus, Voltaire need not be surprised or concerned by the behavior of Othello, for it is entirely within his nature.

We should note that the solidification of race helpfully accompanies the increased exposure and conquest of Europeans in the exterior world. Wheeler, however, argues against a more conventional, nineteenth-century interpretation of race and the colonial paradigm, preferring instead a dynamic model that accounts for the gradual resolution of a multiplicity of racial concepts that slowly bleed into the nineteenth century. Thus, race does not immediately solidify at the moment that Bernier and Voltaire begin to speculate upon the nature of its presence. Instead, we can read race as having formed only slightly, with an uncertain multiplicity of experience still available in a significantly confused notion. So, for example, different narrative strategies were called upon to reconcile racial nuances. As Wheeler suggests, the main three options were lightening a character's complexion, enacting his/her conversion to Christianity, or masking racial difference. Again, within literary convention, we can see racial confusion manifest. Although the Enlightenment increasingly makes race natural, obvious, and undeniable, there are also dramatic moments within the movement that highlight the continued malleability of the term.

Perhaps the most enduring racial exchange from the fiction of the early eighteenth century originates in Daniel Defoe's *Life and Adventures of Robinson Crusoe* (1719). The novel is most often read as a black/white and imperial narrative. Certainly, the interaction between the memorable Crusoe and his "friendly savage" Friday speaks volumes about the eighteenth-century colonial disposition as well as our current conception of race. As compellingly argued by Wheeler, focusing exclusively on this interaction misses a great deal else that the novel offers about the malleability of race. While composing only a brief part of the entire narrative, the often over-looked Morisco Xury adds distinct layers of complexity when reading overly reductive, or overly modern, versions of race into the text. First, the term Morisco denotes the diminutive form of the Spanish Moor. In comparison to the Moor Othello discussed in Chapter 1, Xury offers a characterization both strikingly similar and altogether different. For one, Xury's social position is altogether different than Othello's. We are introduced to him already a slave in North Africa. Also like Othello, Xury's relationship with language is largely precluded by others. At very few points does Xury actually speak, and when he does, Defoe makes a point of noting that his dialect is broken and thick. Little, however, is made of Xury's color, and, likewise, he is never misunder-stood as being in any way conflicted or with noble origins. Thus, far from offering the exact tension we find in the racially over-determined Othello, Xury still demonstrates the natural and relative confusion of racial mobility. Indeed, Xury is neither noble nor in any way privi-leged. As importantly, Xury's literal mobility means that he is afforded the opportunity to interact in a broad spectrum of cultural situations. The narrative scope of the novel no longer centers on the projection of a metaphorical Venice–England experiment. Instead, the narrative's borders, along with England's, extend out into the greater world, for the acquisition of lands and capital. If Crusoe's capitalist adventures into foreign lands represent a shift in attention from the interior to the exterior, his experience of the foreign still betrays an ability to shift registers contextually. Thus, *Robinson Crusoe* can be read as an exper-iment in which categories (racial, religious, class-based) are donned and abandoned in a tour of cultural opportunities.

Now, the Morisco Xury provides the map upon which social and racial difference can be traced. Let us not forget that Bernier's conceptualization of race (1684), as previously described, includes most of North Africa and particularly inclusive gestures toward Spain and Germany as part of his first categorical distinction, the white European race.[3] While Bernier admits that this accommodation must be made in terms of Spain and Germany for fear that the entire system may unravel, it is worth noting the manner in which Moor signifies racial ambivalence through the time of Bernier's publication and beyond. One might expect, therefore, that a Spanish Moor offers a potentially borderline specimen, existing between competing regis-ters of difference. On the one hand, Xury's religious difference makes him a menace to European Christianity at a time when European contestation of land with Islamic empires has only recently begun to settle. As late as 1683, Turkish armies attempted a second and final attempt to take Vienna (Lewis 2001: 41). That an Islamic empire could attempt such a feat testifies to the often-overlooked process of European expansion in the world where it is decidedly not the only significant or dominating aggregate of power. Thus, the title Morisco, although diminutive, still reminds a European audience of Xury's relationship to a declining, but potent power.

On the other hand, Xury remains European and worthy of inclusion into the early racial categories offered by the likes of Bernier and Kant. We can see, therefore, tremendous conflict and contradiction within each aspect of his character, and it is within the friction generated by juxtaposing these contrary markers that Defoe asserts the contextual borders of his subject. Xury is religious, and the imperial implication of that status acts as one level of complexity in the composition of his cultural position. He represents both the religious other and the legacy of a diminishing imperial threat. Likewise, as both Spaniard and Moor, Xury's racial composition is contrasted both to Crusoe's paleness and the blackness of West Africa. Thus, "While Xury is neither as powerful as Crusoe nor as abject as the Africans on the west coast, his status in the novel is not stable, reflecting British uncertainties about difference in the early eighteenth century" (Wheeler 2000: 60). Indeed, Xury's position can be considered highly fluid and contextual.

The interaction between Crusoe and Xury exposes much of the friction between opposing registers of difference. The North African Moors, who enslave both Crusoe and Xury, by proxy focus almost entirely on their European character. In this sense, the relative hierarchy between the two characters becomes a product of their age difference rather than a more superficial notion that might be imposed by Crusoe. That Crusoe presumes his superiority can be seen both in the manner in which he considers his situation and the immediate servitude that is expected of Xury once the pair have secured their freedom. When first contemplating that he should escape, Crusoe laments the fact that he does not have a co-conspirator, stating, "for I had no Body to communicate it to, that would embark with me; no Fellow-Slave, no Englishman, Irishman, or Scotsman there but my self" (Defoe 2001: 18). Only a bit later do we learn of Xury, whom he only reluctantly considers worthy of recognition. When Crusoe's plot comes to fruition, for example, he brazenly considers dumping Xury overboard along with the Moor knowing that only the Moor would survive. Indeed Crusoe suggests that he actually values the Moorish kinsman of his captor more than Xury. Crusoe states, "I could ha' been content to ha' taken this Moor with me, and ha' drown'd the Boy, but there was no venturing to trust him," so that if Xury does not swear by "Mahomet and his father's Beard, I must throw [him] into the Sea too" (Defoe 2001: 21).

Even despite Crusoe's repeated assertion of his superiority over Xury on a number of occasions, their relationship is multifaceted. To Crusoe, Xury initially represents something like a household servant with extended privileges. It is occasionally suggested that Xury's continued servitude is based more on the hierarchy of their age difference rather than questions of racial status. Ultimately, the text undermines this supposition when they encounter a fellow Christian in the form of the Portuguese captain. Thus, the text demonstrates a second shift in the relative value of the boy Xury. As suggested by the diminutive nomination "Morisco," which testifies to the condescending emphasis of his adherence to Islam, Xury's relation to Crusoe alters dramatically in the presence of other European Christians. At this point "The Catholic Portuguese captain treats Crusoe as an equal, even though he possesses only the stolen boat – and Xury" (Wheeler 2000: 61). The immediate bond constructed in the mutual recognition and import of their religion crystallizes the real hierarchical distinction between Crusoe and his "boy." The captain's altruistic rescue of Crusoe immediately constructs a social situation in which Xury's difference is emphasized in its most dramatic European context. That is, his non-Christian beliefs allow the captain to presume Crusoe's possession of the boy, a mantle that Crusoe seamlessly assumes. The significance of the exchange between Crusoe and the Portuguese captain lies in the fact that, once again, Xury's status shifts with his relative position. That he should be sold by Crusoe into indentured servitude based entirely on his religious belief precludes the racial status of slavery. Moreover, Xury's status as an indentured servant comes with conditions. In a rather odd passage in which Crusoe negotiates the price of his possessions, all of which he has stolen from his former master, Crusoe comes to a striking compromise in which the Portuguese Captain offers "the Boy an Obligation to set him free in ten Years, if he turn'd into a Christian; Upon this and Xury saying he was willing to go to him, I let the captain have him" (Defoe 2001:

31). One is left to wonder what real contribution Xury supposedly had in the transaction, despite Crusoe's limited suggestion otherwise. Xury's position, or rather multitude of positions, in the text demonstrates both the malleability of race in early European experience, and the dramatically more important emphasis of religion as a mark of one's participation in humanity. Thus, if Xury does "not fall easily into categories of difference," he does, at least, invoke a hierarchy based on distance and difference from the European clearly demonstrated in the Christian solidarity between Crusoe and the Portuguese captain (Wheeler 2000: 57).

The significance of the supposed Christian ideals of Charity and Justice briefly and persistently force their way into the narrative during Crusoe's interaction with the Portuguese Captain. Of course, these notions are considerably compromised by the nature of Europe's growing imperial project. Thus, although Wheeler argues that "Christian is the only category that is not undermined by its liminality," we can infer some mischief in the cool European civility (Wheeler 2000: 65). The Captain, for example, will not accept direct payment for the handing over of Crusoe's possessions (again, including Xury) on the grounds that he would expect the same. Instead, he ferries Crusoe to their destination exclaiming, "I will carry to thither in Charity, and those things will help you to buy your Subsistence there and your Passage home again" (Defoe 2001: 30). To this Crusoe adds "As he was Charitable in his Proposal, so he was Just in the Performance to a title" (Defoe 2001: 31). Of course, the Captain eventually purchases all of Crusoe's possessions, making the exchange a brief symbolic charade, excusing both Christians from the appearance of anything other than Charity and Justice.

When compared to the undermining of baser, and more distinctly racial, presumptions, however, the illusory nature of Christian charity serves only to highlight one more in a line of troubled preconceptions. In Crusoe and Xury's brief encounter with the black Africans, a scene that foreshadows later encounters with the natives of "Crusoe's" island, Xury supposes that the Africans might be cannibals and warns against venturing too close. Upon first seeing the Africans, he remarks "we saw People stand upon the Shoar to look at us, we could also perceive they were quite Black and Stark-naked" (Defoe 2001: 27). Wheeler suggests that the nakedness may be just as disconcerting to the extensively class-conscious European mind as the supposed savagery (Wheeler 2000: 72). Simply, these individuals defy standard methods of European class evaluation. Ultimately, of course, the text destabilizes the validity of these suppositions with a cautious, but mutually beneficial exchange. Interestingly, given the nature of our discussion above, it is Crusoe's military might that helps accomplish this task. By killing the Lion, Crusoe presents his physical dominance from which we are to intuit his intellectual and cultural prowess, as well. What follows, however, is an exchange where Crusoe accepts "Pieces of dry Flesh and Corn" from the savages despite the fact that "we neither know what the one or the other was" (Defoe 2001: 27). Later, when the Lion's meat is offered, Crusoe politely declines, opting for the skin instead. The exchange once again leaves the supposed racial distance considerably diminished as Crusoe reports, "and leaving my friendly *Negroes*, I made forward" (Defoe 2001: 29). As this scene directly precedes the "liberating" encounter with the Portuguese ship, the text creates a direct juxtaposition between the differences of pagan and Christian forms of charity.

As with Othello, Xury's mobility in terms of his register as Other does not solely operate within the logic of the text itself. In fact, editorial amendments and additions in the publication history of *Robinson Crusoe* also help the reader map racial difference. Interestingly, in a gesture that directly parallels the span of Enlightenment fabrication of distinct racial difference, Wheeler is able to trace the blackening of Xury from his earliest visual representations through later eighteenth-century editions of the text. A London edition from 1726, for example, includes a plate in which Xury mirrors Crusoe both in his complexion and, as importantly, in his style of dress. An edition from 1791, on the other hand, has Xury marked as a black African with a style of dress more closely related to the other African characters pictured (Wheeler 2000: 63–64). Likewise, a Dublin edition from 1774 amends Xury's speech so that it more closely resembles stereotypically fragmented forms of Pidgin English, commonly attributed to black Africans. The blackening of Xury, as it coincides with the construction of racial categories, may be coincidental, but not entirely unrelated to the continuing development of race.

Frankenstein's imperial paranoia

Nearly one hundred years later, Mary Shelley constructs a novel representing English (and European) fears with regard to the social mission of its own supposed progress. Perhaps an unlikely text to be considered in a volume such as this, which focuses exclusively on the varying constructions of race and racial ideology, Mary Shelley's *Frankenstein: or, The Modern Prometheus* (1818) ([1818] 1963) still offers a great deal of insight both into the continued evolution of the term, and the tension that the Enlightenment inspired in the greater community.[4] To this end, we can read a subtle ambivalence among the obvious conflicts in Shelley's text. Traditional interpretations of Frankenstein have spent a great deal of energy noting the tension between man and technology. Indeed, Frankenstein has entered the public conscious as a metaphor for unchecked and irresponsible technological progress. The extent to which Frankenstein remains deeply embedded in the modern conscious is evidenced by the way we worry about "Franken-foods" when discussing genetically modified food; however, through the popularity of film, we are accustomed to the notion of Dr. Frankenstein as the mad scientist surrounded by odd gadgets. These pleasingly silly, but rather unfortunate representations of *Frankenstein* miss the genuine source of Shelley's anxiety, and may lead one to wonder about the relation of this text to our discussion. Granted, there are relatively few distinctly marked characters that overtly embody the developing notion of race in Shelley's *Frankenstein*; however, the obtuse morality of the text takes the fabrication of *a race* of beings as its axis. Mary Shelley helps this discussion not so much in terms of Europe's conflicted experience with the foreign, but rather in terms of Europe's own internalization of its social mission. In the Enlightenment, we witnessed the community effort of la Peyrère, Voltaire, Bernier, Linnaeus, Buffon, Blumenbach, and Kant and the piecemeal construction not just of *a race*, but all races. Frankenstein's experience is not concerned with either the foreign or the explanatory agenda of the natural philosophers, although he claims inspiration from them. In fact, on several occasions, he displays a succinct disinterest in matters outside of Europe. Thus, Frankenstein's creation inherits the racial fetishism of natural philosophy, but operates solely within the European social dynamic. Shelley's critique of the "modern Prometheus" is not based in the tradition of the mad scientist working through the night with mutilated henchmen and technological gadgets; it is based on the rational, albeit over-zealous, investigation of natural phenomena. Above all, Frankenstein is a natural philosopher, one of the exact specimens of men we have just discussed at such length, but instead of taking race to the exterior world, Frankenstein creates race on his own doorstep.

Situated between the Enlightenment and the steady decline of the British Empire, Mary Shelley offers at least two distinct interpretations of her writing. On the one hand, in an uneasy backward glance to the Enlightenment, there is a troubled introspection into the mass project of natural history, which suggests Shelley's distinctly unsettled connection with the more ambitious aspects of the Enlightenment. She has, after all, constructed a dramatically cautionary tale, warning of the dangers of our modern Prometheus. Central to the entire action of the text, therefore, Shelley both explicitly and metaphorically questions the mission of natural history and delivers less than encouraging answers. *Frankenstein* is fraught with anxiety as to the potency and desirability of the project. Instead of bringing the product of natural history to the outside world, Shelley and Frankenstein's monstrous creation comes home.

On the other hand, Shelley also demonstrates a clear understanding and sympathy with the increasingly intense levels of anxiety with regard to the future of humankind, and represents a divide between the growing authority of scientific discourse and the popular notions of a reality quite detached from that scientific authority. A fundamental issue in all of this is the lingering specter of societal decay in the late eighteenth and early nineteenth century mind, as echoed in Blumenbach's theory of degeneration. For the British Empire, one potential cause of the decline ironically finds itself in the source of its greatest triumph. Imperialism brings contact, and contact brings exposure to those unfortunate others whom the Enlightenment theorists have worked so intensely to fix in an identifiable position. Of course, this is a politics of paranoia. Thus Shelley's Frankenstein is caught between the perils of progress and the decline of a society in degeneration. As one might imagine, this is a bleak and fantastic landscape upon which to build a tale of gothic horror.

Despite the rather exhaustive efforts of other Enlightenment thinkers to create a functioning social model of four to five categorical races, Shelley maintains one of the early denotations of the word race, abstractly and literally. Significantly, this demonstrates the failure of the natural philosophers to rigidly define the term, and leaves the several older meanings to resiliently abide in the lexicon for some time to come. For her part, Shelley, in her first chapter, implicitly invokes the sense of race as noble lineage, as opposed to physical difference.

Later, while the purity of his lineage remains a concern, race as physical differentiation becomes preeminent. This, accompanied by the growing anxiety of degeneration, vitalizes the importance of hedging the boundaries between the privileged and dangerous classes. In the subtext of the novel, there is a preoccupation with sustenance of the stock. Elizabeth must be the descendent of a certain "Milanese nobleman," who has fallen on hard times, in order to constitute the appropriate stock for the young, noble Victor Frankenstein (Shelley [1818] 1963: 20). There must be no degeneration of the stock, and the fact that she is rescued from the precipice of disaster only helps to augment the moral potency of Shelley's tale. If the privileged classes are not careful, they risk slipping into the disenfranchised multitude growing throughout Europe. Moreover, it is the political nostalgia for a more civil age that helps her father instigate his, and thus her, ruin. His fixation on the "antique glory of Italy" excites his passions, a weakness to which he ultimately succumbs ([1818] 1963: 20). There is an interesting symmetry in what Shelley communicates here that is not immediately apparent. Later in the novel, during the monster's education, Frankenstein describes a series of steps in his progression. One significant portion of this education includes a cautionary tale about a devious "Turk" who encourages the romantic passions of his daughter only in relation to his own liberation from a Parisian prison (Shelley [1818] 1963: 103–107). True to the cautionary nature of the tale, the moral of the story suggests that no good deed goes unpunished, and that one should never trust the foreign emissary of a once proud and triumphant society that has since disintegrated. In the creature's slow awakening, and specifically in his awareness of human history, he learns of the Romans and "their subsequent degenerating" ([1818 1963: 100). Thus, inscribed in the creature's education is an ominous reminder of the collapse of imperial states through degeneration. The threat is subtle and slow to develop, not unlike the generational progress of societal implosion.

Within the lingering threat of degeneration and the disintegration of the noble classes, we can also observe a fascination with the hypothetical pitfalls of miscegenation indicative of the new racial markers and of colonial conquest. The physical proficiency of Frankenstein's monster represents the fundamental fear inherent in projects of colonial expansion. The contrast between the monster's physicality and Frankenstein's intellect is a fairly standard binary juxtaposition between the savage in need of governance and the cultured

European. Often marked, and never adequately explained, the creature's physical prowess is inversely proportional to Victor
Frankenstein's near constant need to "repose" in the face of any
excitement, a sign of his physical inferiority. The monster's creation,
as Frankenstein frequently reminds us, is an accomplishment of his
own astounding intellectual fortitude. The text however undermines
this achievement by allowing the monster to articulate his own inde-
pendent relationship with knowledge: "Of what strange nature is
knowledge! . . . I learned that there was but one means to overcome
the sensation of pain, and that was death – a state which I feared yet
did not understand" (Shelley [1818] 1963: 101). The monster's humility and fear of death reveal a superior, yet indirect understanding of
Frankenstein's perpetual need to sleep. Thus, Frankenstein's savage
monster surpasses him physically (as expected) *and*, one could say,
intellectually, as his ability to argue reasonably and non-violently with
his creator clearly demonstrates. The monster displays his rational
abilities stating "I am content to reason with you. I am malicious
because I am miserable" (Shelley [1818] 1963: 124).

Frankenstein exhausts considerable effort to make his creature
fantastic, somewhat exotic, and oddly racial in composition: "His
limbs were in proportion, and I had selected his features as beautiful.
Beautiful! Great God! His yellow skin scarcely covered the work of his
muscles and arteries beneath; his hair was of a lustrous black . . . his
shriveled complexion and straight black lips" (Shelley [1818] 1963:
42). If we read the creature as a racialized character, we immediately
recognize the European impression of savage physicality. Linnaeus'
three most bothersome subspecies each attempted to define the
elusively savage and barbarian aspects of the colonized subject.
Linnaeus' *Homo ferus*, *homo troglodytes*, and *homo monstrous* each
attempt to isolate savagery in its most mythological form, as it is
founded in the base physicality of the uncivilized. Frankenstein's
creature embodies a significant portion of this physicality: he is cruel,
endures incredible physical hardship, is largely unaffected by the
elements, and demonstrates little aesthetics. This fact alone makes
him a threat to the languid Frankenstein; however, it is a significant
part of Frankenstein's arrogance, and his failure, that he never once
marks the equally potent mind that he has helped create.

To the direct actions of colonial conquest, Frankenstein remains
largely impassive. When he undertakes the study of Oriental
languages with Clerval, for example, he does so with an apathetic

knowledge-for-knowledge's-sake attitude. This is the indifference of the European dominator who exoticizes the oriental other, but has no genuine interest in a communication or exchange with that being outside of proscribed parameters. Instead, they are there for his "temporary amusement" (Shelley [1818] 1963: 53). That Frankenstein proceeds to contrast the writing of these languages to the "manly and heroic poetry of Greece and Rome" help to feminize and antagonize the Orient (Shelley [1818] 1963: 53). Frankenstein states, "When you read their writings, life appears to consist in a warm sun and a garden of roses, in the smiles and frowns of a fair enemy, and the fire that consumes your own heart" (Shelley [1818] 1963: 53). Thus, Frankenstein's relationship with knowledge is deeply imbued with antagonism and exoticism, but with no hope of genuine interaction or communication. It is tempting to read Frankenstein's engagement with these studies as a sign of his intellectual acuity, but his reluctance to learn these languages to any practical purpose stands in direct contrast to Clerval, whose dream it is to travel to the Orient and, one presumes, to engage in some form of cultural exchange. He will never arrive, of course, because the monstrous race that is the fruit of Frankenstein's earlier studies in natural history will destroy Clerval.

Indeed, Frankenstein's motivation for creating the "monster" in the first place can be easily conflated as an imperial impulse, with the desire to rule over the grateful masses, or the gratefully oppressed in the colonial paradigm. Frankenstein proclaims, "Life and Death appeared to me ideal bounds, which I should first break through, and pour a torrent of light into our dark world. A new species would bless me as its creator and source; many happy and excellent natures would owe their being to me. No father could claim the gratitude of his child so completely as I should deserve theirs" (Shelley [1818] 1963: 38–39). That Frankenstein should expect gratitude from his new "species" for the mere fact of its existence is, in equal measures, paternal and condescending. It is also fundamentally imperial, as demonstrated by his desire to create many more than his single subject. Moreover, Frankenstein specifically announces a refusal to view his creation as anything other than a child. Without any considerable stretch, this admonition can be read as colonial paternalism, writ small. Frankenstein has no time or interest in recognizing the fundamental humanity of his creation. Instead he would have his new species innocently revel in the glory of its existence. Thus,

Frankenstein participates in a Kantian refusal to acknowledge the potency and will of his racialized subjects. Here it is important to note a slight lexical shift. At this point, Frankenstein discusses his creation in terms of specific organization. But later, in his refusal to accommodate his creation, Frankenstein refers to the humanity in which the monster is not included, in distinctly racial terms: "A thousand times would I have shed my own blood, drop by drop . . . but I could not, my father, indeed I could not sacrifice the whole human race" (Shelley [1818] 1963: 164). Frankenstein refuses to deliver a female companion to the monster, professing to prefer death in favor of the consignment of his race. The contest between the monster and Frankenstein, thus articulated, is racial. Consequently, what begins as a distinction of species shifts malignantly once the alleged savage is unleashed.

There is another avenue through which race presents itself in the text. From the outset, when Frankenstein is rescued by his *Doppelgänger*, Walton, the text provides an interesting moment of solidarity between the two men. In an act that ultimately instigates Frankenstein's tale, which would otherwise have remained secret, Walton professes his desire, "One man's life or death were but a small price to pay for the acquirement of the knowledge which I sought, for the dominion I should acquire and transmit over the elemental foes of our race" (Shelley [1818] 1963: 12). Once again a protagonist adrift is summarily reclaimed by a fellow European, and once again, they demonstrate an almost instantaneous bond. Unlike Crusoe and his Portuguese Captain, Frankenstein has nothing to offer Walton in exchange for his Christian charity other than his tale, which he delivers only upon recognizing the blind scientific ambition in his savior. Thus, science replaces Christianity as the authority that inspires solidarity among our European adventurers. At this point, the meaning of "our race" doubles. On the one hand, our race could be the human variety, on the other, the white European. Their brotherhood, therefore, stems directly from their mutual participation and devotion to scientific progress. Likewise, given the speculative nature of the racial project and the scientific progress of the Enlightenment, the juxtaposition of elemental foes with "our race" seems rather suggestive. The elements, we will remember, are an integral component of the natural philosophers' causal mechanism for race. The presupposed role of the elements in the creation of race cannot pass unrecognized by either individual so competent in the field of natural philosophy.

The immediate solidarity between Frankenstein and Walton signals another aspect of the dominant European social network, also evident in *Robinson Crusoe*. Put simply, this is a man's world. In this man's world, physical, ideological and sexual conquests are consistently interchangeable. Frankenstein's desire to create a species becomes not only one based on the mastery of knowledge, but on total domination of it. As with various forms of colonial tropes of attraction and repulsion, Frankenstein's desire endures a painful reversal. His desire becomes dramatically reversed at the exact moment of his accomplishment, as he experiences a near post-coital moment of procreative horror. He states, "I had desired it with an ardour that far exceeded moderation; but now that I had finished, the beauty of the dream vanished, and breathless horror and disgust filled my heart" (Shelley [1818] 1963: 42). Likewise, if we presuppose racial intent in Frankenstein's intellectual mission, we can intuit a dramatic blend of racial and sexual desire. Frankenstein states, "It was the secrets of heaven and earth that I desired to learn; and whether it was the outward substance of things or the inner spirit of nature and the mysterious soul of man that occupied me, still my inquiries were directed to the metaphysical, or in its highest sense, the physical secrets of the world" (Shelley [1818] 1963: 23). Ultimately, however, Frankenstein betrays his preference for the physical aspect of his mission. Often, even the pursuit of knowledge is articulated with ravaging sexual undertones. For example, Frankenstein's "fervent" desire to "penetrate the secrets of nature" leads directly to the "birth" of his passion (Shelley [1818] 1963: 24–25). Frankenstein's fantasy originally involved his reign over contented savages. His desire, however, is a perversion of nature. The text leaves us to wonder whether it is the physical creation of the race, the colonial desire to rule it, or the obsessive, immoderate manner in which it is pursued that demands Frankenstein's atonement.

Transition

As suggested in Chapter 1, the fabrication of race is a communal affair. For the natural philosophers of the Enlightenment, this task was inspired by their fundamental need to classify and organize the natural world. The confidence they exhibit in the enterprise grows considerably as European influence reaches outward across the globe. For Voltaire, Bernier, Linnaeus, Buffon, Blumenbach, and Kant, the world demanded explanation, and their faith in the processes of distanced, reasoned observation suggested to them that they were capable of accomplishing this goal. Moreover, the sheer volume of material fixated toward this goal seems to suggest that this encounter with foreign people called urgently for considerable attention. Once reasonably articulated, the fabrication of race was almost immediately woven into the public conscious.

Race is now natural and obvious. Situated thus, race will not be removed from the European ideological landscape and will accompany Europeans well beyond their borders. But we must remember that, in many ways, the European fabrication of race was natural. As suggested in our discussion of Kant, the Enlightenment needed to explain why Europeans were suddenly capable of dominating the world on a scale that seemed, to them, unprecedented. It is reasonable to suggest that the explanation they found for their dominance lay in the precise explanation that they used to explain other more obvious difference. By articulating race in this manner, the natural philosophers move race well beyond the scope of natural and obvious.

Race is now essential. The Enlightenment did much more than simply explain physical difference. Natural philosophy prepared a society increasingly confident in its domination of the globe, fully cognizant of race, and sincere in its belief that race could describe much, much more about an individual than her skin color. And it is at this point that race becomes potentially quite threatening, because in theory race may be obvious, but in practice it is anything but. As poor diminutive Xury points out, the European world did not operate exclusively upon reason and Christian charity. Moreover, despite the essentially solid notion of race, the registers were (and are still) extremely malleable.

That the natural philosophers should place their faith in reason signals a profound development in the authority of the sciences. Indeed, commentators such as Kant were still intellectually bound by the previous religious authorities that would slowly become antagonistic to the machinations of a nascent scientific discourse. For we know, however, that the unification of religion and science testifies to a dramatically different time. That scientific discourse should gain such considerable and authoritative ground will become dramatically evident in Chapter 3 as we witness competing forms of scientific discourse argue for and against the existence of race. In a gesture nearly identical to Frankenstein's monster once brought into the world, the creation is at once brilliant and obscene.

Notes

1. Repeatedly, we have referred to the "fabrication of race," and we will continue to do so throughout this volume. We recognize that the word fabrication, when applied to linguistic constructions, tends to have the connotation of fallacy. The first connotation that we would like to suggest, however, is that the concept is constructed. Fabrication, in this sense, suggests that process. While we would like to obliquely hold onto the implication that this construction is also to some extent a fallacy, we by no means suggest that the theorists in this chapter felt this way. The construction of race was not necessarily a project undertaken with malice or deliberate falsehood.

2. Interestingly, Kant gets this right. In his cumulative effort, Kant arrives at the deductive leap that Buffon himself fails to make, stating, "If we reflect that anciently animals and humans must have crossed back and forth between Asia and America, so that we meet with the same kinds of animals in the cold atmosphere of both continents" (Kant 1997: 45).

3. We should also note that Kant makes a similar gesture and without the apologetic suggestion that the entire classificatory system might break down as a result of the admittedly tenuous supposition. This demonstrates the resilience that the term Moor displays in the resistance to limiting racial registers.

4. Mary Shelley's *Frankenstein: a Modern Prometheus* is more often discussed in terms of its participation in the Victorian gothic. This, however, may be rather misleading for purely chronological reasons. Victoria Saxe-Coburg was not born until a year after the first publication of *Frankenstein*. Moreover, Queen Victoria did not ascend to the throne until 1837, nearly twenty years after the first publication. While this fact does not necessarily exclude the text from being Victorian in a more general sense of the literary movement, it should be considered carefully in a discussion such as this. To be sure, *Frankenstein* does participate in several tropes that are distinctly Victorian; however, *Frankenstein* is also situated directly between the Enlightenment, with which it takes major issue, and the Victorian periods. As such, it represents a perfect chronological and thematic transition point between this chapter and Chapter 3.

3 Scientific Authority and Appropriation

> The danger, however, to which he exposes himself cannot deter a man from doing that which he regards as his duty. When a scientific truth has been discovered, he owes it to humanity, and has no right to withhold it. (Nordau [1895] 1968: vii)

> Pay no attention to him; he has no common sense: he is all genius. (Anon., quoted in Lombroso [1899] 1911: 33)

Charles Darwin

As we have observed in Chapter 2, the fabrication of race is a community matter, one that requires a momentous effort from a significantly varied population. Likewise, the fabrication of race is not intimately connected in a cause and effect manner to the proliferation of colonial conquest and the slave trade, as evidenced by the imperative role played by nations not participating in either matter, namely Germany. And so, the effort seems one that is both pan-European, and practically grounded in the grand empires which she nourished. As suggested in Chapter 2, Europeans were left wondering as to the reason for their growing, global preeminence. For this explanation, they turned to the imagined authority of scientific discourse. Because scientific discourse claims to merit dispassionate distance and objective observation, the legitimacy of its truth-claims are rhetorically imposing. To be sure, the reach and influence of this discourse certainly benefited from the channels, forced or otherwise, of exchange between previously disparate societies. But within this discourse there are competing avenues of authority.

Certainly, there was at least some relationship between the exposure of European scientists to new information and experience, and the progressive leap of the sciences. As the power and supremacy of the British Empire spread across the globe, the discourse prepared by its most significant scientists gained fortitude in equal measure. This is not to say that the authority of scientific discourse is intimately connected to the ambition of empire. The two activities need not be. This exposure to the exterior world facilitated scientific research for its own sake and the requirement of first-hand collection of data as the grounds upon which one could base a critical assertion, i.e., Darwin's travels on the *Beagle*.

It is an odd and compelling coincidence that as scientific discourse gained authority in the Western mind, the scientific foundation for race seemed simultaneously to crumble and solidify. Indeed, one of the most significant avenues of scientific investigation, supported in this case by Charles Darwin, worked actively against the scientific notion of race. Another scientific perspective concerned with cultural/racial atrophy and deeply embroiled in the imperial project found great recourse in the popular imagination. It is this second school of thought that wholeheartedly believed in the existence of race, and which eventually found popular resonance in its account of the growing European fear of its own repressive, decadent, crime-laden, and urbanized society. This chapter, therefore, begins with Darwin and his systematic refutation of race, and then moves to several more mobile narratives of degeneration and eugenics that appropriate the discourse and ultimately attempt to validate race. The effects of this second strand can be read in the late Victorian literature of Rudyard Kipling, as well as in the more recent quasi-scientific debates of *The Bell Curve*.

With the burgeoning power of scientific discourse in mind, it would be difficult to overstate the contribution of Charles Darwin to the modern intellectual. Darwin's *The Origin of Species by Means of Natural Selection or the Preservation of Favoured Races in the Struggle for Life* (1859) crawled into the consciousness of the Victorian mindscape and remains one of the most significant books to be published with regard to our perception of the world. Although not immediately embraced by many readers, the subsequent force of its rhetoric was such that Darwin's notion of natural selection currently entertains an almost commonsensical status within not only the scientific community, but also significant populations of the world beyond those skilled in the profession. Thus, "During the past hundred years or so evolutionary theory has functioned in our culture like a myth in a period of belief, moving endlessly to and fro between metaphor and paradigm, feeding an extraordinary range of disciplines beyond its own original biological field" (Beer 1983: 17). Certainly, the power of Darwin's narrative was recognized by commentators of his day as well, who often immediately saw the political implications and possibilities offered in his work. Ernst Haeckel ("Darwin's greatest popularizer"), for example, argues Darwin's theory in terms of its political might:

> Evolution and progress stand on the one side, marshaled under the bright banner of science; on the other side, marshaled under the black flag of hierarchy, stand spiritual servitude and falsehood, want of reason and barbarism, superstition and retrogression . . . Evolution is the heavy artillery in the struggle for truth; whole ranks of dualistic sophisms fall before [it] . . . as before the chain shot of artillery. (Quoted in Gould 1973: 217)

Granted, Darwin's theories have not always been received pleasantly or enthusiastically. One need look no further than the Scopes trial in the United States to witness lingering moments of antagonism between the goals of scientific reason and waning fundamentalism in the church. In the context of Chapters 1 and 2, and particularly the discussion of Kant's role in the creation of race, it is noteworthy that the interests of science and religion were not always considered belligerent opponents. And here, race plays a peculiar role. Kant, as we will recall, employed his methodology as a direct response to theories of polygenesis, which contested the literal, biblical story of a single human lineage beginning with Adam and Eve. By the time we get to Darwin, scientific observation has become increasingly, although by no means entirely, secular in its disposition, as well as more formidable in the rhetorical power of its authority. It has also become rather political despite the wishes of many proponents of genuine scientific investigation. The political dimension of science enters the debate when we consider pronunciations about "facts of nature," as we noted with Kant. The problem with such pronunciations is that they tend to remove the speculative nature of genuine scientific investigation and turn, instead, toward the kind of limiting discourse (where experience must meet preconception rather than the other way around) so common in the narrow, cloistered mindset of religious fundamentalism.

Although perhaps best known for his theories of evolution, survival of the fittest, and natural selection, most of which were articulated in his *The Origin of Species*, Darwin's natural theories have had a profound influence over racial thought as well. The sum of Darwin's influence on the subject of race can be expressed in terms of both encouraging and tragic consequences, with equal measure. The encouraging aspect of Darwin's influence stems from his systematic refutation of race in anything other than in its broadest biological sense, which employs the word to denote simple variety in organic life, and not as a distinct signifier of speciation. It is, however, the application of some of Darwin's earlier theories that have tragic consequences. These theories and consequences will be discussed later in this chapter. Now, we will turn our attention to Darwin's link to race. Specifically, Darwin dedicates a chapter of his work *The Descent of Man and Selection in Relation to Sex* (1871) exclusively to the concept of race. In the seventh chapter of this volume, titled "On the Races of Man," Darwin systematically destroys the scientific basis for the distinction between races. Again, having dealt with muddled definitions in Chapters 1 and 2, we should note that Darwin applies the word race in the broadest biological sense. He neither attempts, as with Linnaeus, to reconcile behavioral characteristics with the differentiation of physical features, nor does he allow physical distinction to predetermine mental or particular cultural acuity.

Darwin's mission is to "apply these generally-admitted principles to the races of man, viewing him in the same spirit as a naturalist would any other animal" ([1871] 1998: 55). In this rather lovely moment of egalitarian thinking, Darwin levels the scientific gaze and summarily negates the privilege of humanity's position within the natural system. Early scientific endeavors purported to do the same. Kant, we must remember, was not deliberately malicious or cynical in his "fabrication" of race (Boxill 2001: 19). Darwin's argument against race, therefore, marks a response that counteracts previous claims of objectivity to dismantle the scientific ground for race. Moreover, Darwin does not stop after negating the relevance of color differences. Instead, he systematically works through several other key criteria that had been consistently used to justify the need for distinction and/or speciation, namely skin color, fertility, and climate. This, however, does not preclude or eradicate a more conventional use of the term. Darwin himself saw no real problem with the application of the term race in more traditional, and increasingly rare, social or religious connotations. At times, the mission to isolate scientific discourse from the more general lexicon seems a stretch even for Darwin, who concedes that "from long habit the term 'race' will perhaps always be employed" (Darwin [1871] 1998: 182). Darwin's chapter title, "On the Races of Man," testifies to this precise inevitability. This does not, however, derail Darwin in his attempts to dismantle the scientific viability of the term.

The three most compelling observations for early natural philosophers marshaled in support of racial and special variety in humankind were the obviousness of skin color and other physical differences, particularly pertaining to facial and cranial features, the supposed sterility of mixed-race individuals, and the apparent influence of the climate on skin color. Combined, these three (spurious) distinctions formulated the base theory that then allowed natural philosophers to seek behavioral support to bolster the distinctness of each regional specimen. As we observed in Chapter 2, to these basic concepts they added racial dispositions and, most significantly in the case of Kant, they added the essential notion of seed or germ to fabricate a social unity between the races. With these criteria in mind, then, Darwin set to his task.

From the outset of "On the Races of Man," Darwin clarifies that it will not be his "intention to describe the several so-called races of men," as was the case with the majority of the material published before him (Darwin [1871] 1998: 172). Darwin's shift in approach from the likes of Bernier, Linnaeus, and others is that he does not have a proscriptive or descriptive agenda. His appeal to fundamental observation stands in direct contrast to those who would link race to the analysis of character or behavior. Instead, he announces his intention to test the viability of the distinctions that were already gathering some critical momentum. One of the primary reasons for his initial skepticism of the basis in the speciation of humankind is his recognition of the relativity and arbitrary nature of demarcation. Darwin writes, "Whether primeval man, when he possessed very few arts of the rudest kind, and when his power of language was extremely imperfect, would have deserved to be called man, must depend on the definition which we employ." In fact, "it would be impossible to fix on any definite point when the term 'man' ought to be used" (Darwin [1871] 1998: 187–188). For the evolutionary theorist, boundaries between the categorical distinctions of all life must blend considerably at some point. This explains at least part of the initial resistance to Darwin. The notion that humanity descended directly from apes could reasonably be considered a shock, or at least a social *faux pas*, next to the very recent notion that one's race could denote lineage. The problem for Darwin was the deployment of criteria and the intellectual ground upon which one marked the distinction between species. Now, the quote above does not suggest that because of the blending of species and the difficulty in marking the point at which apes evolved into man that we must also ignore the obvious differences between man and ape. That would be reductive to the point of absurdity. Darwin's argument suggests that the use of speech and tools would not appear as a sudden and clearly articulated leap in the history of humanity unless viewed from a tremendously reductive distance.

With this in mind, Darwin begins his investigation into the demarcation of races with the most obvious and broadly noted difference between human varieties – skin color. The problem that Darwin articulates directly relates to the trepidation we noted in Bernier's digression in Chapter 2. Any classification system of natural, organic, and fluid phenomena will require a certain amount of arbitrary decision-making inspired by practical concerns. For Bernier, the tension between arbitrary and practical decisions leads him to question whether his system would collapse if a race were needed to describe every nation in Europe. Indeed, Bernier's trepidation extends well beyond his own time. Shermer explains that "Part of the problem of race classification is that within-group variability is greater than between-group variability" (Shermer 1997: 248). In other words, the difference between black and yellow is not nearly as profound as the difference within either black or yellow. Adding to this point, Luca Cavalli-Sforza and his colleagues, Paolo Menozi and Alberto Piazza, conclude that "from a scientific point of view, the concept of race has failed to obtain any consensus; none is likely, given the gradual variation in existence" (Cavalli-Sforza *et al.* 1994: 19). Furthermore, Cavalli-Sforza believes that "Although there is no doubt that there is only one human species, there are clearly no objective reasons for stopping at any particular level of taxonomic splitting" (Cavalli-Sforza *et al.* 1994: 19). When viewed from this vantage, race seems highly illogical. The point simply made is that racial groupings consistently refer to their own arbitrary nature by being ineffectual, or inconsistent, in their ability to genuinely articulate difference with any precision or poignancy. Does this situation deny the reality of race? Again,

there are those that would insist that race is immediate and undeniable, but race, as articulated by Darwin, is not a necessary, accurate,
or beneficial method for describing the human subject.

The counterpoint to Darwin's negation argues simply that race is
obvious – black is black and white is white – and to deny the existence
of these races is to ignore, in the most unscientific manner, the empirical evidence. The most basic, objective scrutiny can detect the simple
difference in the binary system. And indeed, Darwin concedes that
"Of all the differences between the races of man, the color of the skin
is the most conspicuous and one of the best marked" (Darwin [1871]
1998: 200). To this, however, Darwin would add that race is not an
empirically supported basis for biological differentiation in the
genuinely scientific sense the word. Let us return briefly to Aristotle's
distinction between species and genus from Chapter 1. In order to
mark a speciation or secondary category for dividing the human
genus, we must also note a difference in function. The demand for
function left many theorists cold, hence the need for subsequent
theories that argued for a germ or seed that could then act as the
causal element and racial essence of that species. But skin color in
itself offers little more in terms of function than, say, eye color.
Moreover, the variation of skin color could be traced to its cause,
climate, but not to its general function if separated from the essential
racial elements. Therefore, as suggested by Gould, "Geographic variability, not race, is self-evident" (Gould 1973: 232). Darwin articulates
the problem as such, "It may be doubted whether any character can
be named which is distinctive of a race and is constant." Darwin adds
that "the most weighty of all the arguments against treating the races
of man as distinct species, is that they graduate into each other, independently in many cases, as far as we can judge, of their having inter-
crossed" (Darwin [1871] 1998: 181). And this is the precise issue that
Darwin takes with theorists who exhausted considerable time and
energy without paying appropriate attention to the fundamental
characteristics of divisionary techniques that go beyond simple
geographic variation.

Perhaps one of the most fundamental criticisms that Darwin levies
is his criticism of the research that has preceded him. Here, Darwin
precisely locates the confusion we detailed in Chapters 1 and 2. In
particular, Darwin was troubled by the inability of his predecessors to
competently fix the object of their discussion, and their general inde-
cision regarding the number of races in existence. Darwin laments

that "all naturalists have learned, by dearly-bought experience, how rash it is to attempt to define species by the aid of inconsistent characters" (Darwin [1871] 1998: 181). In fact, Darwin seems extremely frustrated with the sum of earlier attempts to argue that the subject of humankind should be treated with a poverty of intellectual rigor. In an almost mocking tone, Darwin provides a brief summary of the potential number of subdivisions. Darwin plaintively catalogues the work, regretfully noting that humanity should be "classed as a single species or race, or as two (Virey), as three (Jasquinot), as four (Kant), five (Blumenbach), six (Buffon), seven (Hunter), eight (Agassiz), eleven (Pickering), fifteen (Bory St. Vincent). sixteen (Desmoulins), twenty-two (Morton), sixty (Crawfurd), or as sixty-three, according to Burke" (Darwin [1871] 1998: 181). With this statement, Darwin begins the systematic dismantling of the criteria and evidence generally advanced in support of and offered as an explanation for the existence of race as a viable tool for the differentiation of humankind.

The second major criterion for marking different species is based upon their respective fertility and the ability to successfully breed. As suggested in Chapter 2, the popularity of Buffon's rule marked a fundamental basis for fabricating special distinction. When applied to the human subject, and particularly to the processes of racial categorization, Buffon's rule isolated races through the insistence that individuals of mixed race were either sterile or incapable of generating successive generations. Although apparently missing the highly charged and political nature of what must be considered contentious data, Darwin is willing to consider the inferior vitality of mulattos, who were believed to be increasingly susceptible to disease.[1] Having duly considered the evidence, however, Darwin took exception to the argument, and particularly to the assertion that blacks and whites could/should be considered a separate species based on the asserted potential sterility of their mixed offspring. For his argument, Darwin picks upon the by now tired example of the sterile mule, the offspring of the mixing of a horse and a donkey, and undermines the notion of mulatto invalidity. Darwin states, "The common Mule, so notorious for long life and vigor, and yet so sterile, show how little necessary connection there is in hybrids between lessened fertility and vitality" (Darwin [1871] 1998: 178). Indeed, Darwin asserts the exact opposite of popular notions of racial rigidity, "Hence the races of man are not sufficiently distinct to coexist without fusion; and this it is which, in all ordinary cases, affords the usual test of specific distinctness"

([1871] 1998: 62). That Darwin should insist that the races of humankind are not sufficiently distinct to exist *without* fusion is both compelling and deeply indicative of a social reality that exists in spite of racial demarcation. Miscegenation, in itself, testifies to the impropriety of racial distinction both in the proper application of Buffon's rule, and in the material fact of its existence. Interestingly, Darwin falls in line with the much earlier, greatly misunderstood assertion by Aristotle who insisted that humanity could not be broken down into any increasingly specific distinction other than "man."

Having spent some effort reducing the racial criteria offered by the traditional natural philosophy, Darwin was left with the consensus with regard to the formation of races. As noted with Blumenbach and others in Chapter 2, climate was offered as a useful tool in explaining the darkness of peoples near the equator because it was easily observed that a European would tan in tropical conditions. The presumption, therefore, was that white was the base or original color from which climate could induce variation. By the time Darwin appeared, however, this theory had fallen rather flat for the obvious reason that Africans living away from the equator for several years had not changed in appearance. In a more significant timescale, we might also note that Dutch families did not change race after several generations of life in South Africa. More complex theories were then proffered. Darwin seemingly mocks the opinions of "D'Orbigny in South America, and Livingstone in Africa" who speculated that humidity and dryness in the atmosphere might have a more dramatic role in the alteration or composition of racial characteristics, like skin color, than heat, but who "arrived at diametrically opposite conclusions" with similar information (Darwin [1871] 1998: 201). This leads Darwin to doubt the likelihood of finding a reliable conclusion to the matter, adding that one "cannot account for the difference in color in the races of man, through any advantage thus gained, or through the direct action of climate" ([1871] 1998: 204). To which he adds only that climate should not be ignored entirely, but only insomuch as it may inspire an evolutionary advantage.

One might wonder what Darwin's scientific negation of racial speciation has to do with the popular conception of race, something that Darwin himself was willing to entertain to a limited degree. To respond, let us consider the most profound aspects of Darwin's impact on Western thought, natural selection and survival of the fittest, the latter being a function of the first. Natural selection, in its most basic terms is "design without a designer," it is "the preservation of favorable variations and the rejection of those injurious" (Jones 1999: 70). The key mechanism of natural selection operates in the guise of survival of the fittest. The most successful species will always be those variances found naturally in all communities that respond most preferably to the exterior pressures. Variation appears with constant and more-or-less random consistency, while the most beneficial of these characteristics are offered the best opportunities to perpetuate. This kind of variation allows for tremendous possibilities within a species, without necessarily having a precise or deliberate function. Darwin wonders if it is improbable that given the observation of beneficial variation in humankind, "that other variations useful in some way to each being in the great and complex battle of life should sometimes occur in the course of thousands of generations" (Darwin [1859] 1979: 130). This kind of natural scrutiny allows, indeed encourages, variation in species because such variety promotes the possibility of continuation. And here is where we encounter an opportunity to misrepresent Darwin. What we must not neglect in Darwin's suggestion is that variation occurs without direct reason or purpose, and that it occurs randomly, and with both positive and negative results, and with roughly equal amount of variation in either direction. In other words, selection is impassive. It is more like the designer without a design.

Darwin himself was rather baffled when it came to the processes of natural selection as applied to the potential creative instrument for the multiplicity of humankind. Quite simply, he could not find the mechanism that necessitated the variation. He declared therefore that "as far as we are enabled to judge (although always liable to error on this head) not one of the external differences between the races of man are of any direct or special service to him" (Darwin [1871] 1998: 206). Race was likely a vestigial, obsolete characteristic that had lingered past its use, or an accident of mutation that bore no practical purpose. Both suggestions were unsatisfactory and Darwin was left to presume that there was some element of sexual selection that he had not yet adequately considered inspiring the distinction. Darwin comments, "Variations neither useful nor injurious would not be affected by natural selection, and would be left a fluctuating element" (Darwin [1859] 1979: 131). Darwin's clearly articulated premise is that, as far as could be discerned through rational, considered observation, race is ancillary or otherwise irrelevant to the pressures of evolution.

The presence of these theories signals a fundamental shift in more than the obvious reconsideration of humanity's self-promoted and privileged position in the natural world. Certainly, Darwin's theory advanced Western thought, particularly pertaining to biological mechanisms. An equally profound result of Darwin's thought, however, stems from the perhaps unsolicited theoretical reorientation that occurs as a result of his theory of evolution. As we have seen, and shall see, traditional racial theory focused on a kind of historical archeology, where the past was enlisted to explain the present forms of variety. With regard to race, however, as with Kant, for example, the past was all that was necessary. The present status of humanity was presumed to be stable and fixed. Darwin's increased emphasis on the fluidity of the past, however, also destabilized both the present and the future. Likewise, theories of monogenesis and polygenesis became increasingly alienated from the theory of human evolution, and one of the great rifts between scientific and religious discourses began to open. Although perhaps a shift more subtle than stated here, this movement in disposition had a profound influence on popular interpretation and interaction with racial thought.

Counternarratives, degeneration, and eugenics

Of course, Darwin's theories do not exist in a vacuum, and there are plenty of counternarratives that work against his grain of thought. Arthur de Gobineau is one such theorist, who can be read as assisting in two major shifts in the orientation of racial thought. Gobineau first published his seminal text, *Essay on The Inequality of the Human Races*, between 1853 and 1855. Gobineau has been called the father of racist ideology, a sentiment which may over-state his contribution and misrepresent the totality of his disposition (Banton 1987: 46). Nevertheless, his theories helped establish race as an integral explanatory mechanism for the entirety of human history. When juxtaposed with Darwin, in particular, we can see the dramatic scope of these contending narratives. Darwin argues against the existence of racial speciation in scientific terms; Gobineau employs race as the focal point of all history. As a cultural philosopher, Gobineau could employ the popular notion of race without great fear of intellectual reprisal. Situated thus, Gobineau is free to focus on his second significant development of racial theory. If race is the causal mechanism to be found in the center of all of human history, then a function is needed to explain this mechanism. We must note that the precise function of race was still a mystery to many, including Darwin, at this point. Gobineau attempts to fill that void.

As one might expect, Gobineau faced a considerable task in his attempt to overcome the rhetorical influence of scientific discourse, which he did by offering more of a history of humanity than a rigorous investigation. Indeed, Gobineau's racial taxonomy lacks much of the sophistication, misguided or otherwise, that we witnessed in the Enlightenment. Gobineau divides the races into three major categories: white, black, and yellow. By creating this basic division, Gobineau side-steps the majority of the categorical quagmires that distracted earlier commentators. In order to situate Gobineau's disposition concerning the races precisely, we must also note that he felt that the three basic types were only found historically, and that his contemporary racial position resulted from a mixture of those three types. So, already, Gobineau feels that the processes of miscegenation had moved the races beyond their pure origin and that only the traces of these forefathers remained. By only tacitly offering this definition of race, Gobineau signals to some extent the commonsensical nature the notion had gathered and demonstrates Darwin's acceptance that race would not be an easy concept to detach from the European psyche. However while speaking as a serious social commentator and historian, the fact that Gobineau feels no real need to clarify the foundation for his racial categorizations also indicates the momentum that race had gathered in a broad spectrum of disciplines.

As suggested above, Gobineau felt that original races long since disseminated into the three predominant colors. Here, we must note the decidedly melancholy nature of Gobineau's analysis, as well as his appropriation of Blumenbach's form of degeneration.[2] For Gobineau, civilization remains in continual contest and flows naturally towards a kind of entropy. This entropy, as we might imagine, carries the civilized race away from the triumphs that founded the society and toward a mildly heightened but dramatically diluted state of humanity. Thus, the racial composition of the Roman civilization during its collapse was related to its progenitors only in the most tangential and diluted manner, and it is this dilution that sowed its demise. What makes Gobineau's formulation rather melancholy is that this collapse results from both the triumph of the empire, and the racial dissolution that accompanies such expansion. Gobineau suggests that "the

man of a decadent time, the *degenerate* man properly so called, is a
different being, from the racial point of view, from the heroes of the
great ages" (Gobineau [1853–1855] 1992: 25). Gobineau attributes the
ultimate decline of society to an ambivalent relationship of attraction
and repulsion, as we shall discuss further in a moment. The concept
of degeneration was not entirely new or unique to Gobineau. As
suggested, Blumenbach described a related idea, but one that was not
explicitly or intentionally diminutive or denigrating. Gobineau's
appropriation, in this sense, articulates a paranoia that was steadily
growing, which we indicated earlier in our discussion of Shelley's
Frankenstein. This paranoia posits progression and regression as intimate companions.

In terms of his theory of attraction and repulsion Gobineau, along
with Blumenbach and others, posited white as the original color.
Thus, the Aryans represented the most noble and potent. Gobineau
does not doubt that, without racial mixture, the white race would
dominate and the black and yellow races would ascend to nothing
more than a groveling existence at the feet of the Aryans. However,
Gobineau concludes that the inevitability of Aryan dominance "would
not have been all gain" because certain advantages would have been
forfeited, such as artistic expression, which "is equally foreign to each
of the three great types, [and] arose only after the intermarriage of
white and black" (Gobineau [1853–1855] 1992: 208). Thus the system
works in constant exchange and some small degree of mingling actually helps ignite some mutual beneficence. Racial mixing, therefore,
accounts for both the rise and the ultimate fall of great civilizations.
Gobineau writes, "we must conclude that a part of mankind, is in its
own nature stricken with a paralysis, which makes it for ever unable
to take even the first step towards civilization, [if] it cannot overcome
the natural repugnance, felt by men and animals alike, to a crossing
of blood" (Gobineau [1853–1855] 1992: 27–28). Banton clarifies,
"Gobineau did not think of racial crossing in terms of blending inheritance . . . Rather, he regarded the superior, especially Aryan, as a
catalytic agent, bringing out latent powers in others (as yeast makes
dough rise), or, if it was too strong, destroying them" (Banton 1987:
49). When taken to its logical conclusion, Gobineau's theory makes
miscegenation a fascinating and terrible proposition. If we consider
this theory from its European perspective, Gobineau exposes the
potential for sexual projection onto racial others. In a masculine
controlled society, the European other becomes the site of sexual

desire and repugnance at the same moment. But the sexuality is placed on the other so that the racialized male becomes Othello's over-sexed and ambitious monster who would dilute the purity of a Venetian rose. Likewise, racially distinct women become the alluring temptresses, offering exoticism and conquest in a sexual dynamic rife with tropes of domination. However, while a society might gain from miscegenation, it also forfeits some small part of its noble integrity, and the races become both enticing and threatening with equally terrible consequences. The next logical step then posits the degree of forfeiture against the ultimate gain. And here, the odds are stacked greatly against humanity. Should a social group sacrifice the noble lineage of a great individual by diluting his/her purity in order to elevate the groveling masses to a state of mediocrity? Or is this singular purity precious?

To a limited extent, Gobineau admits some trepidation about the criteria he posits. In particular, Gobineau seems hesitant to embrace the relative nature of his aesthetic hierarchy. Gobineau suggests that "The moment that a decision as to culture becomes a matter of personal feeling, agreement is impossible" (Gobineau [1853–1855] 1992: 81). For this reason, Gobineau's thought depends upon two basic tenets to sustain its imperative. First, racial agency is the catalyst for all grand historical developments. Second, whites have, and continue to, dominate, thereby empirically demonstrating their superiority. But there is a third lingering possibility. European dominance is both a blessing and a curse because the triumph and conquest of other peoples also acts as the catalyst for its collapse. Ultimately, Gobineau delivers a genuine sense of urgency to the understanding of racial interaction because it is primarily the most significant aspect of human civilization. In this manner, Gobineau helps solidify the entire history of humanity as racially determined. All civilization, all art, every achievement, according to Gobineau, can be traced directly back to some form of racial diffusion, or the lack thereof to isolation. Gobineau, therefore, offers a singular fear, one based on a theory of degeneration that threatened to instigate and dilute the grand potential of humanity. If we consider this notion next to the primacy of race as the catalyst and cataclysm for human civilization, as well as Darwin's reorientation of the critical disposition, we can trace a cultural paranoia fixated on its own progress and the potential for its own degeneracy.

Having mentioned the inadvertent effect of Darwin's thought, we might also note that almost as soon as Darwin articulated his theories, they were absorbed and transformed into more digestible, but less accurate, forms. Thus, rather than adhering to Darwin's invalidation of racial categorization, nineteenth-century theorists isolated individual aspects of Darwin's argument to help re-assert what they already held to be true. Thus, "Races were thought to represent different stages of the evolutionary scale with the white race – or sometimes a subdivision of the white race – at the top" (Gossett 1997: 144). That the white race should be placed at the top will undoubtedly raise alarms of inconsistency. When reviewing natural philosophers such as Bernier, Blumenbach, and Kant, we noted the conventional wisdom that suggested that white was the original race. For his part, even Gobineau posited whiteness as dominant, but not necessarily the first among the three more original races. Generally, then, white was considered the most pure, most original, most undiluted of the races. As Darwin reverses the emphasis, however, theorists responded by invoking what amounts to the same observed evidence with dramatically altered implications. Now, white represents the most evolved species, which also implicitly argues that white is the least original species. Instead, whiteness becomes evidence of the most developed and the most accomplished race. Thus, "From a rich body of data that could support almost any racial assertion, scientists selected facts that would yield their favored conclusion according to theories currently in vogue" (Gould 1973: 216). The fundamental inconsistency of this reversal is obvious and spectacular. It also opens the door for a whole new notion of degeneracy, where the degenerate represents a form of evolutionary digression back to primitive and savage forms. Implicated in this regression, by definition, one could also recognize a "backwards" movement in racial progress. Thus, what began with Darwin's radical reorientation of evolutionary perspective gets quickly appropriated into popular notions of racial dominance and actually serves to shift the entire concept of racial thought. Racial purity, in other words, becomes a symbol of how far one has moved from the original type rather than how closely one embodied the dominant and noble lineage.

Working upon both the shift in orientation prepared by Darwin and the dominant fear of degeneracy, Lombroso and Nordau offer a counternarrative to the scientific authority of Darwin and a perspective of humanity's position in the universe that strikes chords more directly in tune with significant portions of the popular conscious. Gobineau, as we have just noted, placed race in the center of the entire span of human history. Moreover, he contemplated the white race as indicative of the most undiluted and therefore culturally potent of all the races. Keeping in step with Gobineau's fascination with race, Lombroso and Nordau respond more directly to a general and growing discontent with criminal and degenerate behavior. While each of these authors views the past as superior to the present and look to race as an explanatory mechanism, Lombroso and Nordau pick upon degeneration and apply it in a more progressively scientific manner. As suggested by the manner with which the term gets appropriated from Blumenbach, Gobineau, and others, it should not seem surprising that the term degeneration "had no single fixed meaning or material referent. Indeed, meaning and referent notoriously changed according to the type of research being done" (Arata 1996: 14–15). Indeed for Lombroso and Nordau, close attention to the evolutionary shift causes the term degeneration to equate more readily to regression than dilution. Discursive mobility is convenient for the appropriation of theory and, to this end, Lombroso and Nordau bring degeneration to anthropology, philosophy, sociology, aesthetics, and most famously, criminology (or criminal anthropology).

Cesare Lombroso pioneered criminology by systematically organizing criminal behavior as the manifestation of inherited deficiencies. Conveniently, these deficiencies were also manifest in a series of physical symptoms that could be readily identified by the skilled interpreter, such as Lombroso himself. His publication of *Criminal Man* (1876), *The Man of Genius* (1891), and *Crime: Its Causes and Remedies* (1899) signaled the opening salvo of his scientific mission. His project appears straightforward enough: observe behavior and measure physical difference. As with several other commentators that we have seen already, however, data mean absolutely nothing until one prepares a theoretical framework through which one can view it and, for Lombroso, this theory is degeneration. Lombroso demonstrates the influence of theoretical disposition on perception perhaps as vividly, if not dramatically more so, than any of the other theorists we have discussed.

Lombroso's conclusions may seem a bit startling, but should not be altogether surprising given the nature of the scientific debate of his time. Lombroso built upon other genuine, popular, but misguided scientific explorations of physical features, race, and character that looked for the biological basis for human behavior, particularly in terms of criminality. As suggested by Gould:

> If Lombroso and his colleagues had been a dedicated group of proto-Nazis, we could dismiss the whole phenomenon as a ploy of conscious demagogues. It would then convey no other message than a plea for vigilance against ideologues who misuse science. But the leaders of criminal anthropology were "enlightened" socialists and social democrats who viewed their theory as the spearhead for a rational, scientific society based on human realities. The genetic determination of criminal action, Lombroso argued, is simply the law of nature and of evolution. (Gould 1973: 227)

For precedent, Lombroso could look to people like Franz Joseph Gall who pioneered phrenology, a quasi-scientific attempt to relate behavior to the features of the skull. Likewise, Lombroso's adherence to the theory of evolution led him to his contentious conclusions. We must not, however, underestimate either the seriousness of his endeavor or the potential that still exists for similarly sincere and damaging errors.

Lombroso asserted unequivocally that criminal behavior could be measured in physical features, and that it was biologically based, predetermined, and heritable. Indeed, by measuring various features, particularly skull size and shape, of known convicted criminals, and prehistoric humans and apes, Lombroso concluded that the modern criminal has quite literally regressed, or degenerated, into a more primeval form. Here Lombroso borrowed quite heavily from essentialist notions of race, which allowed him to contend that a thick forehead or protruding jaw were physical characteristics intimately connected to potentially social and behavioral characteristics. Of course, to some considerable extent, the description of the appropriately simian elements remains subjective, and a great deal has been made elsewhere as to the way in which marginalized "white" cultures were simianized in order to facilitate their denigration. For Britain and the United States during this period, the Irish sufficed as a supposed race worthy of these spurious physical descriptions.[3] But for Lombroso, criminality was not the only form of degeneracy, and in an intriguing shift he also posited genius as a similar form of degeneracy. Thus, any deviation from an imagined normalcy, or purity, signaled a movement away from competency. In this manner Lombroso argued, "that the creative power of genius may be a form of degenerative psychosis belonging to the family of epileptic affections. The fact that genius is frequently derived from parents either addicted to drink, of advanced age, or insane, certainly points to this conclusion, as also does the appearance of genius subsequently to lesions of the head" (Lombroso 1891: 336). Here, we absolutely must think of Othello's military prowess, his epileptic fits, and his murderous temper as being singularly linked. As importantly, these characteristics, according to Lombroso, must also be biologically determined. This presents us with a dilemma similar to that prepared by Gobineau. Quite simply, degeneracy offers both the greatest potential and threat to humankind.[4]

Lombroso described the phenomenon of degeneracy as atavism, a term deployed readily to denote movement into more primitive states. Thus, the criminal could not be entirely blamed for his criminality because his hereditary condition predetermined his savagery. This is not to suggest that criminal behavior or savagery were in any way rendered acceptable, or entirely forgivable, based on these new-found discoveries. In fact, both Lombroso and Nordau were compassionate, perhaps, but also notoriously unforgiving. Indeed, Lombroso felt that over-achievement at too early an age was a sign of potential insanity. An over-achieving child was, therefore, not only destined for the asylum but indicative of savage degeneration: "This precocity is morbid and atavistic; it may be observed among all savages. The proverb 'A man who had genius at five is mad at fifteen' is often verified in asylums" and continues "Among the children of the insane are often revealed aptitudes and tastes – chiefly for music, the arts, and mathematics – which are not usually found in other children" (Lombroso 1891: 16). One significant problem with atavism, and indeed much essentialist thought, is that it allows for very little consideration of environmental factors. This represents a considerable irony given the role that the environment allegedly played in the variation of the races. Once prefigured by essentialist thought, theorists seemed reluctant or incapable of considering the nurturing aspect of environment as well as the climatic variety. This, of course, poses early examples of Lombroso's thought against early Freudianism, which found a considerable sum of an individual's later capabilities in the nurturing environment Lombroso's fears do not need to stretch directly to the influence of environmental factors on behavior (nurture as opposed to nature), despite the fact that he manipulated almost precisely the same logic in his advocacy of "deliberate selection" in his treatment of local criminals (Nordau [1895] 1968: xx). Deliberate selection, of course, meant nothing other than the death penalty.

Max Nordau looked to Lombroso as an inspiration. In his dedica-
tion of *Degeneration* (1895) to Lombroso, an excerpt of which acts as
the epigraph of this chapter, Nordau genuinely believes that his social
mission is one of a gravest and most pressing urgency, and also one of
distinguished scientific authority. Indeed, Nordau's *Conventional Lies
of Our Civilization* (1883) sets the tone for *Degeneration*, both of
which enjoyed tremendous popularity on their publication. Ironically,
however, the reactionary nature of Nordau's philosophy inspired its
eventual decline after the First World War, at which point Nordau
almost summarily disappeared from the public consciousness. In this
sense, Nordau represents a great deal about the age that directly
precedes the turn of the century. His aesthetic criticism, for example,
continuously reacted against new and/or derivative art forms that he
felt indicated the decline of European preeminence. In this sense,
Nordau was a social conformist who admired the heights achieved by
European civilization and adhered to the conservative values of its
middle class. Therefore, when Nordau announces that "The great
majority of the middle and lower classes is naturally not fin-de-
siècle," he aligns himself decidedly with tradition immune from
fashion and modern crazes (Nordau 1895: 7). An individual indicative
of these classes is one who, according to Nordau, prefers "the old and
oldest forms of art and poetry . . . Ohnet's novels to the symbolists . . .
enjoy[s] himself royally over slap-dash farces and music-hall
melodies, and yawns or is angered at Ibsen" (Nordau 1875: 7). The
reactionary nature of his writing, as it operated against the tide of fin-
de-siècle experimentation, prepared his rather dramatic fluctuation
from fame to obscurity. Put simply, Nordau backed the wrong horse,
and his reaction against the growing discontent of young artists ultimately placed him outside the momentum of modernism.

The central tenet of Nordau's philosophy, as with Aristotle, rests
firmly on the notions of altruism and the greatest communal good.
Just as the criminal vagrant must not be allowed to satisfy his perverse
desires, whatever they might be, neither should the vagrant artist be
allowed to fulfill his/her desires in the expression of degenerate art.
The sincerity and urgency with which Nordau turned the fixation of
deviant behavior in criminals toward areas more traditionally considered cultural artistry may seem rather abrupt to the modern reader.
Nordau was not, however, an isolated old curmudgeon waving his
bony fingers at the younger generation. Nordau worked against the
great strain of pessimism that can be read into Gobineau and, to some

degree, Lombroso. The point of his argument reaches toward the advancement of civilization through rigid adherence to the principles that had been so beneficial thus far. The worry, therefore, is that too much frivolity will lead to decline.

Nordau attributed potential decline and "general hysteria" to the fact that the modern individual had become frazzled from excessive excitement of modern urbanization, whereby the brain was stretched to its limitations and where "five to twenty-five times as much work" was demanded of each individual than had been fifty years previous (Nordau 1895: 39–40). Subsequently, in much of Nordau's thought, Mosse (in his Introduction to Nordau) finds a "mighty dose of utilitarianism" in which "A clear-headed poet calls a cat a cat," based upon Nordau's belief that genuine knowledge must be removed from trifles and must also be inherently useful to the progress of humanity (Nordau 1985: xvii). In terms of his aesthetic judgment, then, the eloquence of scientific principle became functionally appealing, which Havelock Ellis articulates in these terms: "Darwin was one of those elect persons in whose subconscious, if not in their conscious, nature is implanted the realization that 'science *is* poetry,' and in a field altogether remote from the poetry and art of convention he was alike poet and artist" (Ellis 1929: 57–58). Again, Nordau's aesthetic alignment works against what he considered a pervasive hysteria. The grand European empires had been built upon the priorities of progress, discipline, and strict adherence to order. An aesthetics of utilitarianism appealed to Nordau for these precise reasons.

On some level, one might consider the sum of Nordau's contribution to aesthetics as his insistence that art is political; Nordau heatedly insists in his cautionary pronouncements that "art is not practiced for its own sake alone . . . but for the satisfaction of an organic want of the artist, and the influencing of his fellow-creatures" (Nordau 1895: 325). Nevertheless, it is difficult not to flinch at the bitter, ominous irony in Nordau's suggestion that "Under the influence of an obsession, a degenerate mind promulgates some doctrine or other – realism, pornography, mysticism, symbolism, diabolism. He does this with vehement penetrating eloquence, with eagerness and fiery heedlessness . . . In this case all participants are sincere – the founder as well as the disciples. They act as, in consequence of the diseased constitution of their brain and nervous system, they are compelled to act" (Nordau 1895: 31). For Nordau, as with Lombroso, degeneracy operates in the frenzied and exhausted minds of the modern urban individual, whose mind has been compelled to atrophy under modern pressures. This fact, however, does not excuse that individual, nor does it assist in reclaiming that individual from the grip of frenzied atavism. Thus, while Nordau seems to insist on the political aspect of art, he does so while insisting that all forms of political thought exterior to his aesthetics are proof of degeneracy and madness.

Indeed, perhaps the most fundamental problem with countering Nordau's scientific and medical claims appeared in the simple accusation of insanity for any/all that might prefer a differing choice of social priority. Again, as his formulation is often based in aesthetic judgments, there remains great opportunity to find oneself on the opposite end of artistic appreciation, a fact that could then be considered a sure sign of essential degeneracy. Ultimately, the attribution of degeneracy to all things different is indicative of a great deal of the European encounter with the foreign during the formation of its empires. However, this also offers a grand narrative of paranoia. Difference, whether it genius, madness, criminality, frenzied aesthetics, or psychosis, lurks not only in foreign lands, but within our own potential for decline. What is more, this potential can go undetected. With this in mind, Lombroso could write with conviction, "It must be added that moral insanity and epilepsy which are so often found in association with genius are among the forms of mental alienation which are most difficult to verify, so that they are often denied, even during life, although quite evident to the alienist" (Lombroso 1891: vii). What Lombroso suggests is that he is privileged in his ability to discern degeneracy among the general population, even when it is disguised to the layman. The power inherent in this form of rhetoric stems from its ability to muster the forces of scientific logic, alongside social fear and commonsense, and systematically pronounce any dissent within the system as indicative of one's own latent degeneracy.

There is a rather astonishing component to both Lombroso and Nordau that bears mentioning here. Both were raised as Jews. How then, one may wonder, could two European Jews be compared so callously to "proto-Nazis"? Indeed, Gould makes a point to mention that they were much less, and much more than mere Nazis. Of course, the psychoanalytic potential in the investigation to their heritage is almost too tragically compelling, if not entirely helpful in this discussion. Their relationship to their Jewishness (in light of both the tradition of anti-semitism in Europe and the growing intensity of that

pressure) offers a great vantage from which we can view the summation of their contribution to European paranoia. For his part,
Lombroso despises difference. His relation to his own Jewish-ness,
therefore, is one based upon the negation of difference. Thus, "The
conclusion reached at the end of his analysis is that assimilation is the
answer to the problem of anti-Semitism – in other words, the total
obliteration of difference" (Harrowitz 1994: 49). Oddly, however,
Lombroso exposes a conflict in his logic on this point. In a derisive
passage, Lombroso articulates the precise problem that he has with
the European Jews: "If all religions have modified their essence, not
just their appearance, according to the times, why can't they at least
modify appearances?" (quoted in Harrowitz 1994: 49). Given our
previous discussion of Lombroso, several matters call for our attention
here. First, note the rhetorical distance that Lombroso gains by postu-
lating the question with the conveniently deployed "they."[5] Second,
Lombroso's accusation appears consistently orientated around his
fixation on physical difference. What bothers him so completely about
the Jews is not so much the religious difference that they represent,
but rather the physical difference that signifies their cultural and religious affiliation. Having stated this, however, we can see that, thirdly,
Lombroso's argument suspends itself between a fear of atavism and a
fear of progress. The Jews, according to Lombroso, need to change at
least their appearance with the times, but not too much, one might
easily gather. We can see quite readily how Lombroso's, and indeed
Nordau's, position quickly becomes untenable.

Nordau offers a much more genial, although still potentially quite
conflicted, relationship to Judaism. For his part, Nordau actively
supported Theodore Herzl and the Zionist movement. Indeed, after
Herzl's death it was widely presumed that Nordau would assume his
mantle. Like Herzl, Nordau recognized that assimilation was failing.
More importantly, assimilation was disingenuous because it involved
denial and potentially hypocrisy. Thus, "As with everything not
genuine, this kind of Jew was offensive to anyone with true aesthetic
feeling" (Nordau [1895] 1968: xxv). And indeed, as with his other
concerns, Nordau's basis for establishing a Jewish homeland
stemmed from pragmatic rather than distinctly religious concerns.
Both Herzl and Nordau saw the Zionist movement in "political and
sociological but not in spiritual terms" (Nordau [1895] 1968: xxv). The
difference between Lombroso and Nordau, despite their intimate
relationship, demonstrates the fissure in their collective thought.

Where does one locate degeneracy? Who decides? For both individuals, however, the essential nature of humankind had not been removed from its preeminent position, as suggested by Gobineau. And taken together, all three theorists spectacularly display the growing force of cultural paranoia.

To varying degrees, Gobineau, Lombroso, and Nordau represent strong counter narratives to the scientific, but largely unpopular, efforts of Darwin. As Western thought turns its attention from an archaic debate of the past to the future of the species, we begin to see how the impetus of Darwin's thought creates yet another example of misappropriation in the assertion of popular ideas about the fundamental significance of race. In one of history's bitter little ironies, the source of this final appropriation comes from a cousin of Darwin, Francis Galton. To arrive at Galton's appropriation of Darwin's thought, we need only apply the theory of natural selection to social issues and we have an obtuse "social Darwinism." Hofstadter states, "Imperialism, calling upon Darwinism in defense of the subjugation of weaker races, could point to *The Origin of Species*, which had referred in its subtitle to as *The Preservation of Favoured Races in the Struggle for Life*, Darwin had been talking about pigeons, but the imperialists saw no reason why his theories should not apply to men" (Hofstadter 1955: 171).The question is no longer where we have been, but where we are going, and this change in disposition dramatically changes our attitude with regard to natural selection. And this question has a brother. Who is the most fit to be selected "naturally"? Of course, appropriating natural selection into the social dynamic removes at least one essential piece of the equation, that is, the natural part of natural selection. We previously mentioned Lombroso's advocacy of deliberate selection as a worthy method of assisting the more natural processes of selection, without necessarily considering this leap of logic to be, by definition, unnatural. The above questions become even more loaded when we add the aesthetic dimension to social achievement. This is no longer the design without a designer, but a programmatic attempt to invigorate the species. The empirical observation of naturally structured selection becomes deliberate, subjective manipulation.

To complete the picture, we must revisit Plato from Chapter 1. In his ideal political community, Plato speculated that the Guardians, the most sophisticated, responsible, and benevolent class, should enjoy primary access to mating with other gifted Guardians. Along with the selective breeding of healthy military stock, this privilege was designed to help maintain and/or advance the natural capacity of the entire political populace, an activity not dissimilar to the way a shepherd might breed his best dogs for the advantage of the offspring. As we remember, this system is brazenly unkind to the individual and supportive of the most divisive inequality. Likewise in our discussion of Plato, we suggested that the society proposed was potentially proto-eugenic, although the term itself did not yet exist. This would not stop later commentators from picking upon Plato. Note also the very similar terms set forth between Galton and Plato. Galton states, in an almost direct echo of Plato's idealized society, "Let us for a moment suppose that the practice of Eugenics should hereafter raise the average quality of our nation to that of its better moiety at the present day and consider the gain" (Galton 2000: 80). The naked ambition in this statement can be interpreted in varying degrees as both optimistic and vulgar.

Francis Galton introduced the term eugenics in his text, *Inquiries into Human Faculty and Its Development* (1883). By this time, his opinions were no secret and had been consistently developed since his publication of *Hereditary Genius*, and his specific article "The Comparative Worth of Different Races" (1869). Galton's introduction of eugenics performs a selective blending of Darwin and Plato to formulate a systematic explanation for the paucity in certain less desirable aspects of the late Victorian world. With Darwin and Plato enlisted as authoritative qualifiers, Galton justifies the doubled action of Plato's proposal, increased breeding among the "fit" and reduced breeding among those less so. Galton would then be operating within the most natural boundaries of the natural world, only in a slightly accelerated manner. As Galton suggests, "What Nature does blindly, slowly, and ruthlessly, man may do providently, quickly, and kindly" (Galton 2000: 83). For many proponents of social Darwinism, the biological landscape came to represent the ultimate destiny of humankind. The authority of science and empirical observation would be employed for the greatest benefit of the entire population. With regard to the reliability of empirical evidence, please note the difficulty in not tripping over the doubled significance of the expression. The evidence gathered by these theorists is indeed empirical in the sense that it directly serves the purposes of the Empire. But the primary focus of eugenics does not exclusively apply to the conquests of Western civilization in the greater world. Eugenics is also an intense inward examination of the components of the society. Note, however, one is never far behind the other; Galton writes, "The general tone of domestic, social and political life would be higher. The race as a whole would be less foolish, less frivolous, less excitable and politically more provident than now . . . We should be better fitted to fulfill our vast imperial opportunities" (Galton 2000: 80).

In its least offensive appeal, eugenics is deeply rooted in racial ambition and the desire to establish the highest stock. This means, quite simply, the deliberate application of what Darwin set out in his basic principle of natural selection and survival of the fittest. The problem, quite immediately, emerges as to the human, as opposed to the natural, analysis and selection of what actually constitutes the criteria for the category of "fittest." The most basic goal is the improvement of human stock. With this in mind, Galton proposes "Historical inquiry into the rates with which the various classes of society (classified according to civic usefulness) have contributed to the population at various times." To this, Galton adds that "We must therefore leave morals as far as possible out of the discussion, not entangling ourselves with the almost hopeless difficulties they raise as to whether a character as a whole is good or bad" (Galton 2000: 79). Wittingly or otherwise, when considered together these statements are indicative of Gobineau's emphasis on racial history and the paranoia such an emphasis instills, Lombroso's quasi-scientific investigation into criminality, and Nordau's utilitarian emphasis on the advancement of civilization. When combined, the result may appear beneficial, but in summation and application, quite terrible. Although not necessarily stated insidiously or with terrible malice, we need not extrapolate to a significant degree to see the impetus of this logic. Galton also betrays a secondary nervousness in his evaluation of the current situation. Galton laments, in keenly felt class paranoia, "It seems to be the tendency of high civilization to check fertility in the upper classes" (Galton 2000: 81). And here he betrays the aesthetics of his prioritization as being one not rooted in Nordau's middle class, but the least "degenerate," and therefore "fittest" specimen of humankind.

As one might expect, it did not take long for the criteria to be established by various and often varying political ideologies that included quite explicit political agendas. It is hardly a wonder, given the concerns of Lombroso and Nordau with regard to the question of Jews in Europe, that the entire social project only needed a modest and persuasive shove to go appallingly wrong. Thus, "In a move that was already an indication of what was to follow, eugenics was known in Germany as *Rassenhygiene*, or race hygiene" (Bernasconi and Loft 2000: 79).

Kipling's duality and degenerative subversion

The theory of degeneration opens profound avenues of investigation into all three texts discussed at length thus far in this volume, and in particular *Othello* and *Frankenstein*. Degeneration helps question the tension between the nobility of Othello's lineage *vis-à-vis* his epilepsy and violence. The concept of degeneration also helps locate the imperial terror in Shelley's *Frankenstein* placed between the paranoia of miscegenation and social implosion while remaining competently inside the European social structure. Likewise, Lombroso's comments on the degenerative link between genius and madness may help interpret Frankenstein's immoderate obsession and ultimate failure. While it is indeed tempting to read the previous texts in this direction, it is perhaps more beneficial to read Lombroso and company as the culmination of the racial seeds that had been germinating in the European consciousness for a considerable length of time, and to interpret Lombroso as the embodiment of their collective, and malleable, racial paranoia.

Rudyard Kipling is generally considered the literary representative of the colonial paradigm *par excellence*. To England he represents in conflicted but compelling measures, both the exotic and the very essence of Englishness. And yet, to some commentators, Kipling is a victim "of unspecified nervous disorders" (Arata 1996: 14). For his part, Kipling is considered degenerate on both social and aesthetic grounds: social, because of his "fleshiness and hooliganism" and aesthetic, because his "fiction perverts the standards of classical realism" (Arata 1996: 14). Undoubtedly this development may surprise those accustomed to a more cheerful, English reception of Kipling's work. This criticism, however, demonstrates the length to which the paranoia of degeneration could extend both outward, to the supposed exterior savages, and inward, into the very fabric of Englishness in England.

The play between the two extremes of exemplary and degenerate also demonstrates how rapidly social registers could change. The judgment of degeneracy, after all, and despite claims to scientific objectivism, was ultimately aesthetic and flawed. Thus, "Dickens was being remodeled into a figure of English solidity, with Kipling as his avatar. At the same time, however, Kipling's work was considered to embody deeply alien tendencies. He may have been the new Dickens, but he was so, paradoxically, because of his distance from the culture" (Arata 1996: 154). When placed under this light, then, Kipling's fiction presents something of a problem. Is he English enough for England? Is his residence in the English canon threatened in any way by his exposure? Or, to the contrary, does the Englishness of England benefit from this experience with its imperial borders?

Certainly, the imperial project, which Kipling has traditionally been mustered to represent, benefits from his uncanny exoticism. However, read in the context of degeneracy, this exoticism must be considered both in terms of its imperial achievement and in terms of the threat that such contact portends. In two extremely different short stories, "The Mark of the Beast" and "A Wayside Comedy," Kipling engages wild exoticism. Indeed, these stories vary even in the form of the exoticism that Kipling provides: one is fantastic, magical, and savage, while the other is civil, farcical, and deviously sexual. Each set in India, these two texts embody paired tropes of imperial impressions of the other as well as the potential threats of degeneration. On the one hand, the exterior and uncivilized world is fraught with violence and brutality, while on the other, the unknown offers a canvas upon which desire may be projected. With regard to degeneration, then, the attraction and repulsion of the imperial project threatens to expose the manner in which the colonizer embodies these "uncivilized" potentials.

"The Mark of the Beast" can be read as a simple magical adventure story with the exception that several key textual omissions suggest much more. On the one hand, the story unfolds as a cautionary tale; a drunken Englishman desecrates a local deity and ridicules the heathen practice, in retribution for which he is cursed by a visiting priest. The curse briefly transforms the overbearing Fleete into a werewolf-like beast until the efforts of Strickland, a local English constable, and the narrator coerce the priest into restoring order. The fantastically magical nature of this story certainly panders in part to the demand for such stories, and echoes the type of fabulous tale related by Sir John Mandeville. For this reason, the story can be read as capitalizing upon the pulp portrayal of the East as the site of wild mysticism and exoticism. On the other hand, Kipling provides a potentially more complex narrative. Fleete's descent into his monstrosity directly demonstrates a base fear of atavistic degeneration. But this fear is coupled with at least one other potential form of savagery. In order to bring Fleete back from his curse, Strickland and the narrator ensnare the prowling leper-priest that has placed the curse and who haunts Strickland's home. In order to perform this coercion, the protagonists get "to work," adding only "This part is not to be printed" (Kipling 1994: 305). The narrator hints at their activities, however, stating, "The dawn was beginning to break when the leper spoke" (Kipling 1994: 305). Of course, we are meant to understand that more than the dawn had been broken. The narrator gives another important clue when, discussing the now transformed Fleete, he comments, "I understood then how men and women and little children can endure to see a witch burnt alive" (Kipling 1994: 304). The text, therefore, hints but avoids the direct attribution of barbarity to the two protagonists. The narrative, therefore, salvages its adherence to civilized decency, even as it betrays that the characters themselves do not. Who, we are left to wonder, has actually regressed into an animal? Upon his salvation, Fleete remembers nothing and continues his "civility" unabated.

Fleete stands alone, then, as the only genuine Englishman in the text. Strickland's position in the text situates him between cultures, in a manner that both preserves part of his Englishness, and dramatically removes him from this possibility. For him, India remains a mystery, distant and unknowable. Despite the fact that he "knows as much of natives of India as is good for any man" (Kipling 1994: 293). Indeed, despite his best efforts he suggests that "in fifteen or twenty years he will have made some small progress" toward unraveling the mystery of his subject (Kipling 1994: 296). For his part, the narrator comments that Strickland has a "weakness for going among the natives" almost in the same breath that he betrays his own adherence to the deity Hanuman whose statue Fleete then desecrates. Likewise, if Strickland remains suspended between cultures, the narrator also awakens to a threshold that he has crossed as well. He states, "Then it struck me that we had fought for Fleete's soul with the Silver Man in that room, and had disgraced ourselves as Englishmen forever, and I laughed and gasped and gurgled just as shamefully as Strickland, while Fleete thought that we had both gone mad" (Kipling 1994: 306). The narrator's identification with Strickland, who has a weakness for going native, and his own realization that he has sacrificed his Englishness, signifies the precise point of their movement away from their cultural and racial purity, their degeneration.

The degenerative moral of the text ultimately remains conflicted. In terms of degeneracy, only Fleete comes away ignorant and therefore civilly pure. And, yet, his physical transformation exposes his own regression and brutality. Fleete's physical transformation directly echoes what we already perceive as his moral and ethical lack of consideration. It is, after all, Fleete who drunkenly desecrates the Hanuman idol. So, Kipling offers a genuine example of English imperial purity while also exposing the soft underbelly of its moral disposition. The two protagonists, however, omit their transgression in an obvious plea for salvation, while at the same moment the narrator confesses their degeneration. Yet we are excluded from the precise information we would need to accommodate their salvation. Instead, we are left with veiled suggestions of violence that ultimately undermine any suggestion that these protagonists, and indeed the imperial project, are not fundamentally violent, cruel, insensitive, and belligerent. And thus, Kipling removes the entire text from a comfortable position that would otherwise situate the narrative as triumphantly English. The narrator's omission and obfuscation of the contentious events of the story do not signify a bold departure for Kipling. On the one hand, the omission operates as an attempt to save the reader from an encounter with savagery by keeping us civilly ignorant, as is the case with Fleete. On the other hand, the narrator's attempt to obfuscate his own potential brutality only serves to demonstrate his degeneration. Such narrative exclusions have a tradition in Kipling for undermining the Englishness of his texts. Kipling often excludes parts of his English speaking readership by privileging his Anglo-Indian audience. As Arata states, "If dialect fiction has traditionally worked to reinscribe the superiority of the reader's norms – norms of language, ethics, cultural literacy, and so on – in Kipling's case the positions are usually reversed" (Arata 1996: 155). Degeneracy, therefore, can be read both in what the text provides and excludes from its English readership. The ultimate effect of these exclusions demonstrates ironically that the idea of degeneracy has in fact transcended both the Englishness of England and the foreignness of its empire.

If religion fails the conquering subjects in their encounter with the foreign in our first text, "A Wayside Comedy" sees the law fail in equal measure. Indeed, Kipling's narrator makes certain to remind us that "laws weaken in a small and hidden community" (Kipling 1994: 392). The narrator continues, "When a man is absolutely alone in a Station he runs a certain risk of falling into evil ways. This risk is multiplied by every addition to the population up to twelve – the Jury number" (Kipling 1994: 392). Kipling seems to suggest here that isolation in a foreign land inspires mischief provided that the potential consequences of transgression are limited. But this is not entirely the case. The story describes a single affair between a young Captain Kurrell and one Mrs. Boulte, the wife of the Engineer. This in itself never presents the slightest problem in the action of the text. In fact, upon its exposure, Boulte and Kurrell continue to enjoy something like a friendship, a circumstance that one might argue is remarkably civil. The lawlessness mentioned above, however, suggests that at least part of the problem for the Kashima Station is a lack of sufficient English presence. The colonizers have arrived in a number that is ultimately ineffectual to inspire genuine civility. To be sure, this is a broad justification for imperialism full stop; we need to embark in numbers to ensure that civilization is adequately demonstrated to the brutes.

The characters quickly undermine the pretense of their decency. The specific lawlessness that Kipling's narrator laments is one of sexual desire, or rather failed sexual desire. The story makes a point, in fact, to limit the threat of violence, which ultimately becomes farcical, in spite of marking several opportunities where decency and honor might demand some form of confrontation. It is Mrs. Boulte's confession of her affair to her husband that instigates the real action of the narrative. In this sense, the text critiques the socio-sexual mission of imperialism from the outset. It is Mrs. Vansuythen, the new English arrival and source of unsolicited attention, who brings disaster to the sexual dynamic of the small outpost, and "all Kashima knows that she, and she alone, brought about their pain" (Kipling 1994: 391). While potentially accurate, this statement also reflects a significant part of sexual projection that imperialism imposes upon its subjects. Mrs. Vansuythen, as the story reveals, does absolutely nothing other than act in a civil, faithful, and appropriate manner. Instead, it is the unsolicited sexual advances of the Engineer Boulte and Captain Kurrell that inspire so much of the apprehension in the text. And yet, she alone has brought misery to the station. There is a peculiar social commentary here, and one that may or may not digress slightly from what one might expect in a tale of imperial desire. Put simply, Mrs. Vansuythen is only contextually exotic. She is fair, and her grey eyes dazzle the men, a fact that precludes them from understanding her faithfulness. From the women of Kashima, however, the most description we get of her amounts to a backwards compliment of "not bad looking." Indeed, for her part, "She merely went through life, looking at those who passed; and the women objected while the men fell down and worshipped" (Kipling 1994: 392). What she brings to the Station, therefore, is Englishness, and a social grace that has become all the more desirable because of its limited availability. Again, her virtue is never compromised, unlike the other significant female of the narrative. She remains an unspoiled English rose.

If we are to suppose that Mrs. Vansuythen represents the civilizing mission of Queen Victoria herself (Mrs. Boulte uses the excuse of borrowing last week's "Queen" when making her visit), then we must also wonder what to make of the attribution of culpability to her. Mrs. Vansuythen does not demand that the Station worship her in this manner and "is deeply sorry for the evil she has done to Kashima" (1994: 392). Kipling offers a lovely conundrum here. To suggest that the civilizing mission embodied by Mrs. Vansuythen is evil inverts the (thin) premise of colonization in the first place. Bringing civility back to these degenerate Englishmen (and women) is ultimately to impose misery and pretense upon them, a fact the text reminds us of on several occasions. On the other hand, we might consider the violence that would erupt were the colonizing presence more numerous, at which point Boulte and Kurrell might have been forced to compete physically for the attention of their oblivious and uninterested icon. Indeed, the increased presence of civility hardly seems a likely remedy when the narrator opens the tale "praying that the Government of India may be moved to scatter the European population to the four winds" (Kipling 1994: 391). Of course, the Queen will spread her influence to the four winds. Kipling, therefore, can be read both in terms of his grand imperial mission, and the subtle manner in which he subverts the purity of that mission.

Transition

We must hope that the end of the Second World War, and particularly the Holocaust, signaled the end of eugenics. While we cannot predict the future, we may at least learn from the past. On this note, however, the prospect appears relatively grim. Lest we fool ourselves into believing that the vulgarity of the past is somehow a distant dream from which we have all long since awakened, we must consider more contemporary applications of misappropriation of evolutionary theory and/or eugenic ideology. Gould warns, "People who are unaware of this historical pattern tend to accept each recurrence at face value: that is, they assume that each statement arises from the 'data' actually presented, rather than from the social conditions that truly inspire it" (Gould 1973: 243). As suggested previously, almost every compilation of data is meaningless without a theoretical framework through which it may be interpreted. The problem, therefore, stems from the scientific observer's ability to maintain the perspective suggested by Gould; we must remain aware of these broad historical patterns. We need simply to consider the manner in which theorists were able to re-orientate the original color of the human species, from white to black, after the theory of evolution gained credibility to see the ease with which identical sets of data may be in interpreted and misused in order to maintain the hierarchical norm.

In 1994, Richard J. Herrnstein and Charles Murray published the conclusions of their divisive scientific research in a volume titled, *The Bell Curve*. Herrnstein and Murray's text was widely disseminated, if not completely embraced, and sparked tremendous controversy for its suggestion that intelligence was the primary motivating factor for modern social accomplishment and class. If this had been the sum of their conclusions, we might easily dismiss the text as unworthy of the exhaustive attention it received. However, Herrnstein and Murray linked their social critique to an essentialist notion of race that exposes the rather troubling tenuousness of their conclusions, as well as their potentially insidious political disposition.

To accomplish their task, Herrnstein and Murray observed the standard measurement of intelligence, the IQ, against a spectrum of social problems, including poverty, crime, fertility, unemployment, and most contentiously, race. Certainly, the nature of their research would strike deep and lasting chords with social scientists like Lombroso. Indeed, Herrnstein and Murray actually deliver extremely similar accounts of social problems. But that is not all. The cornerstone of Herrnstein and Murray's conclusions rests upon the current star of biological determinism, the gene. In a gesture not entirely dissimilar to Kant's "germ," genetic research allows scientists to attribute social and behavioral characteristics to the indefinite network of genetic composition on an unprecedented, and scientifically persuasive, level. Herrnstein and Murray then proceed to link intelligence to "America's most pressing social problems," because, "different levels of cognitive ability are associated with different patterns of social behavior" (Herrnstein and Murray 1994: 117). Thus, Herrnstein and Murray argued that the differences they observed in IQ could be directly linked to race and that, subsequently, blacks were genetically predetermined to be on average 15 points less intelligent than whites. The ultimate conclusion therefore is that blacks are genetically determined to be both less intelligent than whites, and a relative social underclass as a result of this deficiency.

The methods employed to reach the conclusions offered in *The Bell Curve* are astonishingly imprecise. Take for example the first basic tenet of their argument. What exactly do IQ tests measure, and how exactly does one define intelligence? Block notes, "The crucial factor that has enabled the research that Herrnstein and Murray report to exist at all is the fact that one can measure the heritability of a characteristic without even having much idea of what the characteristic is" (Block 2001: 121). Thus, Herrnstein and Murray can measure the manner in which IQ appears to be inherited without actually defining the object of their measurement. This is particularly convenient for Herrnstein and Murray who then use heritability to make the leap to genetic predetermination.

Likewise, the limited scope of Herrnstein and Murray's investigation exposes a fundamental gap in their methodology that is a direct result of their bias. When positing environmental and genetic factors as competing forces for the determination of IQ, Herrnstein and Murray allow for the possibilities that blacks are genetically equal to whites and that any IQ difference may be environmental, that blacks are on equal environmental terms with whites and that IQ difference must be genetic, and that blacks are below white both genetically and environmentally (Block 2001: 115). Block notes, "But their way of putting the alternatives blots out a *crucial possibility*, namely that blacks are *much* worse off than whites environmentally and actually *better* off genetically. Allowing this option, we get a different set of alternatives: *genetically, blacks are worse off – or better off – or equal to whites*" (Block 2001: 115). The fact that Herrnstein and Murray overlook this possibility critically compromises the validity of both their research and their conclusions.

Oddly the disparity appears to be neither constant nor genuinely racial in composition. Boxill notes "The British psychologist H. J. Eysneck has argued that the average Irish IQ is about 15 points lower than the average English IQ, and that environmental causes cannot explain the difference" (Boxill 2001: 26). While we might be tempted to note the atavistic fantasy that suggests that the Irish were more simian and less evolved than their British counterparts, we should also note that this means little in terms of Herrnstein and Murray's research. To their end, both British and Irish immigrants, or descendants of immigrants, would appear white and should not, therefore, demonstrate an almost identical gap between *The Bell Curve*'s conclusions regarding blacks and whites.

Regardless of this, we do know that environment can have a tremendous effect on IQ. For example, Block notes that the average global IQ has increased by about three points every ten years. Likewise, certain countries have demonstrated a profound ability to increase their average IQ. Holland, for example, increased its average IQ by twenty-one points between 1952 and 1982 (Block 2001: 121). Surely, IQ in this example has not increased through pressures of heritability or radically improved genetics? Rather, the statistics would suggest that social pressures can dramatically shape intelligence. Moreover, the dramatic scale of the increase in average IQ suggests that within fifty years, the currently observed gap between black and white IQs can be closed.

Perhaps the most telling problem in Herrnstein and Murray's conclusion, therefore, stems from the direction in which they position their cause and effect mechanism. Rather than suggest poverty causes low IQ, a potentially rewarding line of research, they argue that IQ predisposes an individual to poverty and potentially crime as well. Their conclusions, however, because they are wrapped in the cloak of scientific objectivity and authority, borrow the authority of this discourse in the popular mind. In fact, *The Bell Curve* amounts to little more than misguided social bigotry. Lombroso would be proud.

As we move into Chapter 4, essentialist notions of race and racial determinism begin to take on new and yet familiar guises. Race is not a scientifically sound concept, yet this fact seems to have perhaps ironically encouraged its prevalence in both scientific and popular communities. Having thus noted our reluctance to abandon race, and the traditionally offensive consequences of this stubbornness, we are left to wonder what benefit, if any, we can gather from the concept. In Chapter 4, we shall see an attempt at a response as the empire writes back.

Notes

1. For evidence that Mulattos were potentially weak and/or susceptible to disease, Darwin relies on an anthropological survey from the US military from 1869 ("Military and Anthropological Statistics of American Soldiers," by B.A. Gould). Although the authority of this document is not brought into question by Darwin himself, our reading of the American situation will reveal that the nature of this survey must be considered highly suspect. In Chapter 5 we will discuss the significance of the census and similar surveys. The 1840 census mustered rather contentious data as evidence that free Mulattos were dying at a higher rate than blacks, thereby suggesting that miscegenation was ultimately responsible for a threat of degenerative infertility. The devious agenda behind this research, its timing, and its political significance, should be obvious.

2. B. A. Morel is often cited as having popularized the term "degeneration" as it is used in this context in 1857. In the context of Nordau particularly, Morel's account of the base influences of this degeneration held some appeal for Nordau's causal sense of the modern condition of human deterioration.

3. For a superb account of this phenomenon, see Vincent Cheng's *Joyce, Race, and Empire* (1995) and Noel Ignatiev's *How the Irish Became White* (1995).

4. It is worth noting that Lombroso speculated that Darwin suffered from a form of "*Paraesthesia*," which was the "exhaustive and excessive concentration of sensibility [that] must be attributed to all those strange acts showing apparent or intermittent anaesthesia and analgesia . . . to be found among men of genius as well as among the insane" (Lombroso 1891: 33).

5. Harrowitz brilliantly notes the varying us/them dynamic offered by Lombroso as a form of discursive evasion (1994: 45–49).

4 Modernity, Orientalism, Négritude, and the Phenomenology of Race

No more of that. I pray you, in your letters,
When you shall these unlucky deeds relate,
Speak of me as I am, nothing extenuate . . . (*Othello* V.ii.340–342)

When you removed the gag that was keeping these black mouths shut, what were you hoping for? That they would sing your praises? (Sartre 2001: 115)

At the foot of my Africa, crucified these four hundred years yet still breathing. (Senghor, quoted in Sharpley-Whiting 2001: 98)

Modernism as movement toward the postcolonial

As we move towards the turn of the twentieth century, we also witness the slow but consistent ideological and material collapse of the great empires. By the end of the First World War, Britain was no longer in a position to deny the pressures that had been mounting for some time in the commonwealth. At home, the stagnant ideologies of biological determinism were also slowly grinding to a halt as the theories of Lombroso and Nordau waned in the popular consciousness. Modernism had won the day. Of equal import as the practical demands that Britain's foreign endeavors were placing on the Kingdom, the horrors of the First World War left a visceral emptiness towards the supposed glorious empirical pursuits that had slaughtered a generation in Europe. This change helped to usher in the new voice of modernity with the subsequent catchphrase "make it new." As such, the newness sought by the early moderns marked a fundamental shift in the individual's relationship with his/her social surroundings. Rather than broiled in suffocating and ultimately murderous traditions of nationhood, the "experience of Modernism was, and to some degree remains . . . obscure. It was an art that frequently began in sensation and outrage, or else displacement and exile" (Bradbury and McFarlane 1991: 11). The degeneration from principled, confident, and altruistic homage to scientific utilitarianism, to outrage, displacement, and exile, marked for Nordau, in particular, an unconscionable lapse.

The reactionary disposition of modernity signaled a shift in aesthetic focus. The importance of being outraged, displaced, and exiled in the twentieth century can be read in the "new" English literary mainstream by authorial voices which were speaking and writing in English, but were fundamentally not English in the literal sense of the word. Terry Eagleton comments on this phenomenon when he states that "with the exception of D. H. Lawrence, the heights of modern English literature have been dominated by foreigners and émigrés" (Eagleton 1970: 9). In Eaglton's calculation, six out of the most impressive seven authors in the English-speaking world are/were not from England as such, an inconsistency he claims "is odd enough to warrant investigation" (Eagleton 1970: 9). Displacement and outrage also creates a space for inventiveness, and particularly for an originality that is tied to exiled subjectivity. Peter Nicholls notes that during the early modern period "writers began to adopt a kind of self imposed exile as a necessary condition of creativity, and with that gesture went a new conception of poetic language as something quite distinct from a shared language of communication" (Nicholls 1995: 13). The modern impulse to "make it new" appears to intimately accompany the increased sense of cultural dislocation, as the manifestation of the "new" finds a soft target in cultural fragmentation. And so, authors emerging from both within marginalized communities in Europe and from other, exterior communities stake their claim in a Europe suddenly ready to internalize and celebrate their voices. Consider authors like James Joyce or Joseph Conrad. Conrad's tenuous relationship with his adopted English nation has been the source of much of the commentary that would like to argue for his, at times, disconcerting English brashness, a commentary that perpetually encounters the fabricated nature of his Englishness. Likewise, Joyce's turbulent relationship with Ireland inspired his departure near the age of twenty. Despite his continued literary fascination with Ireland, he lived nearly all the rest of his life in self-imposed exile. Both of these judgments are often employed to bolster each author's position as modern, without even considering the aesthetics that such a discursive move inspires.

But what does this mean for racial thought? Does the significance of the word "displacement" transcend the keenly established color barriers discussed in Chapters 1–3 The answer is "yes" and "no." In Chapter 5 we will discuss the role of modernity in the United States and the shape that reactionary movement takes in post-civil war, post-reconstruction, America. We have already discussed this to an extent in the resurgence of the programmatic and misleading appropriation of science in the *Bell Curve* debate. The nature of that debate did not genuinely engage aesthetic priorities and the "voice" of colonized people speaking as colonized people. In Europe, and particularly in Britain, modernity begins to open up opportunities for a wider disparity of such voices, including melodious accents and disparate colors from the former colonies. This is not to suggest that the English-speaking world woke to a radically altered landscape on the morning of January 1, 1900, nor after the armistice at the end of the First World War. Change is almost always slow, and indeed, some avenues of Modernism still maintain the white exclusivity of high Victorian pretense. And yet, many authors like Joyce were greatly moved by the American popular, artistic expression, like Jazz, which was explicitly racial in composition and gathering considerable attention on the continent. The problem was, at least for the early modern period, that the majority of accented expression could, in the case of Jamaican-born writer Claude McKay, "become beautiful only when touched by the wand of English approval" (North 1994: 102). Granted, aesthetic value was changing, but making it new still needed to be validated under some remnants of old world dogma.

Still, the aesthetics of displacement made considerable room for alternative perspectives. However, there is an irascible irony in the fetishization of displacement, which has rigid consequences for racial thought. Although actively mustering outrage against the standard forms of expression, the reactionary nature of modernism tends to essentialize the subject that it celebrates as contrary. Hence, Joyce's lifelong, antagonistic relationship with Ireland helps to solidify his position as a celebrated Irish writer. The irony, of course, is poetically tangible. But the implication also has an insidious companion. It seems that at the exact moment that the movement towards modernism opens up radically new spaces in which previously ignored people may be included, the scope of what they may articulate also becomes oddly prefigured. Thus, the presentation of this new aesthetic space offers little of substance, hence the first epigraph of this chapter. Othello's triumph was that, in the face of exoticizing rhetoric, he created his own ability to speak briefly for himself. Perhaps an empty victory, but one not enjoyed by the vast multitude of colonial subjects marked by race. Early modern writers working to express themselves racially, rather than being allowed to speak as such, were confronted with something like a script. As suggested earlier, the problem for Claude McKay was the reversal of his anticipated colonial learning. For McKay, education in English schools had taught him that "the Jamaican dialect was considered a vulgar tongue," and the sudden celebration of his accent in works like *Songs of Jamaica* (1912) was a dramatic and counterintuitive shift toward gestures of dialectic authenticity that would earn him critical acclaim (McKay 1979: 67). Unfortunately, there was little room for McKay to work against the grain of this celebrated form, nor was there any real interest in McKay's view of McKay that extended beyond that proscribed by the fetishized celebration of his accent. Thus, there is an awkward ambivalence in the progress of subaltern speech, for on the one hand we must celebrate the fact that such speech is finally audible, yet then regret the programmatic manner in which it is permitted to be spoken. The balance between these two impulses is not an easy one to strike. This phenomenon will be discussed in greater detail in Chapter 5 when we move to America and note a very similar ambivalence in the Harlem Renaissance.

What the advent of modernism signals, if not racial enlightenment or egalitarian thought, is an increasingly precise focus on race as the essential substance of an individual. Linnaean thought, although not articulated as such, re-emerges in its base essentialization of racial and cultural character. Here, it must be added that race preempts culture and largely informs the latter. In modernism, the exoticism of difference is internalized with the desire for a "new" method of expression and brings the exiled, the colonial, the displaced, and the other into the discursive fold. As the most pronounced mark of difference, race becomes everything. As such, we might readily predict the combination of a series of events that helped to further the emphasis on race, and racially based aesthetic and socio-political movements. The fetish of displacement, the fascination with hybridism, the search for aesthetic newness, the increasingly essential and solid notion of race, all assist in the formation of racially based movements. These movements, of course, enjoyed varying degrees of success, as in the case of Négritude, which we will discuss in a moment, and relative failure, as in the case of the Harlem Renaissance, which we will discuss in Chapter 5.

One more introductory comment. In Chapter 3 we discussed competing narratives of authority, one scientific (Darwinism) and one scientifically expressed, although ultimately deluded and thinly veiled in its socio-political agenda (Degeneration and Eugenics). There is an irony to the situation now presented by these two counterclaims. As the twentieth century dawned, several aspects of the degeneration prophesy seemingly came awkwardly to fruition. As posited by Gobineau, certainly, the slow implosion of the British Empire could be read as a direct consequence of its continued exposure and miscegenation to inferior races. Equally predicted by Gobineau, this exposure coincided with a fantastic artistic explosion of creativity that resulted from this racial encounter. For Gobineau, the collapse of traditional empires in this manner, although perhaps unfortunate, would likely pass without much surprise as it would merely fulfill the entropic pattern that he speculated in the first instance. For Nordau and Lombroso, the matter remains much more conflicted. Certainly, their functional aesthetic conservatism washes out to sea under the impulsive wave of modernism. We might expect that their pseudo-scientific rhetoric of biologic determinism might smoothly accompany the decline of their other theories, but history has taught us to know better.

The aesthetic and cultural response to modernity and the ebb of empire seems to react against the most fundamentally solid authority of empirical discourse. As such, Darwin, and his scientific negation of race through the appropriate and accurate use of this discourse seems to get carried along with the tide instead of his pseudo-scientific contemporaries. Indeed, Nordau and Lombroso's more radically aggressive propositions, including Lombroso's advocacy of "deliberate selection," are also "made new," while being appropriated and combined with Galton's eugenic ideal. As suggested throughout this volume, the potential for misappropriation, and the potential for its terrible consequences, follow the development of race from its first inspiration. And thus, as Nordau and Lombroso fade from the spotlight, their worst fears come to pass, realized at least in part, by the monsters they helped to fabricate.

Certainly after the Second World War, the remaining bookends of Empire crumble, and eugenic ideals are exposed for the vulgar Holocaust that they helped, indirectly, inspire. It is at this point that postcolonial agency begins to gather momentum in a previously promised but largely undelivered sense. Despite the appearance of a rather broad and linear narrative presented here, the precise nature and timetable for the postcolonial remains a site of considerable tension. Indeed, the entire shift away from the imperial experience, as well as the modernist fetish of displacement, are by no means as rigidly structured or systematically coherent as they tend to appear in narratives such as this one.

Orientalism

Likewise, to this point, this volume has given considerable attention to the European experience of the outside world, and particularly the European experience in and around Africa. It should pass without comment, although often does not, that the postcolonial space is by no means limited to Africa. While the binary antagonism between black African and white European tends to gather the majority of critical attention, particularly in the United States, we must also note the fundamental role that the Orient played in structuring the colonial conscious. Indeed, from the outset a fundamental component of Europe's experience of the foreign resided in the East, rather than in Africa. Certainly, Europe's encounter with the Orient was consistently more conflicted than its experience of Africa. From the Crusades, the European was faced in the Orient with a sophisticated and elaborate society that was in many cases much more civil and advanced than the intruding Europeans. As we have seen, the superior sophistication and competence of Eastern civilizations, no matter how briefly experienced, offered a considerable challenge to European narratives of preeminence.

Situated thus, it is worthwhile to contrast the Muslim view of the exterior world, after having spent such considerable effort observing the Western construction of racial variation. While Europe has exhausted considerable effort to fabricate rather intricate explanatory theories to account for variation in humans, the early Muslim experience of the mirror image tends to pass without much comment. As suggested in Chapter 4, the European contact with the Muslim world exposed the Europeans to a civilization that was greatly advanced from their own. Perhaps disconcerting to these early combatants, it is quite interesting to note the reception that they inspired from their counterparts. At times, the relative positions of the two competing narratives seem completely foreign, and at others, compellingly familiar. This juxtaposition sums up a key point of what will later be called Orientalism.

But first let us consider the early Muslim experience of the European. Bernard Lewis suggests that unlike the elaborate classification systems designed to describe the natural world, including maps that would clearly delineate nations and political states, the Muslims placed their primary divisionary qualification under a single category. To the Muslim world, "The really significant division of mankind is between Muslims and unbelievers. If the division among Muslims were of secondary importance, the parochial subdivisions of the unbelievers and, particularly, of those who lived beyond the Islamic frontier, were of even less interest or significance" (Lewis 2001: 63). Thus in a reversal of our initial discussion of the Greek political state, in which participation in the political world signaled the most fundamental division of humanity, the Islamic world articulated a similar division, but based almost exclusively on religious terms. As Lewis suggests, the focus on religion often superseded any need or notion of national boundary between Muslim states, relegating further foreign divisions inconsequential.

As the Greek political state precluded the need for racial demarcation, we might wonder whether the same might be said of the Muslim prioritization of religious devotion. Bernard Lewis notes the example of Sā'id ibn Ahmad, Qadi of the Muslim city of Toledo in Spain, writing in 1068 (two years after the Battle of Hastings and thirty before the Crusaders arrived in Palestine), who had compiled a book in Arabic on the "categories of nations" (Lewis 2001: 68). The nations are broken into two major groups, "those that have concerned themselves with science and learning and those that have not" (Lewis 2001: 68). In a description of the second category, Sā'id offers some enlightening observations. Note the tragic irony, and the familiar focal points, in the method in which Sā'id articulates northern, white barbarians:

The other peoples of this group who have not cultivated the sciences are more like beasts than like men. For those of them who live furthest to the north, between the last or seven climates and the limits of the inhabited world, the excessive distance of the sun in relation to the zenith line makes the air cold and the sky cloudy. Their temperaments are therefore frigid, their humors raw, their bellies gross, their color pale, their hair long and lank. Thus they lack keenness of understanding and clarity of intelligence, and are overcome by ignorance and apathy, lack of discernment and stupidity. (Lewis 2001: 68)

To some degree, Sā'id's pronouncement echoes Greek divisions between civilized and cultured people and barbarians, the classic division of peoples of the earth. In many more significant ways, however, we can also see a categorical inversion of the sum of Enlightenment progress in terms of its racial mission. Here, the European becomes the beast-like savage, incapable of learning. Indeed within this quotation, we can see almost all of the central tenets employed in the fabrication of race, from climate, intellect, agency, and temperament, to dehumanization. The totality of Sā'id's inversion, and its tenuous relation to scientific observation, perhaps becomes most revealing in his comment upon the precise racial mechanism that makes much of the Enlightenment speculation so suspect. Note the manner in which the climate is presupposed to produce the exact effect that the opposite condition is thought to inspire by eighteenth-century natural philosophy. Indeed, Sā'id's insight is a perfect inversion of the standard European thought that will emerge 700 years later.

The fact that the significant portion of Eastern societies fell into decline almost in direct proportion to the rise of European nations helps to invert the racial dynamic between the two significantly. Having said this, however, it should be noted that an attempt to barbarize, or make savage, the Orient could not be completed to the same extent that it could be accomplished in either Africa or America. The removal of the Jews and Moors from Spain preceded the Spanish presence in the Americas by an extremely narrow margin. As Hannaford notes, "On January 2, 1492, Granada fell, and the Moors were beaten. Ferdinand and Isabella formally occupied the Alhambra, and almost eight hundred years of Arab occupation effectively came to an end. But even at this late date treaties were made under oath with the Moors giving them privileged status and generous terms, as subjects of the Crown" (Hannaford 1996: 23). Even if the European could willfully deny the accomplishments of the Orient, such facts would stick too close in recent memory to allow such usurpation. This was not the case in either the Americas or in Africa, where evidence of an advanced culture stood sufficiently removed from recent memory to preclude proper recognition. Thus, when confronted with the evidence of ancient Egyptian civilization, like the pyramids, European theorists could achieve a self-fulfilling account by suggesting that they had been constructed by white settlers. Moreover, the fact that the descendants of these white Egyptians could not be found only attested to the degeneration that this mysterious civilization endured through exposure and miscegenation with the savages inhabiting the rest of the continent.

The main purpose of this Chapter is to present the idea of Orientalism. This proposition, however, remains rather problematic. On the one hand, we have already begun to consider both the attraction and repulsion that informs Oriental and Occidental encounters, and we have at least modestly attempted to alter the focus of the debate. These limited gestures, however, do not represent the whole picture, which inspires the second point of discussion for this section.

Edward Said, a coincidental namesake of our commentator above, published his seminal text *Orientalism* in 1979. To a certain extent, discussing the theoretical framework of Orientalism before the publication of Said's text is a bit like discussing gravity before Newton. Yes, the phenomenon existed, but the articulation of the precise phenomenon does not call the exact thing into existence until the point of its utterance. This is strange magic, and such anachronisms figure heavily into the theoretical framework of both apologists and detractors of Orientalism, and to this we will come in a moment. The sum of *Orientalism*'s influence can be seen in the profound influence it had on postcolonial criticism. Put simply, Orientalism "is designed to illustrate the manner in which the representation of Europe's 'others' has been institutionalized since at least the eighteenth century as a feature of its cultural dominance" (Ashcroft and Ahluwaha 1999: 52). In suggesting that the Orient is a fundamental aspect of European dominance, Said exposes an often unspoken fixation. Said suggests:

> To speak of Orientalism therefore is to speak mainly, although not exclusively, of a British and French cultural enterprise, a project

whose dimensions take in such disparate realms as the imagination itself, the whole of India and the Levant, the Biblical texts and the Biblical lands, the spice trade, colonial armies and a long tradition of colonial administrators, a formidable scholarly corpus, innumerable Oriental "experts" and "hands," an Oriental professorate, a complex array of "Oriental" ideas (Oriental despotism, Oriental splendor, cruelty, sensuality), many Eastern sects, philosophies, and wisdoms domesticated for local European use – the list can be extended more or less indefinitely. (Said 1979: 4)

Perhaps the first and foremost construction of Orientalism is nothing other than the object of its study, the Orient. But this task is accomplished only in full recognition of the way in which the Orient has consistently been constructed by the West. Orientalism, then, marks this shift and recognizes the fundamental significance that the Orient has had in both the material and ideological expansion of Europe. The material benefit can be seen in the aggressive manner in which France and Britain, in particular, divided up the vast majority of the near east and Asia, with Britain taking India, China, and Australia, while France took most of North Africa and Indochina. Tracing Europe's ideological benefit might be more complicated, although its influence is certainly felt as intensely.

As a reply to the physical and subconscious attention that is the symptom of Europe's fixation, Orientalism announces a reversal in critical attention. Rather than the Orient acting as the source of wonder and fascination for the leering West, Orientalism stares back. What the Orientalist sees when gazing back is the manner in which knowledge and power are interwoven and how dominant discourses privilege those who wield them with the ability to discursively create. Thus, "The key instrument of power in all these domains is 'knowledge' insofar as the subjects of power are first identified as such, whether, 'deviant' or not, and consequently made available for 're(-)forming'" (Moore-Gilbert 1997: 36). The emphasis, therefore, lies in the constructive power of discourse and its ability to form not only the reality that it describes, but also the object of its attention.

As one might expect from a theoretical pronouncement so radical and influential, there has been no shortage of detractors. And indeed, several detractors take exception to the discursive mechanism between knowledge and power; "there is an at times radical contradiction in *Orientalism*'s discussion of the relationship between discursive Orientalism and the material practices and politics of imperialism, which derives in part from Said's attempt to abolish the distinction between the two terms" (Moore-Gilbert 1997: 41). Moore-Gilbert's theory very closely resembles the analogy made earlier about gravity and Newton, a scenario that suffers from the reductive nature of its protestation. On the one hand, Moore-Gilbert argues that Said suggests that the European fabrication of the Orient can be separated from its material dominance of that same thing. Moore-Gilbert does so without fully acknowledging the simple fact that the material domination of the Orient is simultaneously accomplished with the creation of that object. This is perhaps the most succinct example of the way discourse creates power; there was no such thing as gravity before Sir Isaac Newton.

Here it is worthwhile to note a conflicted aspect of the chronology, ordered as it has been to this point. As suggested by the oddly anachronistic first epigraph of this chapter, there is something gravely erroneous in positing postcolonial as arriving only, and literally, after the colonies. As Robert J. C. Young states, "many South American colonies . . . became independent states before the formation of some of the European states responsible for the high noon of imperialism" (Young 2001: 15). Thus, the need for the oft-cited question "When exactly . . . does the postcolonial begin?" (Shohat 1992: 103). Indeed, we could conceivably argue that the postcolonial began the moment that colonialism began. The issue of timing here is relevant, but not fundamentally so. Objects dropped before Newton; the material consequences of European imperialism were still evident before Orientalism lit a spark beneath postcolonialism.

Young takes note of another inconsistency in positioning the post-colonial. Put simply, the reductive term set forth in the conception of the postcolonial presupposes a single form of colonialism, a form that simply did not exist. Noting the tendency to level all colonial and/or imperial experience into a singular phenomenon, Young makes the simple observation that even the two traditionally leveled European nations like France and Britain, each of whom engages in overwhelming imperial projects, tend to arrive at their goals from distinct ends. Young observes that, "French colonial theorists typically distinguished between colonization and domination, the British between dominions and dependency" (Young 2001: 17). To this Stuart Hall adds, "There are serious distinctions to be made here . . . Is Britain 'post-colonial' in the same sense as the US? Indeed, is the US usefully thought of as 'post-colonial' at all? Should the term be commonly applied to Australia, which is a white settler colony, and to India?" (Hall 1996: 245). Hall pokes fun, but also arrives at several serious questions that have tended to get rolled into the homogenizing influence of what is otherwise an incredibly significant and provocative theoretical revaluation.

This is also precisely the nature of Said's point. Orientalism, by its very name and nature, is dramatically inclusive. Said's enunciation creates Orientalism, and demonstrates the exact process of how knowledge and power become institutionalized in authoritative discourse. To this fundamental proposition, Homi Bhabha and Gayatari Spivak elaborate in differing directions (see Bibliography for more details on Bhabha 1994 and Spivak 1985, 1999). With both theorists, the focus remains on re-orientating the critical gaze. Among a bevy of other critical perspectives, Bhabha uses psychoanalysis to present the mechanism of subconscious and conscious desire. In the same manner, Spivak delivers a multitude of critical dispositions, although perhaps most significantly feminism. Desire and feminism, combined in this manner, bring something to the theorization of race that has largely been missing thus far: sex. A fundamental aspect of Orientalism is the implicitly sexualized attraction and repulsion between the unknowable other and the agent whose articulations are designed to fill that void. For the colonizer, the other is charged with a projected sexual energy that is both threatening and enticing, often at the same time and rarely in between.

Together, these three theorists represent a formidable presence in both American and British academic institutions. Oddly, however, the fact of their institutional presence and increasing influence exposes these theorists to other forms of criticism. Perhaps one of the more aggressive antagonisms levied against the institutionalization of postcolonialism comes from Arif Dirlik, who states, that the "postcolonial, rather than a description of anything, is a discourse that seeks to constitute the world in the self-image of intellectuals who view themselves (or have come to view themselves) as postcolonial intellectuals" (Dirlik 1994: 339). The problem for Dirlik, therefore, becomes one of audience, and Dirlik's argument can be read as a potentially quite damaging assertion. How can one claim status as an exoticized individual, and maintain that distinction while employing, or even in the employment of, the discursive tools of the Orientalist? In a similar vein, bell hooks asked of Cornell West, "Why do you insist on using all that meta-language when you know it serves to put distance between you and the very people who you're talking to?" (quoted in Dalton 1995: 83). Likewise, Homi Bhabha has consistently been taken to task for the unnecessary discursive weight he employs to articulate relatively soft rhetorical points. Thus, as Orientalism has gained institutional recognition, a threat lingers that the "authenticity" (a troubling word if ever there was one) of the movement may be in some manner compromised or infected with the taint of the colonizer. This predicts a question that we will return to at the conclusion of Chapter 5: can we dismantle the oppressor's house with the tools of his making? For Dirlik, the answer appears to be "no." The reason for his trepidation is not singularly related to who speaks, but also what one speaks.

Négritude

In Chapter 3, we discussed the manners in which race is a scientifically and biologically unsound concept. As demonstrated, the scientific refutation of race by no means removed the concept from the popular ideological lexicon, nor from ultimately racist and quasi-scientific programs. The racial power of the scientific appropriation of race lies in its ability to posit essential racial behavioral characteristics. From the Enlightenment "germ" to the modern "gene," biological mechanisms offer evasive and potent explanations for the essence of race that reach well beyond mere physical difference. And indeed part of the strength of such a nebulous racial essence is that attempts to scientifically disprove the essential notion are met either with impenetrable scientific data, or nods of agreement, as there is decidedly no scientific basis for race in the first place.

The next response, therefore, transforms the debate from theories of biological determinism to social and environmental points of determinism (here "environmental" refers to social context and not climate). Biological versus psychological methods for racial construction directly echo the standard nature/nurture debate. Orientalism, for example, is steeped in the psychological renegotiation of the individual in relation to his/her colonizing force. Orientalism returns the gaze of the historical colonizer and by doing so carves out a space for articulation that was previously occupied by the colonizer. This space need not bother with scientific negations as it responds directly to the psyche of the colonial subject. We might wonder, however, whether this negates the need or possibility for essentialized constructions of race. Certainly, Orientalism does not necessarily demand racial essence, as evidenced by the manner in which parts of the Orient were included in the dominant, white category for several early and late Enlightenment descriptions of race. To respond, the colonial subject need look no further than his/her skin. The psychological impact of race remains, quite simply, historically determined. The mark of race, say, blackness, as imposed by the colonial paradigm, acts as the catalyst for this historical determination. With this in mind, then, the racially marked subject can return the dominant gaze not simply as colonial subject, although certainly as that as well, but also as a distinctly racial individual.

The term Négritude was coined somewhere between 1936 and 1937 by Martiniquan poet Aimé Césaire. Of course, the expression Négritude, and the expression of Négritude, did not appear suddenly from this moment, and there is considerable evidence that the momentum of the movement had been gathering for a considerable length of time. Indeed, some might argue that that momentum was growing from the moment the European constructed an African other. Nevertheless, the impetus toward the expression of displacement, as suggested in the broad discussion of modernism above, gathered both from within European colonial disillusionment and from outside European discourse and from the aggressive claim of colonial subjects for their voice. Thus, Négritude came to represent "a poetics, a philosophy of existence, a literary, cultural, and intellectual movement, [that] signified the birth of a new literature among black Francophone writers, a 'New Negro' from the Francophone world, a metaphorically rich pan-Africanism in French" (Sharpley-Whiting 2001: 95). Along with Leopold Sédar Senghor and Léon-Gontron Damas (from Senegal and Guyana respectively), Césaire acted as an instrumental catalyst for the serious, vociferous, and real engagement with modern aesthetics that could be formed into a resistance to European modes of cultural exchange, from the trivial to the most destructive.

Négritude, interestingly, posits a significant portion of its value on the simultaneous denial and embrace of blackness. On the one hand, race is denied fundamentally as a social construct invented by the white colonizer and (de)valued as such. It is, therefore, insubstantial in that a social construction should be, by definition, vulnerable to dismantling. On the other hand, Négritude embraces the fundamental reality of socially constructed worlds. The argument that social constructions are immaterial is largely conceptual and therefore immaterial to the colonized subject struggling to maintain his/her dignity, land, and life. Thus, Césaire states, "I do not in the slightest believe in biological permanence, but I believe in culture. My Négritude has a ground. It is a fact that there is a black culture: it is historical; there is nothing biological about it" (quoted in Arnold 1981: 37). Césaire does not contest the fact that race is a social construct. Instead, he recognizes that construct and insists on the reality that it fabricates because his experience foregrounds the reality of that construction. Césaire states, "We affirmed that we were Negroes and that we were proud of it, and we thought that Africa was not some sort of black page in the history of humanity; in sum, we asserted that our Negro heritage was worthy of respect, and that this heritage was not relegated to the past, that its values were values that could still make important contributions to the world" (quoted in Eze 2001: 119). By engaging Négritude, therefore, Césaire invalidates the hierarchy attributed to his race. Négritude is no longer a condition to be suffered, but rather celebrated.

Césaire's invalidation, however, is not a complete reversal, as has at times been presupposed. In his "Black Orpheus," Sartre calls for a reversal steeped in antagonism and with much higher stakes than those permitted at the outset of the twentieth century. His call for a necessary "anti-racist racism" is deliberately provocative, but also accurate in its call to agency (Sartre 2001: 118). Sartre's use of the expression anti-racist racism did not necessarily rest easily with Senghor, and has acted as a catalyst for a considerable amount of debate since its publication (Sharpley-Whiting 2001: 98). The expression anti-racist racism remains troubling not because of the way in which it threatens dominant discourse, but because it does nothing to dismantle the foundation upon which racism itself is built.

In another potentially disturbing gesture, Sartre articulates at least part of his polemic in the vocabulary of another influential thinker from the previous century. For Karl Marx, as for Sartre's appeal here, the impetus of racial leveling lies in class struggle. For Marx, "Race is merely the manifestation of the class conflict arising from inherent inequalities in the economic mode of production" (Hannaford 1996: 275). The black subject, in this instance, could not simply await liberation from "a distant white proletariat – involved in its own struggles" (Sartre 2001: 118). Agency is the agenda, and Sartre does not mind the appropriation of the tools fabricated in Western practices of racism, including but not limited to racism itself. With Marx, however, race tends to work as a mechanism imposed by the processes of socialization. Thus, argues Marx, "it is not the consciousness of men that determines their existence, but on the contrary, their social existence that determines their consciousness" (Marx 1971). Repositioning this formula allows for the precise manner of psychoanalytic response that prepares the ground for Négritude's awakening of black consciousness. Thus, the phenomenon of agency in the European/ African exchange determines the space through which each subject can gain his/her consciousness. And it is just such a formulation that will become so crucially antagonistic for Franz Fanon in a moment. What Sartre apparently wanted to celebrate in his call to action is precisely that action, agency, and dynamism; however, the imprecision of his speech actually potentially serves either to reverse or to subsume race under the inversion of racist ideology, or class discourses that remove the predominance of race from the equation.

Sartre, then, remains a rather troubling spokesman for Négritude for he manages to insist on the phenomenological primacy of race. For Sartre, "The negro cannot deny that he is negro, nor can he claim that he is part of some abstract colorless humanity: he is black. Thus he has his back up against the wall of authenticity" (Sartre 2001: 118). Sartre's calculation divides black experience into two compelling categories. First, the black subject is marked by his or her race as a primary form of identification. Second, and subsequently, all methods of cultural exchange are tainted by that recognition. Race, therefore, becomes the primary condition of existence, and because the mission of Négritude is to essentialize elements of blackness, race prefigures the disposition of the racialized individual. In terms of his experience of race, then, Fanon corrects Sartre, stating, "Jean-Paul Sartre had forgotten that the Negro suffers in his body quite differently from the white man" (Fanon 1967: 138).

The first section of this chapter suggests that modernism clears a space for relatively marginalized voices and art forms. The suggestion that Négritude merely fulfills the role proscribed by the impetus of European modernism is a contentious and problematic assertion. Certainly, the proposal that one causes the other is reductive and simplistic. Modernism did not "allow" black speech any more than black aesthetics can offer the sum total of modernism. There are several significant ways, however, in which the two movements overlap considerably. Primarily, the modernist fetish with exile and displacement finds a rich garden in the African continent.

As suggested in our closing comments on Orientalism, the process of articulation inspires a significant base for controversy. In other words, the question "who may speak?" only prepares the ground for a secondary question, "what may be spoken?" For a movement that desires fundamentally to articulate black essence, black aesthetics, and blackness full stop, there must also be a question as to what this essential blackness can articulate while maintaining this blackness. The question of authenticity has a potentially narrowing effect on the legitimacy and/or universality of speech. If only blacks can speak as/for blacks, and only the oppressed can speak about oppression, we may quickly find ourselves mired in a cacophony of disparate but legitimated voices, all articulating the premise of their own individuality. In this social formation, the individual drowns in a sea of experience and discursive relativism. Fanon works against the threat of relativism by insisting that there is black speech, albeit multitudinous and disparate, and that this speech is of black experience. Fanon writes, "I sincerely believe that a subjective experience can be understood by others; and it would give me no pleasure to announce that the black problem is my problem and mine alone and that it is up to me to study it" (Fanon 1967: 86). Race is real, and blackness is real. The experience of these two factors need not be a prison that locks the racial subject away in silence even when speaking.

Blackness, for Fanon, is created through contact with whiteness. Fanon states, "As long as the Black is with his own, he will not have to experience his being of the other" (Fanon [1951] 2001: 184). This realization dawns upon Fanon when he hears a white child articulate his color; "Look, a Negro!" (Fanon [1951] 2001: 184). Thus, articulation calls into being the entire history of the European construction of his race. In order to reclaim his being, then, Fanon must also reclaim his blackness from this history; he removes his otherness by not allowing it to be filled by a dominating discourse. Fanon writes, "Still in terms of consciousness, black consciousness is immanent in its own eyes. I am not a potentiality of something, I am wholly what I am. I do not have to look for the universal. No probability has any place inside me. My Negro consciousness does not hold itself out as black. It *is*. It is its own follower" (Fanon 1967: 135). Thus, "Fanon's redemption from the past involves not responding or *reacting* to it. Freedom for Fanon involves the active inflection of the 'now,' rather than a reactive valorization or reproduction of what has been given. History, as the framework of cultural origins . . . , is denied" (Weate 2001: 178). Rather than return the imperial gaze, and confront the proscribed authenticity waiting for him, Fanon moves the discursive field. In this manner, Fanon achieves a power traditionally created and protected by the dominant discourse, the precise field of that discourse.

There has been some debate with regard to the origins and ultimate mission of Négritude. Senghor, for one, emphasizes the role of the New Negro movement in the United States as the American interpretation of modernism and posits Négritude as a profound African counterpart. In 1971, Senghor suggested that "the general meaning of the word [Négritude] – the discovery of black values and recognition for the Negro of his situation – was born in the United States of America" (quoted in Sharpley-Whiting 2001: 96). This is problematic for a number of reasons, not the least of which is the rather limited success of the New Negro movement in the United States. We will discuss the New Negro movement, or the Harlem Renaissance, at some length in Chapter 5. For now, however, we might tentatively suggest that at least part of the failure of the movement stems from its re-exoticization of the black other. Rather than overcoming the framework under which the black subject had been systematically negated for so long, the movement tended to play to the largely white audience in a way that ultimately re-inscribed the black/white binary juxtaposition. In contrast to the discussion of Orientalism, the gaze has not been significantly re-directed, and what begins as an attempt to claim agency slips into staged acting.

There is a difficult and circular logic that runs through the concept of Négritude, as the movement both recognizes and stands in opposition to the racial constructs of Western thought. This has led critics like Kwame Anthony Appiah to seriously reconsider the merit of African nationalism and Nativism. Because the movement fails to deny the wholesale validity of the distinction, nativism fails to substantially move beyond, through, past, or against the structure that created it in the first place. As such, Négritude falls into the reactionary trap, and thus Appiah can convincingly proclaim that "few things are less native than nativism" (Appiah 1992: 60). Mosley continues the thought for Appiah, stating, "The European conceived of the African as 'the other,' the opposite to the domineering and analytical bent of Europe; and Négritude enshrined this view of the African as a virtue, the natural antidote to European militarism and will-to-dominance" (Mosley 1999: 82). In this manner, the entire construction of Africa must be seriously reconsidered. The potential misapplication of this principle will be explored in greater detail in Chapter 5 with the discussion of the troubled Harlem Renaissance.

Appiah has proposed a slightly dissenting opinion in his formulation of racialism. Simply put, racialism acts in the precise manner that race operates but without any hierarchical presumptions, and therefore without any trace of racism.[1] Ultimately, "Appiah wishes to divest the world of the concept of race by denying that the notion plays any constructive part in dealing with the problems Africa faces. Further, since African Americans (such as Blyden and Du Bois) conceived of their relationship to Africa primarily in terms of their belonging to the same race, he considers that relationship to be as tenuous and infertile as the concept of race upon which it is built" (Mosley 1999: 81). Appiah contrasts with Césaire by isolating the agency of blackness as opposed to African-ness. Let us consider, for example, the account of Claude McKay mentioned above. At least part of the problem of locating McKay lies not only in the firmness with which he plants himself, but also in the primacy placed upon his blackness. His discursive mobility within the scope of British postcolonialism or American Harlem Renaissance works only as a secondary consideration of his color. It is this color, the Négritude movement would argue, that also prefigures his relationship to any white mainstream (as with Fanon's encounter with the child), and which prefigures his aesthetic response. Thus, the modernist is black, first and foremost.

An unfortunate turn in this logic, however, stems from the placement of the responsive aesthetic. Aesthetics irreducibly revolve around judgments of value, and to suggest a racialist position that levels hierarchy must therefore level values of beauty and terror. As Mosley argues, "Both racism and racialism require viewing race as a necessary condition for possessing (the potential for) certain traits, in order to achieve selective distribution of traits by race" (Mosley 1999: 77). In this formulation, race is at least an essential pretext that allows access to modes of being, albeit ones that are harmlessly negated by equal status or any such relativity that negates hierarchy. But to presume an aesthetic and biological determination offers a very simple and potentially devastating opportunity to puncture this logic with absurd hypotheticals. Thus, "if the racialism of Négritude is taken literally, then Wordsworth and the romantic poets of Europe must be regarded as Africans" (Mosley 1999: 77). Although deliberately reductive and ultimately absurd, the point that Mosley raises illuminates the meaninglessness of moving the logic of Négritude outside of Négritude itself.

In his discussion of Appiah and racism, Mosley clarifies a secondary piece of racial logic that floats precariously between sociological and biological conceptualizations of race. Mosley argues against Appiah's notion of "intrinsic racism," as a bogus concept. The problem centers on Appiah's description of African nationalists such as Sartre, and the subsequent formulation of an anti-racist racism. Appiah describes this form of racism as intrinsic because it does not posit the hierarchy essential to standard examples of racism. In order to explain we can consider the old adage that posits the difference between a patriot and a nationalist; a patriotic man loves his country, while a nationalist hates everyone else's. The patriot is not a traditional extrinsic racist, although he may demonstrate qualities of excluding and preferential behavior, because he has not devalued other nations and his prefer-ence stems only from his imagined community with his nation. Thus, his preference, privilege, and favor for that nation may result from nepotistic altruism and not superiority. The nationalist is an extrinsic racist because the value of his country is gained specifically from the devaluation of others. Intrinsic racism is thus considered racialist, by Appiah, because a community need only structure itself and mutually appreciate that bond. When applied to race, this formulation loiters between sociological and biological concepts because it recognizes the value of socially constructed, but biological, units. Say, for example, a family structure: Treating your sister preferentially may not necessarily represent racism, unless you exist in a social commu-nity where that "familial" relation is not biological.

Mosley argues against the notion of intrinsic racism because "it contains no suggestion that valuable social qualities are selectively distributed between groups" (Mosley 1999: 76). Mosley continues, "On the other hand, Crummell, Blyden, Du Bois, and Senghor were racialists because they did believe that the African harbored special talents which made possible certain contributions to world civiliza-tion that only the African could provide" (Mosley 1999: 76). Therefore, "contrary to Sartre and Appiah's claims, Senghor and Du Bois – with Crummell, Blyden, and Césaire – opposed racism, not with another form of racism but with racialism"(Mosley 1999: 85). The ultimate triumph or failure of Négritude will not be decided; however, the invalidation and return that it signals has undoubtedly stirred the discursive waters that had, until this point, been deviously monochromatic. Taken together, Orientalism and Négritude offer a significant vantage from which to view Western discourse, and a voice with which to speak alongside it. In the next section, therefore, we will read an example of how this visage and voice reacts and revalues a standard text of Western domination.

Encounters with racism: Achebe, Conrad, and Kane

Thus far, we have been tracing the history of the word race and the conceptual frameworks within which it has been employed. In observing the tragi-comic efforts of several individuals to taxonomically define the races, and by proxy the word race itself, we have outlined the basic tenets underlying their interpretation, definition, and application of the word. From this theoretical vantage, however, we perceive the lingering question as to the practical application of the word race. It is one thing to theorize in the abstract, and another entirely to apply the term. And there is a problem here. It would be unrealistic and unfair to suggest that the word "race," plain and simple, is overtly employed nearly as often as the previous sections of this book seems to imply. This is perhaps one simple split between the theorists and practitioners of the term. Rather, the concept of race represents a more common sense and intuitive kind of understanding. As suggested in the introduction, we believe in race and the site of its power lies not in its overt pronouncement and application, but in the lack of need to do so. One would, for example, rarely approach a new acquaintance and ask "what race are you?" in the same manner that you might ask an acquaintance's nationality. In theory, and in practice, one would already have some tangible clues as to the former, while the latter need not be quite so obviously marked. The fact that we do not need, nor even really consider asking, is the mark of the profundity of our investment in the term. This is the phenomenology of race. Again, beneath the masquerade of civility hides the power of the childish presumptions of our common sense. So, where might we look if we wanted to remove the veil from the concept of race? Against what standard might we test the obviousness of our common sense? There is one specific manifestation of race that appears repeatedly and with significant effect.

Embodied in the word "racism," we can more readily appreciate the meanings (mostly derogative) that have come to trail the word race, which is the precise condition that movements like Négritude try to counteract; the mere utterance of the word highlights some rather telling aspects of our relationship with the concept. In particular, the accusation of racism has profound political power (we need consider only Sartre's reversal for evidence). With this in mind, it seems wholly worthwhile to investigate a more material manifestation of the word race as it is thus applied. The mission here lies in locating the circumstances that make the accusation utterable, observing what occurs as a direct result of the pronouncement and tracing backwards from the accusation the inherent meaning of the word race as it is applied. And to be sure, the accusation of racism has tremendous socio-political power. Is this because the word race itself seemingly must not be spoken? Moreover, why is the mere threat of such an accusation so terrifying to the liberal sensibilities of many academics? What conditions must be prevalent to warrant a valid accusation? Finally, as we must have a clear notion of race to administer the accusation of racism, what does the accusation allow us to infer about the subtle and inarticulate concept of race? And so with an attempt to answer these questions and more, we can begin, if not to bridge, at least to map the aforementioned crevasses between the theoretical and the practical.

Let us look at a specific moment where the accusation "you are a racist" opened a maelstrom of debate and recrimination. Not too long ago, the Nigerian novelist Chinua Achebe single-handedly opened and galvanized the critical debate around what was by then a pivotal novel in the western canon, Joseph Conrad's *Heart of Darkness* (1899). As important as the debate surrounding the novel itself, however, was the implication of the argument to both authors. Quite simply, Achebe's reading of *Heart of Darkness* led him to a singular indictment against Conrad and his, by now famous pronouncement that "Joseph Conrad was a thoroughgoing racist" (Achebe 1989: 11).[2] Put simply, Achebe takes Conrad to task for several reasons: the absence of real Africans within this supposedly triumphant novel, the derogatory, dismembered, and limited descriptions of Africa(ns) such as they are, the condescending use of Pidgin English when African individuals are actually allowed to speak, and the explicit questioning of African humanity that results from the above. These were strong words and in many ways were designed to elicit an intense response. Achebe got exactly that.

Undoubtedly, the accusation came as something of a shock to Conrad's more steadfast apologists. After all, a significant vein in the traditional reading of Conrad suggests that he was an ar   ⹃erialist and deeply critical of Europe's supposed enlighᵗ   ions in Southeast Asia and Africa. Indeed, Marlow's   ⹁⹃⹄⹃lamation "And this also . . . has been one of the dark places of the earth," has been read as a demonstration of a revelation concerning the fluidity of race and empire (Conrad 1973: 29). When combined with Kurtz's fatal proclamation, "Exterminate all the brutes!" and the lingering question as to which brutes he means, those wearing the mask of civilization or savagery, Conrad seems to entertain only the most tenuous relationship to the imperial project (Conrad 1973: 87). This skepticism combined with Conrad's stylistic novelty secured *Heart of Darkness* a tremendously important place in the advent of Modernism and the canon of English literature. To those apologists, Conrad represents the perfect proto-Modernist. He appeals to the Victorian masses with the bold adventurism of his sea-going tales. In this regard, he is a champion of Britannia, ambitiously ruling the waves. And yet, he is also a subtle skeptic. He is a transplant, feeding the Modernist need for exile and displacement. This exile allows Conrad to ambivalently embrace the forms of his art and the culture that enforces it. In many ways, Conrad was in the right place at the right time.

On the other hand, Conrad was in the wrong place at the wrong time, and his skepticism with regard to the imperial project does not preclude a racist disposition. When placed under this light, Achebe's indictment seems extremely fair. Our previous discussion of the Victorians and their racist ideologies apply to Conrad in more ways than many would like to admit. There are several simple layers to Conrad's defense on this issue. One such layer stems from the critical misapprehension concerning the time during which Conrad was writing. Achebe himself allows that "It was certainly not his fault that he lived his life at a time when the reputation of the black man was at a particularly low level" (Achebe 1989: 13). To some moderate extent, we can read a critique of what Conrad seems to acknowledge as ridiculous conventions of his time. Before Marlow leaves, for example, the disheveled doctor who ominously requests "in the interests of science" to measure Marlow's head is dismissed as a "harmless fool" (Conrad 1973: 37). Of course, Marlow comments upon the apparent foolishness of the behavioral sciences, like phrenology, discussed in Chapter 3. For this reason, Conrad prepares a protagonist who appears at least mildly skeptical of the apparent authority of scientific discourse. Indeed, the doctor concedes that "the changes take place inside" (Conrad 1973: 38). We are left to wonder what scientific merit, therefore, these measurements could possibly provide. This, however, does not sufficiently accommodate Conrad's ambivalence, nor does it absolve him from the fire of Achebe's accusation. Achebe can thus applaud Conrad for condemning the "evil of imperial exploitation," while lamenting that he "was strangely unaware of the racism on which it sharpened its iron tooth" (Achebe 1989: 19). After all, as we have seen repeatedly, one need not be malicious to be racist.

In order to achieve his aggressive reading, Achebe must work to combine Marlow with Conrad, a feat which Conrad's stylistic maneuvers deflect at several opportunities. The ability to discursively equate a character with an author interestingly stems from the manner in which many of Conrad's apologists have interpreted his work. There is a troublesome double-bind in heralding Conrad as a critic of the imperial impulse, while choosing to distance the man himself from some of the less progressive aspects of his writing. To be sure, Conrad takes great lengths to separate himself from Marlow. Many of Conrad's supporters are keen to note that a reader must be acutely aware of Conrad's obtuse relation to storytelling in his creation of a character whose story comes to the reader through another narrator. Moreover, Conrad's explicit criticism of appropriate articulation, accurate representation, and reliable replication are all manifest in Marlow's acknowledged methods of storytelling. Achebe exploits this act, however, to demonstrate a narrative cowardliness from Conrad. The distance, quite simply, acts as a screen behind which Conrad can mutter anything he wants with impunity. It is a screen that barely conceals, in Achebe's mind, the intimacy enjoyed between Marlow and Conrad. Of course, this is problematic interpretive ground, but not foreign to both sides of the debate.

There are also, admittedly, several simplistic layers to the indictment of Conrad. To begin, there is Conrad/Marlow's apparent fetish with the highly sensitive term "nigger," a sore and problematic epithet to be sure. A flaw in this logic, however, emerges when we consider the practical function and viability of removing a term from the lexicon. It seems highly probable that if the word nigger were never uttered again by a member of any race, class, or political disposition, racism itself would persist without any real obstacle. Moreover, the precise method of racism would also continue unabashed. This is a fairly soft point but the implication, particularly in terms of this discussion of Achebe, has much farther reaching ambition. Conrad's potential racism need not apply where an epithet is leveled against a black African; rather, Achebe posits a significant part of his accusation in the absence of real Africans at which he could hurl these insults.

A primary point in Achebe's argument is that *Heart of Darkness* does not deserve its position, or any position for that matter, within the Western canon. Achebe states, "And the question is whether a novel which celebrates this dehumanization, which depersonalizes a portion of the human race, can be called a great work of art" (Achebe 1989: 12). First and foremost, Achebe levels his accusation because of the notable lack of real Africans present in the novel. For example, as Marlow approaches Africa he encounters a French "man-o-war anchored off the coast. There wasn't even a shed there, and she was shelling the bush . . . there she was, incomprehensible, firing into a continent. Pop, would go one of the six-inch guns; a small flame would dart and vanish, a little white smoke would disappear, a tiny projectile would give a feeble screech – and nothing would happen" (Conrad 1979: 40–41). Achebe wonders, quite rightly, what this scene must have looked like not just from the absurdly gigantic continent, but from the specific area where the "tiny" shells were landing. Certainly, it was not "nothing" that happened from that perspective. In his *Ambiguous Adventure*, Cheikh Hamidou Kane fills in this blank by providing a brief account of that encounter. Kane writes, "Strange dawn! The morning of the Occident in black Africa was spangled over with smiles, with canon shots, with shining glass beads," and later, "Some among the Africans, such as the Diallobé, brandished their shields, pointed their lances, and aimed their guns. They were allowed to come close, then the cannons were fired" (Kane 1963: 48). The outcome of the encounter has not been rewritten, nor has Kane exhausted himself on chronicling the fall of Africa. This brief account, however, provides the humanity that receives the cannon shot. Kane adds to this by juxtaposing this encounter with Samba Diallo's first meeting of the French Lacroix family, a story "of which the profound truth is wholly sad" (Kane 1963: 51). That Kane should combine these two encounters brings life to both the white and the black aspects of the colonial agenda, both the colonizer and the "continent." By comparison, Conrad never prepares the moral confliction that genuine, human engagement with a black African would propose.

When Conrad writes, or Marlow recognizes, a black African, his presence is almost always set up as a counterpoint to the imperial project; Achebe describes this as "the desire – one might indeed say the need – in Western psychology to set Africa up as a foil to Europe" (Achebe 1989: 2–3). That is, when Conrad does provide a concrete example of a black African, the image is generally piecemeal, fragmented, reductive, or imprecise. While this may be read as a fundamental flaw in the character of Marlow, it is also indicative of the reductive and dehumanizing narrative space allowed in imperial discourse for the African. Thus, Marlow's first sight of black Africans leaves him amazed at how natural they seem, or rather, how far removed they are from the "humanizing, improving, instructing" mission of the European engagement with Africa (Conrad 1979: 65). Marlow, therefore, sees precisely what he has come to expect, authentic and dehumanized Africans. To respond to the expected atavism, Achebe quotes Janheinz Jahn; "Only the most highly cultivated person counts as a 'real European.' A 'real African,' on the other hand, lives in the bush . . . goes naked . . . and tells fairy stories about the crocodile and the elephant" (quoted in Achebe 1989: 27). Likewise, when not anticipating atavistic savages, Marlow encounters black Africans only in pieces. As he organizes his trip inland, therefore, Marlow addresses "the 60 pairs of eyes" in front of him rather than sixty individual humans (Conrad 1979: 49). While perhaps a minor example, the continued repetition of such fragmented synecdoche throughout the text betrays the undercurrent of dehumanizing discourse in Conrad's narrative.

So, Conrad initially denies African presence in Africa. Subsequently, he provides limited and/or entirely piecemeal representations of African individuals, suggesting that they are either as natural and savage as the great European atavistic fantasies, or profoundly disconnected. Of course, neither option is remotely satisfactory for Achebe. Achebe writes, "In confronting the black man, the white man has a simple choice: either to accept the black man's humanity and the equality that flows from it, or to reject it and see him as a beast of burden. No middle course exists except as an intellectual quibble" (Achebe 1989: 23). As suggested in our discussion of Orientalism and Négritude, one of the most fundamental methods for achieving this humanity stems from the act of speech. Again, in this department Conrad appears notably lacking. When allowed to speak at all, Conrad's natives are limited both in the scope of their dialogue ("Catch 'im. Give 'im us. Eat 'im!"), and the Pidgin English with which they are allowed to speak (Conrad 1979: 4). And note the disturbing duplicity in a term like "allowed," deployed with apparently disinterested ease, from the previous sentence. Does Conrad really allow his Africans to speak, and would Marlow understand them if they did? Thus, the act of speech becomes the site for an awkwardly contested performance.

The legacy of imperialism, however, has created a situation in which the colonial subject can be understood by the colonizer, a fact loaded with bitter and sweet irony. The real power of imperialism lay not only in military might, but in the processes of reconstruction and forced assimilation that replaces the chaos that the cannons created. Kane writes, "The new school shares at the same time the characteristics of cannon and of magnet. From the cannon it draws its efficacy as an arm of combat. Better than the cannon, it makes the conquest permanent" (Kane 1963: 49). When placed in this light, the act of speaking becomes a peculiarly doubled gesture. Much in the manner of the criticism lobbied against the third world intellectuals of Orientalism, Samba Diallo's speech only serves as testimony to his imperial past. In this sense, and in a cynically ironic gesture, the more articulate he becomes, the more he is removed from what Conrad would consider his authentic and "natural" state. His speech, in other words, testifies with every breath to the imperial legacy that has marked him as a racial and colonial subject. We are reminded of our earlier question. Can we use the oppressor's tools to dismantle his work?

To be fair, it is unclear whether Conrad, regardless of the benevolence of his representation, could actually represent the African in a manner that is satisfactory to all, and particularly to those on the receiving end of the imperial impulse he both embodies and criticizes. Interestingly, Achebe suggests that "the story we had to tell could not be told for us by anyone else no matter how gifted or well intentioned" (Achebe 1989: 38). The whole story of Africa is simply not Conrad's to tell. The very serious joke in all of this lay both in Achebe's stated aim and in the horror that his accusation inflicted upon the political sensibilities of the academy. The intellectual response to the accusation is quite telling. It seems that many on either side of the debate worry that to defend Conrad is to endorse racism. In a stunningly brilliant maneuver, the disposition opens up a Pandora's Box of trepidation. Was Conrad a racist? Could he have been one without realizing it? If the answer is "yes," does this excuse the crime? Could I be a racist without realizing it? Does my defense of Conrad expose my ideological flaw? And so on. The answers to these questions need not appear immediately, but the silence that they inspire not only gives pause for the sound of other voices to be heard, but demonstrates the power that such articulations wield when they do (solicited or otherwise).

And in the end, quite simply, the experience of reading Conrad is all the poorer without Achebe; the two seem, borrowing from Achebe's image, to be standing on two possible corners of a multiple intersection looking at each other not from opposing, but contingent perspectives. The irony here is that despite Achebe's stated desire to remove Conrad from the canon, no other single individual has helped reenliven the debate that surrounds him. After all, Achebe's own figures suggest that Conrad is doing extremely well compared to Achebe's relatively modest, and disappointingly localized, success. Achebe's indictment appears to have had the opposite result than the one he desired. But this is not entirely the case. Reading Conrad is a wholly different experience after Achebe (and Kane) than before; the consideration of opposing narratives, the sound of an African voice, the possibility of response, has changed the possibilities offered in reading Conrad's text.

Transition

A point that has been deliberately overlooked thus far in our discussion of Conrad and *Heart of Darkness* is the prevailing threat of degeneration that floats through the text. Marlow's exclamation that starts the entire narrative ("this also has been one of the dark places of the earth") and the disintegration of Kurtz both actively work to pose the possibility of civilization's fluid and tenuous nature.

But what does degeneracy mean when considered next to Orientalism and Négritude?

The imposition of voices from the margin may be at least partially predicted by the machinations of modernism. The advent of movements like Orientalism and Négritude, however, radically displaces and reinterprets that margin. If we genuinely recognize black consciousness and postcolonial agency, Marlow need not concern himself that London was once barbaric, only that it still is. And so when Achebe argues that "We know the racist mystique behind a lot of that stuff and should merely point out that those who prefer to see Africa in those lurid terms have not themselves demonstrated any clear superiority in sanity or more competence in coping with life," we must recognize the responsibility that dominating discourses have to repeatedly demonstrate their value (Achebe 1989: 34). And if we consider the degenerate fears expressed by Kipling, and perhaps several other writers mentioned in this volume, we must also note the manner in which their fears no longer matter. What Europe could degenerate into is beautiful, active, poetic, and everything that Said, Achebe, Césaire, Senghor, Fanon, and Kane suggest that Europe's other can achieve. Race has transformed from a biologically and tenuously scientific concept into one that takes its initial mark as the recognition of difference and works toward the essence of that difference. This difference is not threatening, a fact that Appiah strives to make us recognize.

Let us return briefly to racism. In apparent agreement with more contentious elements of Négritude, Achebe declares, "we may need to counter racism with what Jean-Paul Sartre has called an anti-racist racism, to announce not just that we are as good as the next man but that we are much better" (Achebe 1989: 45). Should the West feel threatened by Achebe's proclamation? Only if one feels that he has genuinely done a disservice to Conrad by accusing him of being a thoroughgoing racist.

And thus, we conclude this chapter relatively ensured of a genuine social progress. The scientific basis for race has unraveled, and in its stead we can hear the voices of postcolonial individuals, albeit with great struggle, reclaiming their agency by awakening the consciousness of their race. As we move to the United States, however, we should prepare ourselves for another song entirely.

Notes

1. The term racialist as developed here is not always deployed with this exact connotation. D. A. Washbrook, for example, posits racialist as an "attempt by one group to legitimate claims to political dominance or superior social status over others" (Washbrook 1982: 143). The definition proffered by Appiah fundamentally contradicts this usage because of its placement of superior social status. Likewise, Louis Snyder suggests, "Racism assumes inherent racial superiority or the purity or

superiority of certain races; also it denotes any doctrine or program of racial domination based on such an assumption. Less specifically, it refers to race hatred and discrimination. Racialism assumes similar ideas, but describes especially race hatred and racial prejudice" (1962: 9–10). The need to distinguish between plain hatred and a doctrine of that hatred seems rather redundant. Appiah's formulation, however, offers a much more dynamic system where one might recognize racial difference, as one will, but without the racist implications attached to such identification.

2. It should be noted that Achebe's first indictment of Conrad was articulated in a much more abrasive manner, suggesting instead that Conrad was a "bloody racist." The quotation above comes from the printed version of his original speech.

5　America

We are split men, disconnected from our own resources, almost severed from our *Selves*, and therefore out of contact with reality. Not altogether so, else we would not live, or, if we did, there would be no question about our plight, no contradictions between our actual behavior and the ideal state of being. (Toomer 1980: 423)

I tell her if she don't look out, she'll wake up one of these days and find she's turned into a nigger. (Larsen 1986: 171)

Placing race: the one-drop rule

The American experience of race has undoubtedly been, and arguably continues to be, one of abject failure. The breadth of American failure extends through the tragic consequences of the conquistadors, the massacres of Cortes, the legacy of slavery, the eradication of the Native American in the north, the Civil Rights movement, and the list could go on for quite some time. Perhaps because of the dubious nature of the concept, perhaps from the purposes for which it was readily adopted and applied, race has left an indelible and brutal legacy in the Americas. From the first European encounter with the new world, the role of race seems an intimate counterpart to the entirety of its history, although not yet articulated as such. While the struggles of Bartolomé de las Casas, discussed briefly in Chapter 1, were useful in structuring the contemplation of race around the narrowing parameters of the biblical narrative, las Casas ultimately failed to prevent a significant portion of the devastation within his time and after. His failure is endemic among those who subsequently cover similar territory, so much so that race appears as a particularly disturbing feature etched in North, Central, and South American history. Moreover, there is a fundamental failure within American discourse to maintain the consistency of the register. Keeping with one of the central tenets of this volume, America represents a location where race remains almost perpetually in motion, and this mobility does not necessarily portend genuine progress. Instead, the American relationship with race is fundamental, but also deeply ambivalent. It embraces the pleasant fiction of melting-pot beneficence and the violence of radical bigotry in the same breath, and almost always with tragic consequences.

For the United States, in particular, the legacy of slavery and the failure to recover from that legacy continues to dominate significant portions of the public discourse. Despite the prevalence of the United States' melting-pot mythology, an observant anthropologist might have a difficult time producing a nation more fully convinced of the commonsensical validity of race and the structural legitimacy of the extremes it delineates. To be sure, the racial history of the United States is deeply ambivalent to the point of confusion. Likewise, the pervasive presence of American capital and the sheer scale of its academic input on the subject have ensured that the majority of discussion, with regard to the concept of race has been filtered through the vocabulary of the United States. A brief trip to the library will reveal the multitude of volumes published on race, and the limited number of those books that look beyond U.S. borders. One consequence of this limited vocabulary plays out in reductive, yet pervasive, media coverage that simply reiterates American discursive failures. Moreover, American insularity seals the discursive borders from any disconcerting foreign influence. Those few that do reach outside of the United States often relate the subject to, or articulate within, the American situation. This is by no means a positive state of affairs. The racial experience has been, and again continues to be, one of conflation, misunderstanding, misappropriation, antagonism, and almost anything other than civil, ordered, and mature. One need not look any further than the manner in which any rigid or structured concept of race has muddled with the vaguely intelligible ethnicity into the nearly indecipherable code of the new catch-all phrase "identity." Oddly, and perhaps ironically, the discursive poverty of such terms derives primarily from the "American" concept of the individual's role in the political state, and from the mobility that such terms are allowed to denote. More will be made of the American perception of individual agency within the state in a moment.

The cataclysmic tribulations caused by slavery and its legacy have been explored at great length, and with more direct purpose, than can be accomplished in this volume. However, the legacy of slavery and the singularity of the slave trade have helped galvanize the nature of racial conversation into expansive polarities, and for that reason alone, it merits some discussion. Indeed, slavery has forged the concept of race in the United States into an almost exclusively black and white dynamic, and only relatively recently have commentators worked to expand upon this. The pervasive extent of the program-matic, binary extreme can best be summed up in Suzanne Yang's jocular-serious question: "*What is the opposite of an Asian woman?*" (Yang 1998: 141). There is none. The pregnant pause at the end of the sentence is indicative of racial formulations left over from the colonial self/other dynamic. This silence is broken only in the American context with the word ethnicity, where race and ethnicity can be used at times interchangeably, although with ethnicity representing the more inclusive signifier. The word originally denotes a heathen or pagan, generally someone who has not converted to Christianity. More conventionally, however, the ethnic denotes "having or origi-nating from racial, linguistic, and cultural ties to a specific group" (Webster's 1993: 781). So, ethnicity can either be synonymous with race, or it can conveniently blend race with a variety of cultural choices including nation and religion, particularly if those factors are outside the anticipated norm, or are in any other way connected to the foreign, and strange. The offices of slavery have played a dramatic role in orchestrating binary racial dispositions in the United States, and this binary system leaves very little room for the invisible but present multitude of "mixed" race individuals. Indeed, Wheeler laments "the current political hegemony in the United States that encourages the construction of only one Other at a time" (Wheeler 2000: 53). Perhaps the most decisive example of the limitation can be seen in the relatively minor presence of the Native American in the popular racial or ethnic psyche of American popular culture, and who is almost completely subsumed by the limited scope of the debate.

For this reason, ethnicity has been adopted as the ubiquitous cousin of race, conveniently expanding the scope of racial identity through the blending of culture (already a loose term) with race. As an example of this point, it is worth considering the most recent census taken in the United States (2000). At times celebrated as a triumph of modern tolerance and compassion, the 2000 census offered Americans a unique choice in the history of their census. That is, they were allowed to choose more than one race. In fact, a respondent

"could select more than one race – and up to six – in addition to indi-
cating Hispanic origin. Instead of 12 possible racial and ethnic combi-
nations, then, there are now 126" (Osnos and Mendell 2001). While it
is improbable that many individuals would actually check six racial
and ethnic categories, the possibility highlights the fact that the
boundary of race/ethnicity has become hopelessly blurred. The
respondent was asked to check one or more of the following boxes:

> White
> Black, African American, or Negro
> American Indian or Alaskan Native (print name of enrolled or
>   principal tribe)
> Asian Indian
> Chinese
> Filipino
> Japanese
> Korean
> Vietnamese
> Native Hawaiian
> Guamanian or Chamorro
> Other Pacific Islander
> Other Asian
> Some other race

The potential offered by these choices is staggering, to be sure, and
we must stifle an awkward chortle when reading the final category in
light of our previous discussion of Orientalism and the other. In these
categories, however, we also scrutinize the practical blending of racial
and ethnic concepts. We have already established convincingly that
race is a social category and not a biological one, but we must confess
to great difficulty in identifying the logic operating behind these divisions.

The general effect of such ambitious and ambiguous blending,
however, more closely resembles an unintelligible mess and leads to
those comic–serious encounters where, say, a European is confronted
by a truly emblematic, melting-pot American of Nigerian, Irish,
African-American, Native-American, Russian Jewish, and Polish
Jewish decent. This example directly contradicts the possibility that
few Americans would check six categories if allowed to articulate their
race, but the above example is not merely anecdotal. Instead, this

manner of ethnic/racial muddling tends to articulate race in hauntingly imprecise registers within the average American. Ask the majority of citizens in the United States: "What are you?" and the least likely answer one will receive is "American." A 2000 *Newsweek* article, "The New Face of Race," celebrates this fact and includes the exact combination of racial, cultural, and religious possibilities mentioned in the previous example. Next to this is a pair of children of "Chinese, Irish, French, German, Swedish, Italian, Irish, and Japanese" decent (Campo-Flores *et al* 2000: 39–40). While we may get the general picture, we are left to wonder where exactly *race* fits into this popular conceptualization of race.

What becomes so damaging in this formulation is that within the opportunistic ethnicity, race becomes culturally obvious. Race becomes "readily apparent, a surface reflecting light and color . . . warmth or absence, silence and mystery, friend or foe. Race is an outfit like clothing involving no decisions every morning" (Yang 1998: 140). By articulating race thus, Suzanne Yang demonstrates the manner in which race is asked to signify more than race can. This clothing, a distinct cultural signifier, is presumed to communicate much more than it should about registers that have very little to do with the substance of an individual.

Moving backward considerably from the most recent poles, we should consider the role that the census has played in the structuring of the debate in the United States, and particularly the polarizing effects that we mentioned earlier. We must not forget that the United States has been the site of cataclysmic meetings between massively disparate and multitudinous groups of people. Moreover, the melting-pot mythology may not be mythology in practice the same way that it is in theory. Again, this has to do with the statistical probability created not only by the census, but also by popular imagining. The *Newsweek* article, again triumphantly, notes that "there used to be three categories; now there are 30, with 11 Hispanic subsets" (Campo-Flores *et al* 2000: 40). It is difficult to imagine a more telling lapse in statistical representation than that produced by such a mobile register. The adage about lies and statistics comes to mind. If we observe the same population as created by several different censuses, from several different times, we will also be watching the fabrication of several very different communities. In Chapter 1, we mentioned the common inability for an individual to perceive anything other than what he/she is prepared to perceive. This is almost laughable in the case of Odoric and Sir John Mandeville's fabulous encounters with the bizarre discussed in Chapter 1. This more modern example provides a lesson, like Mandeville, in what little distance we have traveled. The lesson learned, however, is that an individual can be created, mutated, and, as we shall see, even made to disappear when viewed through the filters of abstract racial discourse. Indeed, the bizarre history of the United States census, and its ability to make people appear and disappear, is a kind of magical realism worthy of Mandeville.

To be sure, the superficial celebration of racial diversity mentioned above seems to contradict a significant aspect of the commonsense construction of race in the United States. Here it is worthwhile to elaborate upon the implication of what has been coined the "one-drop rule." The one-drop rule makes race visually obvious and unambiguous. Put simply, the rule suggests that if an individual has even "one drop" of black blood in his/her veins, despite the initial appearance of complexion, then that individual is black. The primacy of blackness, therefore, preempts genuine integration or racial adaptation. Mulattos, in this formulation, are considered substantially black first – the significance of their whiteness being sublimated within the mixing of races. The convenient logic of this formulation has helped maintain (some would suggest create as well) the divisive cultural polarity between racial groups in the United States irrespective of its own mythologies. Admittedly, the one-drop rule allows that a certain percentage of mixing should ultimately negate the blackness, which in turn has led to a bizarre preoccupation with percentages. For example, an individual who has one black grandparent out of eight would be considered an "octoroon." However, a loosely acknowledged tenet suggests that one would have to be $1/32^{nd}$ black to shift, unblemished, back into the white category. Stated thus, the one-drop rule can be seen clearly for its absurdity. And yet the ideology remains somehow fixed, again, within the commonsensical notions of race. This becomes all the more important when we consider that for the vast majority of the existence of the United States census, an individual was not allowed to check his/her own race.

Counting the individuals within the nation has played an integral part in the unification of the disparate states from their earliest history. To be sure, the history of the United States is absolutely riddled with instances of counterintuitive and opportunistic racial logic. Take, for example, the notorious three-fifths compromise in the

United States constitution where five slaves were considered three free individuals when tabulating the representation allotted each state in the federal government. Here we have pro-slavery states explicitly arguing for the humanity of the slaves in order to inflate representation in the federal government and to gain political leverage in the formation of national policy. That slave owners should argue for the humanity of their "property" is an odd proposition at best and deeply opportunistic at worst, given that the practice of slavery was one of systematic dehumanization, and that such dehumanization was a fundamental aspect of pro-slavery arguments. The result, however, had direct political consequence in which the southern representation was inflated by 25–33 per cent for the years between 1790 and 1860 (Weyl and Marina 1971: 51). From the outset, we can see the political relevance of how, where, and who is counted in the United States census.

As important to the calculation of the individual presence of races is the criteria set for locating those individuals. Again, the structure of the categories we observe often tells us exactly what we are capable of scrutinizing in those categories, without necessary regard to the material object being scrutinized. In the dominant American discourse, both popular and academic, there is generally little room for nuance, imprecision, and blending. That such little space should be available for amalgamation, no matter how misguided, stands in direct opposition to the melting-pot mythology. For one, the melting-pot mythology is a proud piece of Americana, albeit ambivalently so. This pride is conflicted by the fact that so much of the miscegenation that has occurred in the United States happened because of the systematic rape of slave women who were often brought into the household to help facilitate that service. This remains a significantly divisive issue in the exchange between the poles of America's binary racial formulation for the mulatto represents a transgression for either side of the racial divide. For white Americans, the presence of mulatto acts as a reminder both of the guilt of a terrible transgression and, more overtly, of the threat of degeneration. For black Americans, the presence of the mulatto represents years of systematic dehumanization and oppression of the most intimate nature. It is no wonder, then, that within both extremes we can find either an active effort to erase, or a more passive effort to deny the existence of this portion of the population.

The frequency with which slave owners raped or otherwise procreated with their slaves suggests a profound diffusion of human types, as evidenced by the continuing debate between the descendants of Thomas Jefferson and Sally Hemming with regard to the grounds at Monticello.[1] And indeed, this is precisely the case for the "open secret" of individuals of mixed race in antebellum and reconstruction America. Scruggs and VanDemarr argue that the mulatto families were a growing and surprisingly accepted aspect of southern life in the antebellum south (1998: 9–32). There are several reasons for this perhaps unexpected assertion. First, the pervasive rape of slaves created a mildly (emphasis on mildly) privileged class of mixed race individuals. This class of relatively educated mulattos stemmed from the obvious moral complexity offered by the slave owner's conflicted treatment of his children, who had been conceived through forced concubinage. Subsequently, in a classic reversal of colonial desire, the rape of slave women also helped fabricate a mythical licentiousness attributable to black women, thereby absolving the slave owner from his transgression. It is not until nearly the turn of nineteenth century and the presence of Jim Crow that miscegenation becomes a more dramatic taboo, both publicly and privately: "The mixed race relationship was disappearing because the conditions that favored it – rural isolation of white planters and, perhaps, a 'tradition' of such relationships – were changing" (Scruggs and VanDemarr 1998: 22). Scruggs and VanDemarr argue that after the collapse of Reconstruction, zero tolerance of racial intermingling became a more prominent and increasingly more violent aspect of southern life (1998: 25–32). Scruggs and VanDemarr cite an example from 1910, where a commentator lamented that there were "two million deplorable reasons" to doubt the validity of racial distinctions. The reasons were, "of course, the estimated mulatto population" (1998: 26).

But there is an inherently problematic side to this debate. All of our information about the number of individuals pertaining to one race or another has been filtered through the census. The first census recognized two kinds of individual in the United States, "free whites" and "slaves." The odd adjective before whites suggests that slavery was not a black-only institution at the time, else the word "free" becomes redundant. The first line of reasoning in this chapter suggests that the official discourse created in the census has the ability to make people appear or disappear, seemingly at will. The second suggests that America has consistently worked to polarize racial discourse. There is perhaps no less concise example than that of the Native American and the 1790 census. Even if we blur the color exclusivity of slavery, we are still left to wonder where all the Indians went. A significant part of Scruggs and VanDemarr's theory about a growing mulatto class stems from the fact that the 1850 census listed "mulatto" as a category, but only in an effort to measure the rate in which they were "dying off, believing them susceptible to disease" (Associated Press 2001). In the previous census, this category was folded into the general heading "free colored persons." Interestingly, it is not until 1860, on the cusp of the American Civil War, that "Civilized Indians" appear alongside "Chinese" as inhabitable categories in the census. To add to the general confusion, the 1890 census added the categories "octoroon" and "quadroon" to account for the varying percentages of racial mixture in an individual. Octoroon described an individual with one in eight ancestors who were of "non-white" heritage. Again, the need to qualify in precise degrees demonstrates not only the American fetishization of identity, but also the unease with which the mulatto was regarded. What is more, it was not until 1930 that the "one-drop rule" was abandoned, and not until 1960 that respondents were expected to answer the race question themselves with the advent of the mass-mailed census.

Categorical denial was not the only manner in which theorists speculate the erasure of any middle ground between the binary poles in the American racial, political landscape. Science, once again, played a brief role in fabricating or otherwise supporting a significant myth of the mulatto character. Upon observing the census of 1840, Dr. Josiah Nott noted that there were "twice as many deaths for the free group than for the enslaved," where the "free colored" category used between 1820 and 1860 included an aggregate of free mulattos and free blacks (Tenzer 1997: 96).[2] Nott then sought to explain the cause of this discrepancy in pseudo-biological terms. As one might expect, Nott's methodology and presumptions twist under the pressures of his political and bigoted predisposition. Nevertheless, Nott is a particularly compelling voice to many of his time and his interpretation of census figures further helps to eradicate any common ground between the polar extremes of the American racial conscious. In an appropriation of Darwin and the tenets of Gobineau's degeneration, Nott is able to speculate three specific characteristics of racial mixing. First, Nott asserts that the races were distinct species and that their offspring must be sterile, likened to the mule offspring of the donkey

and the horse (we have already seen Darwin's refutation of Buffon's
rule when applied to humans in Chapter 3). Second, when empirical
evidence clearly demonstrates that mixed race individuals were
capable of producing children, Nott suggests that the condition is
degenerative in subsequent generations so that mixed race individuals would ultimately breed themselves into sterility. Here, Gobineau is
particularly helpful in outlining the gradual disintegration of racial
competence and authority. Third, Nott blends other bigotries to speculate that as the percentage of white blood rose in the mulatto, so too
does intelligence, for which virility suffers in trade. Again, the mind
boggles at this kind of opportunistic logic, which Nott borrows, albeit
indirectly, from Blumenbach, Gobineau, Darwin, and colonial
mythology to fabricate a narrative of his pleasing.

To be frank, the number of racially mixed individuals is ultimately
impossible to discern, either today or a century ago, regardless of who
is asking or who is answering the questions. As discussed in Chapter
4, from a scientific perspective, the differences within racial groups
are often more varied and substantial than those existing between
races. There are certainly factors in the history of the United States
that suggest that there is a tremendous wealth of mixed race individuals, not pertaining to those mentioned above. We must be skeptical
about inferring a wide population of mixed race individuals based
simply on literary trope, but during the late nineteenth and early
twentieth century, the mixed race individual was compelling enough,
either through experience or fanciful imagination, to become a literary type. The "tragic mulatto" is not a figure that sits well with many
critics, but the prevalence demonstrated something of the obscenely
attractive nature of the topic. This is a fascination born out of repulsion, both too gruesome and too good to miss. In Sterling A. Brown's
analysis of the "Tragic Mulatto," he isolates as a literary stereotype the
representation of mixed race individuals who become "clichéd, unrealistic, nonindividualized, and unoriginal" (quoted in Sollors 1997:
223). While on the one hand arguing against the proliferation of literary "types," Brown manages to ground his refutation, at least in part,
upon the lack of any substantially observable counterpart in the real
world. Brown intercepts and derides the mulatto figure in fiction as
unrealistic, commenting that the focus on such characters announces
the "absence of statistically more representative characters" (Sollors
1997: 223). Brown's displeasure with unrealistic, unrepresentative
characters, however, rests uneasily with the conversation above, and

it would appear that if anyone is unrealistic here, it is Brown. If, as Scruggs and VanDemarr argue, the demarcation of the color line was continually raised during the period immediately before the American Civil War through the First World War, one is left to wonder if individuals of mixed racial heritage might become "statistically more representative" in terms of the one-drop rule. Within the census parameters, the mulatto simply disappears. The melting-pot seemingly stops melting.

The Harlem Renaissance: black art and the disappearing trope of race

While commenting upon the fabrication of imagined racial polarities in the United States, it is also worth noting the moments where race plays a significant, and relatively distinct, function. The Harlem Renaissance of the early 1920s–1930s heralded the arrival of black America in the artistic cultural mainstream. Put simply, the Harlem Renaissance was "black America's first self-anointed, self-justifying, and self-propagandized artistic and cultural movement" (Andrews 1994: 3). To its greatest proponents, such as Alain Locke, the Harlem Renaissance signaled a time for artists to write "as" Negroes rather than simply "for" them (Bryant 1997: 128). The Harlem Renaissance can be interpreted as having adopted the mission of Modernism. "Make it new" within the American context means, simply, discover what has already been on the doorstep or working in the fields. There is an apparent, loaded accuracy and irony in Alain Locke's manifesto in which he describes what would later be termed the Harlem Renaissance. Working towards a kind of realism, or at least authenticity of self-representation, Locke writes, "[the Negro] has had to subscribe to the traditional positions from which his case has been viewed. Little true social or self-understanding has or could come from such a situation" (Locke [1925] 1986: 4). Locke describes the authors in his compilation as the "advance-guard" in the "Spiritual Coming of Age" for the African experience of the twentieth century (Locke [1925] 1986: 14, 16). Although Locke traditionally receives most of the critical attention, we must also remember that W. E. B. Du Bois' *The Souls of Black Folk* (1903) was instrumental in configuring the phenomenological articulation, recognition, and creation of the black American experience. Thus, the Harlem Renaissance is born out of a heightened fascination with the emerging aesthetic that had been a fundamental, and fundamentally silenced, part of America since its earliest conception.

In an effort to fill this void, then, Jean Toomer, Zora Neal Hurston, Claude McKay, Ralph Ellison, Charles Chestnut, Rudolph Fisher, Nella Larsen, and Wallace Thurman, among others, each compose a significant facet of the Harlem Renaissance. Increasingly, however, the mission and success of the Harlem Renaissance has been questioned by a number of prominent scholars. These critics distrust the "cultural elitism" of the movement because of its need to sell blackness to a predominantly white audience. The nature of this criticism represents a bitter conflict between a mainstream that is white and the sudden appearance of black artists representing "authentic" blackness within it. The irony in this situation stems from the fact that when viewed from outside of American borders, black contributions to American culture constitute the most fundamental aspects of American culture (e.g., blues, jazz). Given the mobile nature of the racial landscape cited above, one might readily wonder how any racially based movement could possibly offer any viable account of the racial landscape. To be sure, the Harlem Renaissance suffers from its position in the odd polarity of American racial categories, one that, in many instances, the Renaissance itself does very little to genuinely expand or redefine within the American context.

Oddly, the first major writer (although by no means the most significant writer in the movement) to appear chronologically enjoys an extremely tenuous relationship with the Harlem Renaissance. Indeed, Jean Toomer published *Cane* (1923) before the publication of Alain Locke's "showcase" manifesto *The New Negro* (1925). More than mere chronological incongruity, there are quite a few scholars who question Toomer's participation in the movement at all. Moreover, the question of participation is not one unique to Toomer. Even supposedly more radical participants in the movement such as Claude McKay, when viewed in a broader context, appear incredibly mobile in their social and literary activities. While Andrews portrays McKay as the most "radically militant and politically radical of the literary leaders," citing his poem "If We Must Die," several questions linger concerning the extent to which this label may be overly reductive (Andrews 1994: 101). In the brief discussion of Claude McKay in Chapter 4, for example, he readily fits in the context of a discussion of British postcolonial literature. At times, his specific cultural position

applies much more directly to the Jamaican as postcolonial subject
vis-à-vis Britain than it represents African-American experience. To
this end, McKay remains impressively dynamic. North writes that the
"fact that McKay is now so hard to place – novelist or poet? Jamaican
or American? Harlem Renaissance or Lost Generation? – may be due
to the fact that he was so firmly placed every time he settled" (North
1994: 104). If McKay represents the ambivalent individual both fixed
and mobile, other writers are equally fluid. For her part, Nella Larsen
represents a similar form of stealth in identification. Although not
quite as mobile as McKay, Larsen performs another kind of integration (or rather disintegration) by disappearing almost immediately
after the success of her first two novels, *Quicksand* (1928) and *Passing*
(1929). After fleeing the public sphere, and the Harlem Renaissance,
Larsen lived in almost complete obscurity for the remainder of her life
until the Thadious Davis publication of Larsen's biography, which
shed light on questions as basic as the date of her birth. In the context
of the first portion of this chapter, it is worth noting that Larsen's
family, reformed and apparently shamed by the youthful indiscretion
of Larsen's mother, did not even report her existence in the 1910
census (Davis 1994: 27).

Likewise, Jean Toomer offers absolutely nothing to the Harlem
Renaissance after the initial acclaim of *Cane*. As products of this
climate, these authors lived in what was still predominantly an almost
exclusively black and white world. The "New Negro" then, embraces
the opportunity to create authentic self-representation in his or her
work. This authenticity, however, seemingly refuses to stick to an
author such as Jean Toomer. Sollors concludes, "What makes the situation even more complicated is the fact that, given the way in which
'Mulatto identity,' mixed-race self-images have in many cases been
'themed away' . . . any representation of biracial characters appear to
be 'unrealistic' and potentially dangerous heterostereotypes" (Sollors
1997: 232). Put simply, the tragedy of the mulatto figure emerges
through a genuine reluctance, on both sides of the color line, to
acknowledge the mulatto as a tenable racial position. If a fictional
character could not be "realistically" mulatto, what room, one is left
to wonder, could there possibly be allowed for a "real" mulatto, as
such. In these formulations, the third option becomes tragically
untenable. We have already seen how the mulatto was systematically
removed by notions of degeneration, infertility, and census figures
designed to prove and explain the phenomenon. The success and

failure of this movement can be observed microcosmically in the relationship between Toomer and the Harlem Renaissance.

As one might expect, Toomer's adolescence was spent wandering
the various class and racial avenues before him. He was raised with
his grandfather P. B. S. Pinchback, a prominent figure in the political
landscape of post-Reconstruction New Orleans. Of his youth Toomer
remarked, "Fourteen years of my life I had lived in the white group,
four years I had lived in the colored group. In my experience there
had been no main difference between the two. But if people wanted
to isolate and fasten on those four years and to say that therefore I
was colored, this too was up to them," adding, "As for people at large,
naturally I would go my way and say nothing unless the question was
raised" (Toomer [1923] 1988: 125). There were, however, very few
opportunities for Toomer to go his own way, and the question always
seemed to be asked. In his autobiographical writing, Toomer cites an
anecdote in which he came to a fundamental disagreement with
Horace Liveright over his featuring of Toomer as a Negro for the
promotion of *Cane*. Toomer writes, "I answered to the effect that, as I
was not a Negro, I could not feature myself as one. His reply to this
did nothing else than pull my cork. He said he didn't see why I should
deny my race" (Toomer [1923] 1988: 145). Indeed, many reviews
contemporary to the publication of *Cane* further mix what was, in
Toomer, an already muddled individuality. In his article titled "Self-
Expression in *Cane*" (1923), Montgomery Gregory rather effusively
and inaccurately places Toomer in the black southern tradition with
specific interpretive goals at the back of his analysis. Gregory writes,
"thus his childhood was spent in a home where dramatic incidents of
slavery, of the Civil War and Reconstruction, were household traditions" (Gregory [1923] 1988: 165). One is left to wonder how the Civil
War specifically became a household tradition at the Pinchback
estate, which was set comfortably within the affluent middle class of
New Orleans. This strategic placement of Toomer in a precisely
located black environment, however, allows Gregory to validate
Toomer's representation of the South, and particularly southern
blacks, through the supposed authenticity of Toomer's own experiences. Gregory continues, stating that *Cane* "is not OF the South, it is
not OF the Negro; it IS the South, it IS the Negro," adding as a careful
afterthought "– as Jean Toomer has experienced them" (Gregory
[1923] 1988: 166). The accuracy of Gregory's analysis remains ques-
tionable in more than these moments (at one point he suggests that

Toomer is Pinchback's nephew when Toomer is in fact his grandson), but the direct purpose of his observations cannot be mistaken. In order to mark *Cane* as a significant Negro text, critics demanded that Toomer himself was a sufficiently "authentic" black (and southern black, for that matter) who could substantiate the representation of an otherwise unknown and therefore intriguing quantity. However, Toomer could not *be* authentically black in terms of his *cultural* perspective in the same way in which he could not *be* white from a *racial* perspective. In this sense, Toomer's manner of passing, a term used to describe a racial masquerade of fair-skinned blacks in white society, represents a threat to the understanding and conventional wisdom that demands the undeniability of one's race. This assumption supposes that race must ultimately be an obvious and perceivable characteristic, making Jean Toomer's passing reach well beyond the simple subterfuge which is conventionally associated and identified as the purpose of passing. What is more, Gregory's need to place Toomer as an intimate with the rural southern United States, the region which is his subject matter, stems from his desire to authenticate the text both in terms of Toomer's experience of the southern black tradition, and in his reluctance to accept any pretext of miscegenation that might question that authenticity. In a gesture hauntingly reminiscent of essentialist racial thought, Gregory's proposition is only "natural."

If there was an affair of the artistic heart between Toomer and the Harlem Renaissance, the glamour quickly wore off and Toomer was soon dissatisfied with his identification with the "Negro" race. His protestations, however, fell on deaf ears and the text continued to be read almost exclusively in the context of the movement. The fact of his inclusion, therefore, became an increasingly insensitive courtship, and the conditions imposed by those who desired to involve Toomer in the Harlem Renaissance often deliberately misread Toomer and simplified his racial status "so that his books could be sold" (North 1994: 164). Michael North cites an example in which the advertisements for *Cane* released by Boni and Liveright featured the text as an example of "Negro life whose rhythmic beat, like the primitive tom-tom of the African jungle, you can feel because it is written by a man who has felt it historically, poetically, and with the deepest understanding" (North 1994: 164). There is an undeniable vulgarity to the base bigotry that describes *Cane* in terms of the primitive tom-tom of the African jungle, if for no other reason than Africa, as such, is not anywhere in *Cane*. As we have argued already, the inaccuracy of this advertisement can not be understated. And yet these were the terms outlined in the participation of a literary movement apparently as much based in an atavistic and savage romanticism as it was in racial progress.

The placement of Toomer within limited racial paradigms was not simply a mission of conspiring publishers and the interests of commercial viability. Sherwood Anderson, one of Toomer's early mentors, also frustrated Toomer with his inability to grasp Toomer as such. With his own dynamic racial mobility in mind, Toomer wrote "Anderson limits me to Negro. As an approach, as a constant element (part of a larger whole) of interest, Negro is good. But try to tie me to one of my parts is surely to loose [*sic*] me. My own letters have taken Negro as a point, and from there have circled out. Sherwood, for the most part, ignores the circles" (Kerman and Eldridge 1987: 97). North notes the "especially cruel irony that [Toomer's] literary success should have robbed [him] of this essential right of self-definition and more ironic still that he should have suffered thus at the hands of a literary movement that was at that very moment advertising the sparkling newness of its approach to race" (North 1994: 164–165). Ultimately, Toomer's refusal to participate in any activity which foregrounded the notion of his négritude, combined with his refusal to simply write and rewrite versions of the same explicitly "black" texts, isolated him from the Harlem Renaissance, as he no longer qualified for participation in a movement based on "racial advancement." One doubts that Toomer missed the echoing tom-toms. Moreover, with all of this in mind, one might wonder in which direction Jean Toomer "passed," either racially or ethnically. It is a fair guess that the many respondents would answer differently to the two muddled registers (race/ethnicity) offered in the question. The absurdity of this oxymoron only clarifies the impossibility of Toomer's presence in a binary society.

Likewise, and despite conflicting claims by Toomer himself, these continual declarations problematize any reading of *Cane* that foregrounds the possibility of Toomer's reconciliation with black culture, and call into question the very suggestion that Toomer ever even participated in the Harlem Renaissance. One response to this question is to suggest that Toomer did not, in fact, participate in the Harlem Renaissance, while *Cane* did. While this may be a pleasant resolution of an odd conundrum, it also neglects several of the major themes in *Cane*. If we read Toomer as a man struggling with the ambivalence of his racial and cultural positions, we must not ignore the prevalence of these themes in *Cane* itself. As one might by now expect, traditional criticism has not always been particularly helpful in this area. William Andrews introduces Jean Toomer as the first author of the Harlem Renaissance simply because *Cane* chronologically appears as the earliest text in his compilation of exemplary renaissance writers. Although innocent, insofar as *Cane* does appear relatively early in what comes to be known as the Harlem Renaissance, the placement of Toomer at the beginning of the movement can only be understood as radically misleading for both Jean Toomer and the movement itself. Put simply, reading *Cane* into the Harlem Renaissance depends on the content of the text itself, as it revolves around predominantly mulatto themes and characters, while overlooking the racial location or attitudes of its author. The irony here, then, becomes the fact that biographically motivated readings of Toomer and *Cane* as participating in the Harlem Renaissance infer an inaccurate version of Toomer's life and skim past the central themes of dislocation and miscegenation in the text.

Cane and *Passing*

Although "black" in effort and perhaps in substance, the confusion and mixture of races in *Cane* are prevalent themes throughout the text, often with dramatic or tragic events. In the first section there are a series of short sketch stories, all of which revolve around a female in or around Toomer's fictional Georgian town, Sempter. In sequence, the stories "Karintha," "Becky," "Carma," "Fern," "Esther," and "Blood-Burning Moon," each define a small poetic cycle of the town. Each story, however, also takes great care to note the skin of each character that is named in the title. Karintha, for example, has "skin like the dusk on the eastern horizon" ([1923] 1988: 3). Becky is "a white woman who had two Negro sons," a transgression for which she is publicly shunned by either binary extreme, while privately sustained by each ([1923] 1988: 7). Carma has a "mangrove-gloomed, yellow flower face" ([1923] 1988: 12), while Fern is the "soft suggestion of down slightly darkened," "creamy brown" and whose nose is "aquiline, Semitic" ([1923] 1988: 16). Esther looks "like a little white child, starched, frilled," and Louisa from "Blood-Burning Moon" has skin "the color of oak leaves on young trees in fall" ([1923] 1988: 22, 30). Thus, Toomer's characters, both black and white, demonstrate the gamut of complexions that have been delineated within either extreme of the binary trope. Karintha's dusk on the *eastern* horizon represents the extremity of the dark end, while Becky and Esther represent two facets of the white end. To overlook the significance of these very deliberate details is to ignore Toomer's fascination with miscegenation and the abundance of it that he found in Georgia. Read in this manner, Toomer's text is "of the south and of the negro" as much as it is a direct negation of extremes.

Toomer's undermining and negation of binary antagonism does not appear without consequence, however, in a social structure that will not recognize miscegenation. Thus, Becky must disappear with her two black sons to the outskirts of town. She must become invisible. Perhaps just as tragically, the competition between binary antagonists leads to one extreme becoming dominant. Toomer does not deny the one-drop rule and each of the characters risks more dramatic disintegration if he or she does not fall into the appropriate, or available, category. Louisa's two competing lovers, one black and one white, destroy each other in a collision of sexual rivalry. Likewise, Toomer's poem "Portrait in Georgia" draws the fine portraiture of a southern lady out of her antithesis. The symbolic equation and negation in this poem has often been read as a criticism of the high southern society and the base bigotry and violence upon which it rests. Fair enough, but by reading only the societal hypocrisy of southern society into the equation, we miss the profundity in Toomer's poem:

> Hair-braided chestnut,
>   coiled like a lyncher's rope,
> Eyes-fagots,
> Lips-old scars, or the first red blisters,
> Breath-the last sweet sent of cane,
> And her slim body; white as the ash
>   of black flesh after flame.   ([1923] 1988: 27)

If miscegenation, forced or otherwise, is the primary fear of the Jim Crow era, then the prevalence of lynching is the destructive counterpart to that history. The balance between the two self-negating impulses resonates in "Portrait in Georgia" as the white woman is constructed piecemeal through the dismantling of her other. The action of the poem linguistically mimics the presence and erasure of miscegenation and lynching. As George Hutchison states, "By super-imposing the images of the white woman, the apparatus of lynching, and the burning flesh of the black man, Toomer graphically embodies both a union of black male and white female and the terrifying method of exorcising that union to maintain a racial difference the poem linguistically defies" (Hutchison 1993). The intense intimacy between this pair acts as a grand statement when read back into the rest of the first section of *Cane*. Miscegenation becomes the standard for the southern society, and through the portraiture all of the fabrication and negation implicit in the earlier poems and story fragments are clarified into their distinct societal places. The tension between presence and absence, life and destruction, beauty and torture all remark upon the binary system enacted in the Jim Crow era (specifically) and the United States (generally). Toomer's genius here resides in the fact that he articulates the pressures of the binary system and also undermines those pressures so completely by implying the miscegenation through the intimacy that the white woman and black man share.

Toomer's portrait therefore embodies, quite literally, a slip in the validity of at least two systems of identification and categorization. He invokes, in other words, an active shift which confounds hermeneutic systems. As mentioned, in Toomer's formulation there was simply "no main difference between the two" ends of the racial spectrum allowing for a broader understanding of what were typically viewed as irreconcilable positions standing in polar opposition. Toomer's response here might be read as the "don't-ask-don't-tell" method of racial identification, but actually reaches further than merely an avoidance of the polemic. Toomer's response, "naturally I would go my way and say nothing unless the question was raised," may appear to amount to being no real response at all, but is instead an absten-tion from a form of identification that ultimately reaffirms the validity of the distinction. This resistance therefore attempts to enact subver-sion without friction by passing, literally by moving beyond.

The final section of *Cane* re-introduces the southern society of Sempter, Georgia, but through a markedly different style and perspec-tive. The direct implications of miscegenation are no longer the foun-dation for the tension in the text. Rather, Toomer's one-act play confronts another quandary resulting from essentialist formulations of a binary socio-racial existence. Toomer's text returns to the south, after a central section echoing black migration to northern cities, from a decidedly northern and middle-class perspective. Thus, Toomer doubles the gesture of return by creating a character, Kabnis, who journeys (back) to the south, the place of his implied cultural home, a gesture he enacts alongside the text. It is no wonder that Kabnis is often read autobiographically by critics. Even Kabnis' isolation is significantly doubled. He is an outsider not only because he is northern, urban, and confused, but he is also glaringly middle class, a fact that is at least as significant as his literal displacement. Thus, Kabnis' return to "roots" is marred by his general non-participation in any of the cultural dynamics that would realistically make the southern tradition his own.

As suggested above, neither Jean Toomer's racial mobility, nor his uncomfortable fit in the Harlem Renaissance was by any means a unique phenomenon. Nella Larsen, for example, echoes Jean Toomer both in her troubled relationship with a racially "pure" identity and also in the brevity of her literary career. Larsen's *Quicksand* (1928) was followed almost immediately by *Passing* (1929). Both novels involve a social realism which depicts a kind of tragic mulatto woman, but which plays to the expectations of neither black nor white critical expectations. As with Toomer, we see very little room for such figures in this social order and Larsen eventually died in obscurity. The similarity does not end there, and the connection between authors must also extend through their central themes of miscegenation and the practical results of racial mobility in a polarized discursive landscape.

Both *Quicksand* and *Passing* take racial masquerade as the central point of tension in the text. Likewise, each posits the polarity of racial structures as an ultimately destructive quality. Unlike the violent lynching of Toomer's "Portrait in Georgia," Larsen invokes violence that is internalized, and therefore more completely destructive. As the metaphor quicksand supposes, racial mobility is a cure that slowly envelops the individual in a suffocating element. In a similar vein, the metaphoric title *Passing* poses a tragic word game between the practice of racial masquerade and the euphemism for death. The pun on the euphemism for death is doubled because the white middle class society, within which the two central females fear exposure, would use this expression. With this gesture, Larsen works two forms of passing into the fabric of the text. The first involves the immediacy of racial recognition, a constant fear for the protagonists. The second involves the cultural passing that must follow suit. This passing involves a series of mannerisms, aesthetics, and social values that are distinctly middle class and are distinctly white. Like Toomer's Kabnis, therefore, Larsen isolates the class tensions operating within these imagined communities and then strongly criticizes the pressures that would essentialize them.

The grotesque joke that acts as the second epigraph of this chapter comes at a precarious moment for the protagonists. When Bellew greets his wife with the diminutive and demeaning moniker "Nig," her two friends silently suspect exposure. They wonder, "So he knew, then, that Clare was a Negro?" (Larsen 1986: 170). Bellew's expression, of course, is completely demeaning, Irene notes immediately, irrespective of Clare's race. Moreover, Bellew cannot possibly mean the term affectionately because, as he later explains to the group, he despises the other side of his imaginary divide; Bellew states, "They give me the creeps. The black scrimy devils" (Larsen 1986: 172). In a moment of base honesty, Bellew plays his opinions to what he believes to be a consenting and concurrent audience. Thus his petty nickname for Clare, "Nig," reveals a terror with which Clare perpetually lives. When Bellew informs the two other passing women, Irene and Gertrude, that his wife is "gettin' darker and darker," he sees no problem in warning that "if she don't look out, she'll wake up one of these days and find she's turned into a nigger" (Larsen 1986: 171). The fact that he reveals himself to three black women is washed under the sound of his laughter, and of course, the threat is empty in its significance because his joke is already a reality known to everyone in the circle but himself. The active threat of Clare's (or Irene's, or Gertrude's) exposure, therefore, serves only to expose Bellew. Told in the presence of what he believes to be an exclusive, white audience, Bellew's joke rebounds absurdly onto him, as does his laughter. For his part, Bellew's roaring mirth testifies both to the extent of his foolishness and to the imagined clarity with which he observes the racial world. To Bellew and the white community at large there is simply no room for error with the one-drop rule making race obvious, and by proxy, with race making culture obvious and predetermined; the first qualifier determining the other.

For Clare, the threat is not entirely that she will wake up to discover she is marked for racial exclusion from the society in which she otherwise belongs. Irene's overreaction can be read as, in part, overcompensation. She must find the joke funny in order to circumvent suspicion. But the absurdity of the joke may also be genuinely terrible and funny to Irene, and thus the joke turns in its value until a silent gesture on Clare's face informs Irene of "the need for a more quiet enjoyment of this priceless joke, and for caution" (Larsen 1986: 171). As Bellew continues, Irene must expend concerted "effort to fight back her disastrous desire to laugh again" (Larsen 1986: 171). Clare's unspoken silencing reminds Irene of the essential quiet with which they must conduct themselves.

Although the passage cited above tends to inspire critical attention for its forthright vulgarity, the continuation of Larsen's thought is equally significant in terms of the tension that she creates in her text. The absurdity of Bellew's racial paradigm only increases as he continues. Bellew exposes the oxymoronic nature of his ideology by contradicting his own aesthetic. By doing so, he demonstrates a confused notion of race that is at once binary and awkwardly essentialized. Bellew acquiesces by allowing, "You can get as black as you please as far as I'm concerned, since I know you're no nigger" (Larsen 1986: 171). Here, Bellew appeals to the double register that is race and ethnicity in the United States. Clare's color should be the standard by which she is measured by conventional fabrications of racial identity, but what Bellew suggests is that the genuine residence of race lies outside, or rather inside, the skin. This appeal is hauntingly familiar to the essential "seeds" that are the secondary causal mechanism for race, as suggested by Bernier and particularly Kant. Here, race is inspired by an internal essence. With Kant, we will remember, this mechanism, once activated, cannot be altered. Thus, the subtext of Bellew's warning to his wife also exposes his own repressed trepidation that race is not an external register. Of course, Bellew is self-assured of the compliance of his audience to the extent that we can fancifully read nervousness in his overcompensating protestations. Bellew is fundamentally incapable of appropriately reading what has been proscribed as his other. When commenting upon his hatred, he mistakes Clare's unwillingness to hire a black maid for fear of exposure as a symptom of her complicity. Assured of his and her rational contempt he states, "And so does Nig, for all she's trying to turn into one" (Larsen 1986: 172). The irony in the entire exchange is tangible.

The impossibility of an American race

Returning briefly to Jean Toomer and the color consciousness of American politics, the question that must by now be overly apparent asks whether he belongs within a racially motivated movement, as such. Likewise, can we imagine a situation in which the text of a given author participates in a literary movement while the author him/herself does not? Arguably, Toomer brings a distinctly "American," and specifically American-modernist, slant to the discussion and to the quality of the composite novel genre. The term "American" here, we must note, acquires an odd political significance when used in connection with Toomer, resulting largely from his own active and frustrated creation of an American identity. Moreover, even the term "modernism" acquires a curious political significance given the suggestion, which was presented in Chapter 4, that modernism helped facilitate racially motivated literary and political movements.

A significant part of the problem in Jean Toomer's quotation that acts as the first epigraph to this chapter appears through the fact that Toomer was not being "read" as participating in either the white or black cultural sphere while the middle ground disappeared completely. Despite his disclaimers and desires otherwise, the responsibility of racial assignment could not exist as a one-way street in which one could simply prescribe or project racial identity, in the same manner that a text cannot automatically prescribe a single meaning which is then interpreted by faithful readers. In order to pass, as Toomer prepared the term, i.e., to move beyond the racial question, Toomer must be read as doing so. In other words, he must be interpreted in a way which few readers were or are prepared to acknowledge, that is, without the traditional binary markers of racial identification. What remains tragically impressive in Toomer's response, then, is the manner in which he places the onus for identification primarily in the hands of those who would read such barriers. The fundamental nature of the problem, as suggested, is that Toomer's identity is being read. Toomer is not willing to give anything away, an act which continues to make his racial and cultural mobility all the more threatening to the relevance of both methods of identification. His not saying, however, did not stop the processes of interpretation.

In the context of this discussion of the American blending of race and ethnicity within a dynamic strongly fixated on identity politics, the question that is Jean Toomer remains somehow suspended between the undeniability of racial characterization and the invalidity of those distinctions as they are articulated on a cultural basis. The problem becomes the reconciliation of not only fundamentally diasporic cultural influences, but also of the registers upon which these

influences work from both inside and outside an imagined community. Is this a fundamentally "American" characteristic? Certainly
some cultural critics of/in the United States have suggested that such
is the case. In a fairly standard response to such questions, Vévé Clark
writes, "I would argue that all cultures in the 'New World' are diasporic. The singular memory that we 'Americans' share in the hemi-
sphere originates from histories of resettlement, emigration, and
displacement" (Clark 1991: 53). The term displacement, in particular,
seems an oddly appropriate word for the description of Toomer both
in terms of his near constant (literal) mobility and his inability to
locate a stable American identity while remaining within the
American cultural economy. There remains a fundamental paradox
here. Clark argues, as do many proponents of American individual-
ism, that the unifying principle of this American identity resides
entirely in the terms of its own disparity. It should go without saying,
then, that unity through disparity is an oxymoron.

Toomer himself had a fair bit to say in this matter. In a sequence of
disclaimers, Toomer famously formulated his version of what he
called the "new American" race, the culmination of which is
contained in his long poem "The First American" (1921) which eventually became "The Blue Meridian" (1936). Vauthier argues that the
"concern with mulatto characters may therefore imply awareness of
the multiracial character of *American* society" which they spectacularly embody, of the United States, the land in which "there is no
unmiscegenation" (quoted in Sollors 1997: 236). Reading the
American text as such, mulatto becomes representative of the most
common attribute of American-ness. The point then, both in the aspi-
rations of Jean Toomer and his attempt to become American, lies in
his desire to be read as somehow outside the relativity of the racial
binaries, as a subject which reconciles disparity into a functional and
viable model of interaction. The failure, as mentioned, rests in the
inadequate readerly response to this proposition. As Wheeler
suggests, "A corollary to acknowledging one Other at a time is that if
the black/white color binary breaks down, it tends to be in racist
ways, such as in the construction of a 'model minority.' An important
implication is that, in general, only one group at a time is positioned
as Other, marginalized, or disenfranchised from a white norm in the
contemporary moment" (Wheeler 2000: 53). The reading of the
"American" in these texts, then, can be perhaps substituted with the
less ambitious but more accurate employment of a strategy which

views miscegenation as the basis from which one reads the irreconcilable and impossible nature of Modern belonging. What remains
tragic in Toomer's case is that in a society which claims to create its
unity from disparity, a society based on not fitting, Toomer still
manages not to fit. What is more, the main impulse of Toomer's
failure to appropriate an American identity stems largely from his
overwhelming willingness to create one. It is a particularly bitter type
of irony which allows Toomer, in his attempt to recognize a fundamentally American form of discontinuity, to remain a relatively
obscure outcast of that very same society.

Transition: conclusion, introduction, and return

Perhaps it would be best to conclude with the retracing of our steps,
an introduction, and a cyclical return to our first false point of origin.
From the outset of this volume, we have shadowed race through a
myriad of forms and shapes. The Greeks, we argued, represent something like the prehistory of race. To be sure a significant portion of
their theoretical social dynamic suggests that race was not far off from
their conceptual landscape. Their borders were drawn, however, not
by physical difference, but by an individual's ability to participate and
dissolve in the interests of the political state. This disposition
precluded the need for race, as subsequent divisions of humanity
became ancillary to the primary accomplishment of politics.

In the beginning of the word's appearance in the West, we
discussed race as imprecise and muddled in a manner that more
readily applied to noble lineage than to a form of race that we could
recognize and identify. The imprecision with which the term operated
was a direct result of the limited resources and experience with the
foreign. The Enlightenment picked upon the Greek ordering of the
natural world and used it as a means for articulating the observed
differences that the natural philosophers encountered during
Europe's slow rise to preeminence in the world. Natural philosophy,
therefore, formed race into a condition immediately recognizable
today, as both physically obvious and essential. A more fully developed science does not help the matter entirely. On the one hand, the
authoritative discourse of science did not recognize race as worthy of
viable biological distinction. On the other, nobody seemed to have
noticed. As the grand European empires moved into decline, their

conquests were left to respond to the oddly figured duality of race. Exploration of the nature of race was therefore abandoned seemingly on account of the fact that the West had nurtured this concept for such an extended period of time that the question no longer genuinely mattered. Race was finally and fully realized as real, obvious, historical, and psychologically stilted.

And finally, we move to the United States for our introduction and cyclical return. There has been a tremendous amount of literature and scholarship on the subject of race produced from within the great American academic industry. There remains, however, a genuine jaundice in the scope and ambition of the majority of this publication. To begin with, the inspiration for much of the material is nothing more, and certainly nothing less, than America's tragic racial history, and its continued failure to adequately address this history. This is not to say that Americans should not write about America, or that the American dilemma is not unique, grand, and terrible. But there is a failure within the greater portion of this research to look beyond immediate American borders and to think about race in a more ambitious context (which is a rather obvious goal of this volume). While this criticism can be lobbied against American culture on more levels than simply the content of its scholarship, it seems particularly counterproductive to allow scholarship to slip into the self-obsessed, aggrandizing, and Jerry Springer mentality that dominates American public discourse. Nor would it be worthwhile to ignore the sheer volume and weight of American culture being exported around the globe. Indeed, there can be no denial of the impressive dominance of American cultural capital at the moment.

But let us not think that America is a great monster either, and in this conclusion, we will now consider a moment of potential triumph in the continued transition of race and race theory. Perhaps the most compelling modern theorization to emerge from the United States in recent years is that of Critical Race Theory. Although the initial impetus of the movement has been generally attributed to Derrick Bell, Jr., Critical Race Theory is a profound network of diverse scholarship that stretches across an equally broad spectrum of ideological landscapes. The inclusiveness of the program, however, hangs upon its central concern for the way in which theory and practice combine in discourses of social power.

In this sense, Critical Race Theory recognizes the profound failure of official (i.e., state) American discourses on race. Critical Race

Theory, therefore, radically renegotiates the structuring of discourse, not only from a liberal or specifically reactionary perspective, but from its entirety – from top to bottom. While embracing the stated aims of the Civil Rights Movement in the United States, Critical Race Theory severely criticizes the methods and results of that movement. In particular, Critical Race Theory launches its criticism through the discourse of legal studies. This is a rather unlikely, but extremely appropriate, arena for the contestation of socio-political ideologies. By staging its criticism as such, Critical Race Theory immediately acknowledges the rift between theory and practice. That is, Critical Race Theory is acutely aware of the difference between the academic in his/her ivory tower, who speculates that race is an arbitrary cultural construction, and the black man on the pavement with a policeman's boot over his neck.

The law is the most appropriate place to instigate this form of cultural criticism as it encompasses both the theoretical and the practical application of ideology. The law embodies the intersection of ideology and the individual at the same moment that it is embodied by the public. In his Introduction to the volume, Cornell West laments that, "one cannot help but conclude that this has been a barbaric century for the legal academy, which has, wittingly or not, constructed for the justificatory framework for shameful social practices that continue to this day" (quoted in Crenshaw *et al* 1995: xii). Likewise, "It was obvious to many of us that although race was, to use the term, socially constructed (the idea of biological race is 'false'), race was nonetheless 'real' in the sense that there is a material dimension and weight to the experience of being raced in American society, a materiality that in significant ways has been produced and sustained by law" (Crenshaw *et al* 1995: xxvi). Thus, official forms of discourse, like the United States census for example, intersect with the "real" lives of the citizens that it creates/describes in potentially quite oppressive ways. Critical Race Theory, therefore, works "not merely to understand the vexed bond between law and racial power but to change it" (Crenshaw *et al* 1995: xiii). The law's relationship between theory and practice, in this sense, is both institutional and malleable, and therefore the relationship between the individual and the law is one of imposition and fabrication. In other words, the law represents a socio-political contract in which the individual submits to its authority, but also participates in the construction of the legal entity to which he/she submits. This is not to suggest that huge populations of the United States have not been historically excluded from, and subjected to, the imposition of the law; this chapter certainly demonstrates the exclusionary nature of this problem. Rather, Critical Race Theory recognizes the present opportunity to actively engage the institutional distance of the law and, as Crenshaw suggests, change it. In other words, Critical Race Theory recognizes its own political agency.

Critical Race Theory also attempts to reanimate racial conscious-ness, as discussed in this chapter and Chapter 4. In two very different forms of establishing racial consciousness, we have seen both a contentiously dynamic form of historical negation and appropriation of power (in Négritude), and a dynamically reductive attempt at consciousness that failed to account for the genuine racial fluidity of several individuals who were mustered for the effort (Harlem Renaissance). If race, and racial essence, is a fundamental component of each movement, we may wonder why the two movements failed so completely. The difference resides in the manner in which the racial mark rests on the conscious figure. For this reason Critical Race Theory remains significantly critical of the way in which racial consciousness was apparently abandoned "when integration, assimi-lation and the ideal of color-blindness became the official norms of racial enlightenment" (Crenshaw *et al* 1995: xiv). In particular, the critique of color-blindness seems oddly appropriate given our above discussion of Toomer and Larsen. The problem for these two individ-uals was not entirely that the society in which they lived failed to be adequately color-blind, but rather that there was little room for the nuanced positions they offered; they were, simply, off the chart.

In terms of a hypothetical color-blindness, we should note that Critical Race Theory has inspired the creation of a sister theoretical maneuver, Critical White Studies. The need for Critical White Studies testifies to the extent that race remains polarized in the United States. Now it is hardly surprising, given the nature of this discussion and the racial polarity it describes, that the United States should also help to sire the study of whiteness. The theoretical advantage of this move-ment, which was inspired by many of the same individuals who have given so much momentum to Critical Race Theory (Richard Delgado, in particular), realizes what a broad spectrum of postcolonial renego-tiations have not fully accomplished. Although perhaps disconcerting in its title, the study of whiteness is ultimately an egalitarian leveler, designed to turn the critical gaze, which has been mostly constructed by whites, back onto whiteness. This is the inverted call that inspired Fanon's racial awakening, "Look, a white person!" Put simply, the discipline attempts to mark whiteness in a similar manner in which blackness has operated as a mark for a significant portion of the population. Undoubtedly, the historical significance of this investigation will be to note the manner with which privilege protects privilege that is inscribed in whiteness, rather than from the other end where one would investigate the manner in which privilege suppresses its others. To be sure, white is no longer the blank page or rather the presumed condition of normalcy from which all digressions stem. Instead, Critical White Studies investigates the material mechanisms of privilege that such presumed normalcy encourage. Critical White Studies bring whiteness into the arena of identity politics where it may be treated on a, hopefully, level playing field. By positioning white as ubiquitously leveled, we could postulate a time in which Critical White Studies was not a necessary distinction and in which Race Studies implied *every* color, and not (as it often still does today) *other* colors.

With Critical Race Theory, then, we arrive at a point astonishingly near to our point of departure. In the beginning of this volume, we suggested that the Greeks did not have race because their social dynamic was organized so that importance of political participation superseded the need for race. The Greeks, as we should recall, laid the theoretical groundwork for theories of race, but did not build upon that ideological landscape. As we have seen in Chapters 3 and 4, there is neither a need nor a possibility for the complete eradication of race. To suggest otherwise would be to participate in the misguided fantasy of color-blindness. Race exists. Race is real. But the fact that race exists does not preclude our return to a social dynamic that looks back to the Greeks.

While we will obviously want to discard the more obvious and disconcerting aspects of Plato and Aristotle's social hierarchy, the basic disposition proposed by Critical Race Theory remains one of engagement that significantly echoes Greek political engagement. At its finest moments, Critical Race Theory gestures away from the American discourse of Jerry Springer and the public espousal of pain, one that inversely fabricates the authority to speak with individual acuity, and moves toward a consideration of the individual's relationship *vis-à-vis* the government discourse that shapes her world. What Critical Race Theory asks, therefore, is that we reconnect the political and the individual in a direct dialogue that has been largely absent without falsifying our racial history, or trying to deny its existence. Mari Matsuda wittily describes a potential scenario where race could meet the political intersection of theory and practice:

> When you are on trial for conspiracy to overthrow the government for having taught the deconstruction of law, your lawyer will want black people on your jury. Why? Because black jurors are more likely to understand what your lawyer will argue – that people in power some-times abuse law to achieve their own ends, and that the prosecution's claim to the neutral application of legal principles is false. (Matsuda 1995: 63)

Matsuda calls into being our cyclical return, with a significant amend-ment. While the Greeks could use political agency to side-step race, we cannot. We can, however, blend racial consciousness, once leveled, into a secondary political re-awakening. Whether this will provide genuine respite from a brutal racial history or metamorphose into a new monster remains to be seen. The possibility is here, however. The jury is still out.

Notes

1. As the historical home of Thomas Jefferson, the Monticello plantation remains one of the most important architectural features in the United States; it is the only house in the United States protected under the United Nation's World Heritage List. As one might expect, the 5,000 acre grounds have been, and continue to be, a source of great pride among Jefferson's descendants. The current debate between the direct descendants of Sally Hemming and those of Thomas Jefferson stems from recent proof that Jefferson sired children with Hemming, a black slave. As such, Hemming's descendants should be eligible for burial on the prestigious Monticello grounds. The assertion was initially met with formidable resistance from Jefferson's white descendants, although there are signs that such resistance is rapidly diminishing.
2. In 1856 Josiah Nott and Henry Hotz published a highly doctored version of Arthur de Gobineau's *Essay on the Inequality of the Human Races*. This aggressively edited text included an added Appendix, numerous additional notes, and the summary removal of the laws of attraction "which were at the heart of Gobineau's account of the role of

race-mixing in the rise and fall of civilizations" (Bernasconi and Lott 2000: 45). The reasons for Nott's extraction can be speculatively attributed to his utter aversion to the concept of racial mixing.

Annotated Bibliography

Banton, Michael. *Racial Theories.* Cambridge: Cambridge University Press, 1987.

Banton's *Racial Theories* is a comprehensive and compelling volume. In it, Banton describes five variations of racial thought: race as lineage, race as type, race as subspecies, race as status, and race as class. The convenience of this structure may be, at times, anachronistic as it shifts back and forth between theoretical allocations, but the benefit of this approach lies in Banton's ability to account for the multitude of pretenses under which race has been marshaled. Posited thus, Banton can trace race thematically, as the term moves from the connotation of lineage to subspecies, but also geographically, so that he can describe the nuances between, say, British and South African notions of racial class. Banton's racial history comprehensively organizes a web of sense that is not reductive and remains worthy of the imprecise history of the term.

Bernasconi, Robert and Tommy L. Lott (eds.). *The Idea of Race.* Indianapolis: Hackett, 2000.

The Idea of Race is a brilliant reader for the student interested in a comprehensive view of the Enlightenment creation of race as well as modern commentators. Although any compilation of texts in this field must walk a precarious tightrope between inclusion and reduction, Bernasconi and Lott manage to include concisely abridged texts that still allow the reader to experience a tremendous variety of authors, who demonstrate a variety of theoretical vantages. Numbering eighteen in all, Bernasconi includes names that will be familiar from this volume: Bernier, Voltaire, Kant, Blumenbach, Gobineau, Darwin, Galton, Du Bois, Appiah, Senghor as well as several others. For a brief introduction to the texts that ultimately create and then revaluate race, this volume provides a superb first look. In particular, the text succeeds in presenting otherwise obscure or unavailable texts from the Enlightenment. These texts are helpful on account of both their relative rarity and their easy assimilation into compilation. Later texts, such as Du Bois and Appiah, are less wieldy in this context quite simply because they demand more space, but are also more readily available elsewhere.

Crenshaw, Kimberlé, Neil Gotanda, Gary Peller, and Kendall Thomas (eds.). *Critical Race Theory: The Key Writings that Formed the Movement.* New York: New Press, 1995.

Critical Race Theory is by far the most promising racial discourse to emerge from the United States. Although difficult to summarize, Critical Race Theory renegotiates the intersection between racial theory and practice as it is embodied in legal discourse. In this sense, Critical Race Theory can engage in sophisticated and abstract legal and theoretical arguments without sacrificing those arguments to pure abstraction; it is ultimately a practical criticism. Critical Race Theory challenges the manner in which legal discourse has been used historically in the United States to protect the privilege of white society, and to systematically oppress peoples of color. Critical Race Theory also renegotiates/revaluates the Left and the Civil Rights Movement in terms of its accomplishments. The political agency of Critical Race Theory, therefore, recognizes the failure of color-blind assimilation and brings color-consciousness back into the American lexicon.

Fanon, Franz. *Black Skin, White Masks*, trans. Charles Markmann. New York: Grove Press, 1967

In *Black Skin, White Masks* Fanon articulates his experience as a black subject in a world created by/for whites. In particular, Fanon investigates the consequences that the ideological structure has on the mind of the black subject who must confront his/her historical creation by the white society. To some, *Black Skin, White Masks* is a manifesto of postcolonial psychology. To others, it is a profound analysis of the double register that Fanon encounters after recognizing his suspended position as black African, French, Martiniquan, and intellectual. Thus, Fanon is psychologically suspended in the construction of a white world that imposes his blackness upon him first and foremost.

Gates, Henry Louis, Jr. *The Signifying Monkey: A Theory of African-American Literary Criticism*. New York: Oxford University Press, 1988.

Gates' theory of Signifyin(g) traces the Africa into the term African-American. The concept is designed as the 'trope of tropes' for African-American literary criticism. Gates focuses on finding a unifying theoretical premise that could isolate, and then bind, a black American aesthetic to a tangible African cultural foundation. By doing so, Gates dramatically links African and black American linguistic traditions, of doubled and protectively evasive speech. The concept of Signifyin(g), despite showing a flair for the jingoistic conventions of the American Academic industry, describes the duplicitous and subversive rhetorical strategy that is essentially African and American.

Gould, Stephen Jay. *Ever Since Darwin: Reflections in Natural History*. New York: W. W. Norton, 1973.

The late Stephen Jay Gould is an icon and a landmark in the natural sciences. His contribution to science rests not only in his piercing intellect, but also in his ability to communicate science to the uninitiated without compromising the rigor of the subject, as he does in *Ever Since Darwin*. Gould's re-articulation of Darwin brings clarity to what many moderns who have read Darwin find obtuse or awkward. More than merely repeating Darwin's theories in a modern prose, Gould applies those theories to a score of modern misconceptions. For this reason, Gould's text does not limit itself to racial discourses, as one might expect in this context, but covers a broad span of scientific interests. For the individual with only an armchair appreciation of Darwin's relevance in the fabrication of the modern ideological landscape, and for the engaged intellectual, Gould offers a sharp analysis of such topics as human evolution, patterns, and punctuations in the history of life, theories of the earth, the science and politics of human nature, and others.

Hannaford, Ivan. *Race: The History of an Idea in the West.* Washington, D.C.: Woodrow Wilson Center, 1996.

Ivan Hannaford's *Race* is an impressive contribution to the archeology of racial thought in the West. The foundation of Hannaford's argument rests on his interpretation of early Greek texts and his conceptual repositioning of the cultural disposition in early exchanges between the West and its exterior. Hannaford argues that for the Greeks, and well beyond, the primary division of people in the Western mind was between political and barbarian humans. This dynamic, according to Hannaford, preempted the need for race. It is not until much more recently, as aesthetic concerns became the foundation for the theorization of culture, that race became a primary point for dividing humankind. Hannaford's line of argument is fundamental to the arguments advanced here. In particular, Hannaford's revaluation, and ultimate negation of Greek racial thought is the cornerstone of both his and this discussion. Hannaford's argument is exhaustive in its scope and significantly inclusive. As it progresses, however, Hannaford's history shows the strain of maintaining thorough investigation with the sheer volume of material produced with regard to race. For this reason, the first half of his argument is perhaps a bit more fluid and cohesive than the later material. This detracts from the quality of his argument only in that it must become slightly hurried.

Lewis, Bernard. *The Muslim Discovery of Europe.* New York: W. W. Norton, 2001.

In this text, Lewis traces the history of exchange between Europe and the Islamic world. Lewis, however, inverts that standard Western representation by focusing on the Muslim response to European presence. Lewis, therefore, provides exceptional Islamic sources for a rare perspective of familiar historical events, from the Crusades to the fall of the Ottoman Empire. By situating his discussion from the Muslim perspective, he undermines the too often held conviction of Western preeminence. Lewis' breadth of knowledge is both impressive and well needed in a time in which, even among a vogue of postcolonial study, the history of European and Islamic exchange remains remarkably overlooked.

Nordau, Max. *Degeneration* [1895], trans. Gerorge L. Mosse. Lincoln: University of Nebraska Press, 1968.

The fact that Nordau enjoyed a profound popularity during the turn of the twentieth century until the advent of the First World War calls for some attention. Likewise, the fact that the demand for his once influential writing seems to have collapsed almost entirely by his death in 1923 remains disconcerting. Nordau's theory of degeneration will no doubt rub many contemporary intellectuals up the wrong way. Undoubtedly, his theories helped to inspire ultimately conservative and fascist concepts of race and

European preeminence. But this makes his popularity and subsequent dismissal all the more compelling. To be sure, his suggestion that his contemporaries suffered from a nervous exhaustion inspired by the frenetic pace of his time resonates with many modern trepidations. His strong aesthetic reaction against now-celebrated artists, like Oscar Wilde, and his accusation that such artists suffered from neurosis, may seem misplaced, but the sincerity with which the argument was leveled should make us stop and consider modern theories of the same.

Said, Edward. *Orientalism*. New York: Vintage, 1979.

Said's *Orientalism* remains the seminal text in postcolonial theory. Although by no means without detractors, the influence of this text is so pervasive that it is often attributed as the inspiration, or starting point, for postcolonial criticism. Said's criticism realigns the colonial perspective to note the manner in which the West constructs the Orient with an obsessive and reductive gaze. His critical goal, therefore, is to return this gaze and open an ideological space for the postcolonial subject to speak back to the West. Thus, Said instigates academic and institution resistance to the imperial project and the cultures that helped promote it.

Bibliography

Achebe, Chinua. *Hopes and Impediments*. New York: Anchor, 1989.

Andrews, William L. (ed.). *Classic Fiction of the Harlem Renaissance*. Oxford: Oxford University Press, 1994.

Annas, Julia. *An Introduction to Plato's Republic*. Oxford: Oxford University Press, 1981.

———. "Race." *Critical Terms for Literary Study*, 2nd edn. eds. Frank Lentricchia and Thomas McLaughlin. Chicago: University of Chicago Press, 1995, 274–287.

Appiah, Kwame Anthony. *In My Father's House: Africa in the Philosophy of Culture*. Oxford: Oxford University Press, 1992.

Appiah, Kwame Anthony and Amy Gutmann. *Color Conscious*. NJ: Princeton University Press, 1996.

Arata, Stephen. *Fictions of Loss in the Victorian Fin de Siècle: Identity and Empire*. Cambridge: Cambridge University Press, 1996.

Aristotle. *The Basic Works of Aristotle*, ed. Richard McKeon. New York: The Modern Library, 1941.

Arnold, A. James. *Modernism and Négritude – The Poetry and Poetics of Aimé Césaire*. Cambridge, Mass.: Harvard University Press, 1981.

Ashcroft, Bill and Paul Ahluwalia. *Edward Said*. London: Routledge, 1999.

Associated Press. "Race Question Vexed Census Takers Through History," March 27, 2001.

Banton Michael. "Epistemological Assumptions in the Study of Racial Differentiation," in *Theories of Race and Ethnic Relations*, eds. John Rex and David Mason. Cambridge: Cambridge University Press, 1986, 42–63.

———. *Racial Theories*. Cambridge: Cambridge University Press, 1987.

———. "The Idiom of Race: A Critique of Presentism," *Theories of Race and Racism: A Reader*, eds. Les Back and John Solomos. London: Routledge, 2000, 51–63.

Barnes, Jonathan (ed). *The Cambridge Companion to Aristotle*. Cambridge: Cambridge University Press, 1995.

Beer, Gillian. *Darwin's Plots: Evolutionary Narrative in Darwin, George Eliot and Nineteenth-Century Fiction*. London: Routledge, 1983.

Benjamin, Playthell. "Did Shakespeare Intend Othello to be Black? A Meditation on Blacks and the Bard," in *Othello: New Essays by Black Writers*, ed. Mythili Kaul. Washington, D.C.: Howard University Press, 1997, 91–104.

Bernasconi, Robert. "Who Invented the Concept of Race?: Kant's Role in the Enlightenment Construction of Race," in *Race*, ed. Robert Bernasconi. Malden: Blackwell, 2001, 11–36.

Bernasconi, Robert and Tommy L. Lott (eds). *The Idea of Race*. Indianapolis: Hackett, 2000.

Bernier, François. "A New Division of the Earth," in The Idea of Race, eds. Robert Bernasconi and Tommy L. Lott. Indianapolis: Hackett, 2000, 1–4.

Bhabha, Homi K. The Location of Culture. London: Routledge, 1994.

Block, Ned. "How Heritability Misleads about Race," in Race and Racism, ed. Bernard Boxill. Oxford: Oxford University Press, 2001. 114–144.

Bloom, Alan (ed.). The Republic of Plato, 2nd edn. New York: Basic Books, 1968.

Blumenbach, Johann Friedrich. "On the Natural Variety of Mankind," in The Idea of Race, eds. Robert Bernasconi and Tommy L. Lott. Incianapolis: Hackett, 2000. 27–37.

Boxill, Bernard (ed.). "Introduction," in Race and Racism, ed. Bernard Boxill. Oxford: Oxford University Press, 2001.

Bradbury Malcolm and James McFarlane (eds.). Modernism: 1890–1930. London: Penguin, 1991.

Bryant, Jerry H. Victims and Heroes: Racial Violence in the African American Novel. Amherst: University of Massachusetts Press, 1997.

Buffon, Georges-Louis Leclerc, Comte de. "The Geographical and Cultural Distribution of Mankind," in Race and the Enlightenment: A Reader, ed. Emmanual Chukwudi Eze. Malden: Blackwell, 2001, 15–28.

Butler-Evans, Eliot. "'Happy, for I am Black': Othello and the Semiotics of Race and Otherness," in Othello: New Essays by Black Writers, ed. Mythili Kaul. Washington, D.C.: Howard University Press, 1997, 139–150.

Campo-Flores, Arian et al. "The New Face of Race," Newsweek, September 28, 2000, 38–41.

Cavalli-Sforza, L. L., P. Menozi, and A. Piazza. The History and Geography of Human Genes. Princeton, N.J.: Princeton University Press, 1994.

Cheng, Vincent J. Joyce, Race, and Empire. Cambridge: Cambridge University Press, 1995.

Clark, Vévé K. "Developing Diaspora Literacy and Marasa Consciousness," in Comparative American Identities: Race, Sex and Nationality in the Modern Text. ed. Hortense J. Spillers. London: Routledge, 1991, 41–61.

Coetzee, J. M. Foe. London: Penguin, 1987.

Conrad, Joseph. Heart of Darkness. New York: Penguin, 1973.

Crenshaw, Kimberlé, Neil Gotanda, Gary Peller, and Kendall Thomas (eds.). Critical Race Theory: The Key Writings that Formed the Movement. New York: New Press, 1995.

Dalton, Harlon L. "The Clouded Prism: Minority Critique of the Critical Legal Studies Movement," in Critical Race Theory: The Key Writings that Formed the Movement, eds. Kimberlé Crenshaw et al. New York: New Press, 1995.

Darwin, Charles. The Origin of the Species [1859]. New York: Gramercy, 1979.

————. The Descent of Man [1871]. Amherst: Prometheus, 1998.

Davis, Thadious M. Nella Larsen: Novelist of the Harlem Renaissance: A Woman's Life Unveiled. Baton Rouge: Louisiana State University Press, 1994.

Defoe, Daniel. Life and Adventures of Robinson Crusoe [1719]. New York: Modern Library, 2001.

Delacampagne, Christian. "Racism and the West: From Praxis to Logos," in Anatomy of Racism ed. David Theo Goldbergh. Minneapolis: University of Minnesota Press, 1990, 83–8.

Delgado, Richard and Jean Stefanic (eds.). *Critical White Studies*. Philadelphia: Temple University Press, 1997.

Dirlik, Arif. "The Postcolonial Aura: Third World Criticism in the Age of Global Capitalism," *Critical Inquiry*, 20 (Winter 1994), 328–356.

Du Bois, W. E. B. *The Souls of Black Folk* [1903]. New York: Bantam, 1989.

Dunbar, William. *The Poems of William Dunbar*, ed. James Kinsley. Oxford: Clarendon Press, 1979.

Dyer, Richard. *White*. London, Routledge, 1997.

Eagleton, Terry. *Exiles and Émigrés: Studies in Modern Literature*. London: Chatto & Windus, 1970.

Ellis, Havelock. *The Art of Life: From the Works of Havelock Ellis*, ed. S. Herbert. Freeport: Libraries Press, 1929.

Eze, Emmanuel Chukwudi. *Achieving our Humanity: The Idea of the Postracial Future*. New York: Routledge, 2001.

————— (ed). *Race and the Enlightenment: A Reader*. Malden: Blackwell, 1997.

Fanon, Franz. *Black Skin, White Masks*, trans. Charles Markmann. New York: Grove Press, 1967.

—————. "The Lived Experience of the Black" [1951], in *Race*, ed. Bernard Bernasconi. Malden: Blackwell, 2001, 184–201.

Ferguson, Robert. *Representing "Race": Ideology, Identity and the Media*. London: Arnold, 1998.

Galton, Francis. "Eugenics: Its Definition," in *The Idea of Race*, eds. Robert Bernasconi and Tommy L. Lott. Indianapolis: Hackett, 2000, 79–83.

Gates, Henry Louis, Jr. *The Signifying Monkey: A Theory of African-American Literary Criticism*. New York: Oxford University Press, 1988.

Gobineau, Arthur de. *Essay on The Inequality of the Human Races* [1853–1855]. New York: Howard Fertig, 1992.

Gossett, Thomas F. *Race: The History of an Idea in America*, 2nd end. Oxford: Oxford University Press, 1997.

Gould, Stephen Jay. *Ever Since Darwin: Reflections in Natural History*. New York: W. W. Norton, 1973.

Gregory, Montgomery. "Self-Expression in *Cane*," in *Cane* [1923], ed. Darwin T. Turner. New York: W. W. Norton 1988, 165–168.

Habib, Imtiaz. *Shakespeare and Race: Postcolonial Praxis in the Early Modern Period*. Lanham: University Press of America, 2000.

Hall, Stuart. "When was 'the Post-Colonial'? Thinking at the Limit," in *The Post-Colonial Question*, eds. Iain Chambers and Lidia Curti. London: Routledge, 1996, 242–260.

Hannaford, Ivan. *Race: The History of an Idea in the West*. Washington, D.C.: Woodrow Wilson Center, 1996.

Harrowitz, Nancy A. *Anti-Semitism, Misogyny, and the Logic of Cultural Difference: Cesare Lombroso and Matilde Serao*. Lincoln: University of Nebraska Press, 1994.

Herrnstein, Richard J. and Charles Murray. *The Bell Curve: Intelligence and Class Structure in American Life*. New York: Simon & Schuster, 1994.

Hill, Thomas E., Jr. and Bernard Boxill. "Kant and Race," in *Race and Racism*, ed. Bernard Boxill. Oxford: Oxford University Press, 2001, 448–471.

Hofstadter, Richard. *Social Darwinism in American Thought.* Boston: Beacon Press, 1955.

Hulme, Peter. *Colonial Encounters: Europe and the Native Caribbean, 1492–1797.* London: Routledge, 1986.

Hutchison, George. "Toomer and American Racial Discourse," *Texas Studies in Literature and Language* 35 (Summer 1993), 226–250.

Ignatiev, Noel. *How the Irish Became White.* New York: Routledge, 1995.

Jones, Steve. *Darwin's Ghost:* The Origin of the Species *Updated.* New York: Ballantine, 1999.

Jordan, Glenn and Chris Weedon. "The Celebration of Difference in the Cultural Politics of Racism," in *Theorizing Culture: An Interdisciplinary Critique after Postmodernism,* eds. Barbara Adam and Stuart Allen. London: University College London Press, 1995, 149–164.

Jordan, Winthrop. *White Over Black: American Attitudes Towards the Negro 1550–1812.* Chapel Hill: University of North California Press, 1968.

Kane, Cheikh Hamidou. *Ambiguous Adventure,* trans. Katherine Woods. Oxford: Heinemann, 1963.

Kant, Immanuel. "On the Different Races of Man," "On Natural Characteristics, so far as They Depend upon the Distinct Feeling of the Beautiful and Sublime," and "On Countries that are Known and Unknown to Europeans," in *Race and the Enlightenment: A Reader,* ed. Emmanuel Chukwudi Eze. Oxford: Blackwell, 1997, 38–64.

Kaul, Mythili. "Background: Black or Tawny? Stage Representations of Othello from 1604 to Present," in *Othello: New Essays by Black Writers,* ed. Mythili Kaul. Washington, D.C.: Howard University Press, 1997, 1–22.

Kerman, Cynthia Earl and Richard Eldridge. *The Lives of Jean Toomer: A Hunger of Wholeness.* Baton Rouge: Louisiana State University Press, 1987.

Kipling, Rudyard. *Selected Stories.* New York: Alfred A. Knopf, 1994.

Kraut, Richard. *The Cambridge Companion to Plato.* Cambridge: Cambridge University Press, 1992.

Larsen, Nella. *Quicksand and Passing,* ed. Deborah E. McDowell. New Brunswick: Rutgers University Press, 1986.

Las Casas, Bartolomé de. *In Defense of the Indians* [1552], trans. Stafford Poole. DeKalb: Northern Illinois University Press, 1966.

————. *A Short Account of the Destruction of the Indies,* trans. Nigel Griffin. Penguin: London, 1992.

Lewis, Bernard. *The Muslim Discovery of Europe.* New York: W. W. Norton, 2001.

————. *What Went Wrong? Western Impact and Middle Eastern Response.* Oxford: Oxford University Press, 2002.

Locke, Alain (ed). *The New Negro: An Interpretation* [1925]. Salem: Ayer, 1986.

Lombroso, Cesare. *The Man of Genius,* ed. Havelock Ellis. London: Walter Scott, 1891.

————. *Crime: Its Causes and Remedies* [1899], trans. Henry P. Horton. Boston: Little, Brown & Company, 1911.

Long, A. A. (ed). *The Cambridge Companion to Early Greek Philosophy.* Cambridge: Cambridge University Press, 1999.

Mandeville, Sir John. *The Travels of Sir John Mandeville,* trans. C. W. R. D. Moseley. London: Penguin, 1983.

Marx, Karl. "Preface to the Critique of Political Economy," in *Karl Marx and Friedrich Engels Selected Works*, Vol. I. Moscow: Foreign Languages Publishing House, 1962.

————. Preface. *A Contribution to the Critique of Political Economy*, trans. S. W. Ryanzanskaya, ed. M. Dobb. London: Lawrence & Wishart, 1971.

Matar, Nabil. *Turks, Moors, and Englishmen in the Age of Discovery*. New York: Columbia University Press, 1999.

Matsuda, Mari. "Looking to the Bottom: Critical Legal Studies and Reparations," in *Critical Race Theory: The Key Writings that Formed the Movement*, eds. Kimberlé Crenshaw *et al.* New York: New Press, 1995, 63–79.

McKay, Claude. *The Green Hills of Jamaica*, ed. Mervyn Morris. Kingston: Heinemann, 1979.

Milton, Giles. *The Riddle and the Knight: In Search of Sir John Mandeville, the World's Greatest Traveler*. New York: Farrar, Strauss & Giroux, 1996.

Montefiore, Janet. "Latin, Arithmetic and Mastery: A Reading of Two Kipling Fictions," in *Modernism and Empire*, eds. Howard J. Booth and Nigel Rigby. Manchester: Manchester University Press, 2000.

Moore-Gilbert, Bart. *Postcolonial Theory: Contexts, Practices, Politics*. London: Verso, 1997.

Mosley, Albert G. "Négritude, Nationalism, and Nativism: Racists or Racialists?," in *Racism*, ed. Leonard Harris. Amherst: Humanity Books, 1999, 74–86.

Mosse, George L. (ed.) (1968). Introduction. *Degeneration*. Lincoln: University of Nebraska Press.

Nicholls, Peter. *Modernisms: A Literary Guide*. London: Macmillan, 1995.

Nordau, Max. *Degeneration* [1895], ed. George L. Mosse. Lincoln: University of Nebraska Press, 1968.

North, Michael. *The Dialect of Modernism: Race, Language, and Twentieth-Century Literature*. Oxford: Oxford University Press, 1994.

Ogude, S. E. "Literature and Racism: The Example of Othello," in *Othello: New Essays by Black Writers*, ed. Mythili Kaul. Washington, D.C.: Howard University Press, 1997, 151–166.

Osnos, Evan and David Mendell. "New Racial Choices in Census Pose Tricky Issue," *Chicago Tribune* February 5, 2001.

Peters, Edward (ed.). *The First Crusade: The Chronicle of Fulcher, of Chartres and Other Source Material*. Philadelphia: University of Pennsylvania Press, 1971.

Plato. *Republic of Plato, Book V, Book VII*, 2nd edn., ed. and trans. Allan Bloom. New York: Basic Books, 1968.

Posnock, Ross. *Color and Culture: Black Writers and the Making of the Modern Intellectual*. Cambridge, Mass.: Harvard University Press, 1998.

Potter, Nicholas. *William Shakespeare: Othello*. New York: Columbia University Press, 2000.

Said, Edward. *Orientalism*. New York: Vintage, 1979.

————. *Beginnings*. New York: Columbia University Press, 1985.

Sartre, Jean-Paul. "Black Orpheus," in *Race*, ed. Robert Bernasconi. Malden: Blackwell, 2001, 115–142.

Scruggs, Charles, and Lee VanDemarr. *Jean Toomer and the Terrors of American History*. Philadelphia: University of Pennsylvania Press, 1998.

Shakespeare, William. *William Shakespeare: The Complete Works*, ed. Alfred Harbage. London: Penguin, 1969.

Sharpley-Whiting, T. Denean. "Paulette Nardal, Race Consciousness and Antillean Letters," in *Race*, ed. Robert Bernasconi. Malden: Blackwell, 2001, 95–106.

Shelley, Mary. *Frankenstein: or, The Modern Prometheus* [1818]. New York: Signet 1963.

Shermer, Michael. *Why People Believe Weird Things: Pseudoscience, Superstition, and Other Confusion of Our Time*. New York: W. H. Freeman and Co., 1997.

Shohat, Ella. "Notes on the "Post-Colonial,'" *Social Text*, 31/32 (1992).

Snyder, Louis. *The Idea of Racialism: Its Meaning and History*. Princeton, N.J.: D. Van Nostrand, 1962.

Sollors, Werner. *Neither Black Nor White Yet Both: Thematic Explorations of Interracial Literature*. Oxford: Oxford University Press, 1997.

Solomos, John. 'Varieties of Marxist Conceptions," in *Theories of Race and Ethnic Relations*, eds. John Rex and David Mason. Cambridge: Cambridge University Press, 1986, 84–109.

Spivak, Gayatari Chakravorty. "Can the Subaltern Speak? Speculations on Widow Sacrifice," in *Wedge*, 7/8, 1985, 120–130.

Tenzer, Lawrence R. *The Forgotten Cause of the Civil War: A New Look at the Slavery Issue*. Scholor's Publishing House, 1997.

Toomer, Jean. *The Wayward and the Seeking: A Collection of Writing by Jean Toomer*, ed. Darwin T. Turner. Washington, DC: Howard University Press, 1980.

————. *Cane* [1923], ed. Darwin T. Turner. New York: W. W. Norton 1988.

Van den Berghe, Pierre L. "Ethnicity as Kin Selection: The Biology of Nepotism," in *Racism*, ed. Leonard Harris. New York: Humanity, 1999, 50–73.

Voltaire, François-Marie. "Of the Different Races of Men." in *The Idea of Race*, eds. Robert Bernasconi and Tommy L. Lott. Indianapolis: Hackett, 2000, 5–7.

Washbrook, D. A. "Ethnicity and Racialism in Colonial Indian Society," in *Racism and Colonialism*, ed. Robert Ross. The Hague: Martinus Nijhoff, 1982, 143–181.

Weate, Jeremy. 'Fanon, Merleau-Ponty and the Difference of Phenomenology," in *Race*, ed. Robert Bernasconi. Malden: Blackwell, 2001, 169–183.

Webster's Third New International Dictionary. Springfield: Merrian-Webster, 1993.

Weyl, Nathaniel and William Marina. *American Statesmen on Slavery and the Negro*. New York: 1971.

Wheeler, Roxann. *The Complexion of Race: Categories of Difference in Eighteenth-Century British Culture*. Philadelphia: University of Pennsylvania Press, 2000.

Winant, Howard. "The Theoretical Status of the Concept of Race," in *Theories of Race and Racism: A Reader*, eds. Les Back and John Solomos. London: Routledge, 2000, 181–190.

Yang, Suzanne. "A Question of Accent: Ethnicity and Transference," in *The Psychoanalysis of Race*, ed. Christopher Lane. New York: Columbia University Press, 1998, 139–153.

Young, Robert J. C. *Postcolonialism: An Historical Introduction*. Oxford: Blackwell, 2001.

Index